haldol

and

hyacinths

To Beth,
In hope + solidarity!

haldol
and
hyacinths

A BIPOLAR LIFE

Melody Moezzi

AVERY

A MEMBER OF PENGUIN GROUP (USA) INC.

NEW YORK

Published by the Penguin Group
Penguin Group (USA) Inc., 375 Hudson Street,
New York, New York 10014, USA

USA · Canada · UK · Ireland · Australia
New Zealand · India · South Africa · China

Penguin Books Ltd, Registered Offices:
80 Strand, London WC2R 0RL, England
For more information about the Penguin Group visit penguin.com

Most Avery books are available at special quantity discounts for bulk purchase for sales
promotions, premiums, fund-raising, and educational needs. Special books or book
excerpts also can be created to fit specific needs. For details, write
Penguin Group (USA) Inc. Special Markets, 375 Hudson Street, New York, NY 10014.

Library of Congress Cataloging-in-Publication Data

Moezzi, Melody, date.
Haldol and hyacinths: a bipolar life/Melody Moezzi.
p.   cm.
ISBN 978-1-58333-468-3
1. Manic-depressive illness—Cross-cultural studies.   2. Manic-depressive
persons—Family relationships.   3. Iranian Americans—Psychology.   4. Psychiatry,
Transcultural—Case studies.   5. Moezzi, Melody—Mental health.   I. Title.
RC516.M62   2013   2013008224
616.89'5—dc23

Printed in the United States of America
1 3 5 7 9 10 8 6 4 2

BOOK DESIGN BY AMANDA DEWEY

In the name of God,

Most Gracious,

Most Merciful

ALSO BY MELODY MOEZZI

War on Error:
Real Stories of American Muslims

For Matthew

In Memory of

Mamaan Koochooloo

Mamaan Shekoo

Tom Lenard

Farid Jafarian

Willie Knight

Alexis Rose Walker

DISCLAIMERS AND THE LIKE

Any prosecutor or criminal defense attorney will tell you: eyewitness testimony sucks. It's notoriously unreliable, while simultaneously giving the impression of fact.*

This book is my eyewitness testimony. That said, I know what I saw, and I didn't make this up. Then again, that's what all eyewitnesses say. I don't share this because I plan on lying. I share this because I plan on telling the truth, and acknowledging the inherently dangerous nature of such testimonials is part of that.

In some cases, I've changed the names of certain people and institutions out of respect for privacy. In an effort to maintain anonymity and avoid introducing way too many people, a few figures represent composites of several individuals. Also, edited portions of two previously published pieces appear herein, one

---

* Hal Arkowitz and Scott O. Lilienfeld, "Why Science Tells Us Not to Rely on Eyewitness Accounts," *Scientific American*, January 2010, http://www.scientificamerican.com/article .cfm?id=do-the-eyes-have-it.

from the *Yale Journal for Humanities in Medicine***** and another from CNN.com.†

Insomuch as the structure of this book parallels that of my own mind, it boasts about as much order and linearity as a hallucination. If you're expecting fluid transitions or traditional chronology, you can stop reading now.

Finally, psychosis, mania, depression and tons of the medications used to treat them can seriously damage and distort recollection. Where my memory has failed me, I've interviewed other eyewitnesses—mostly friends or family members—to fill the gaps.

As for me, save the disclaimers above, I'm telling the truth as I remember it.

---

* Melody Moezzi, "Half a Pancreas Later, Some Things Are Still Hard to Digest," *Yale Journal for Humanities in Medicine*, November 26, 2002.

† Melody Moezzi, "Embracing Life After Suicide Attempt," CNN.com, September 12, 2010.

CONTENTS

part
one

one

no good reason

There are plenty of respectable reasons to kill yourself, but I've never had any. I've never been in constant uncontrollable pain. I've never lost a child. I've never killed or irreparably harmed anyone with fewer than six legs. I've never fought in a war or witnessed a massacre. I've never *irretrievably* lost my mind. And I've never been raped.

I can't say the same for the bulk of my former companions on the Stillbrook Institute's women's psych unit. If I gained anything from my first inpatient psychiatric stay, it was a deep appreciation for the potential morality of murder. After hearing countless women share their excruciating experiences being tortured and violated, most often as children and by family members, I gained a new appreciation for my legal education. Instead of spending group sessions contemplating my own despair and the pathetic suicide attempt that had landed me in a room full of rape victims, manic-depressives, anorexics, bulimics, schizophrenics, drug addicts and self-mutilators, I spent those sessions contemplating ways to get away with murder. I'm confident that no responsible mental health professional would endorse homicidal ideations as an acceptable cure for suicidal ones, but I'm equally confident that my budding interest in killing rapists drastically curtailed my interest in killing myself. Nevertheless, I'd attempted suicide less than a week before, so I couldn't be trusted. Hence my residence at Stillbrook.

Despite our differences, my fellow prisoners and I had a great deal in common. We were all seriously ill; we all desperately needed help; and we all resented the fact that we needed it. What's more, we were all acutely aware of the classified nature of our conditions and whereabouts. This wasn't paranoia. It was self-preservation. People tend to look unfavorably upon the mentally ill, especially those of us who've been hospitalized.

Losing your mind is indeed traumatizing, but doing so in front of a supposedly sane audience is mortifying. It's not like getting cancer. No one rallies around you or shaves her head in solidarity or brings you sweets. "Normals" (or "normies," as some of us "crazies" affectionately refer to them) feel uneasy around those of us who've lost a grip on reality. Perhaps they're afraid we might attack them or drool on them or, worse yet, suck them into our alternate universe where slitting your wrists and talking to phantoms seem perfectly rational. Lucky for me, my initial audience was limited to my husband, my psychiatrist and a few strangers in the latter's waiting room.

As an Iranian-American Muslim in the buckle of the Bible Belt at the start of the twenty-first century, I've been intimately acquainted with stigma, scorn and isolation for quite some time—long before and since Stillbrook. But this was different. This stigma was far more suffocating, this scorn more subtle, this isolation more literal. A brutal species of shame set in, so vicious and insidious it easily could have starred in its own series on Animal Planet. *Shark Week* would pale by comparison.

I've never been ashamed of my background, and I've never tried to hide it. I'm proud of where I'm from. But I wasn't proud of where I'd arrived. There's no pride in being a mental patient. We have no especially loud and high-profile advocates. No Michael J. Foxes, no Christopher Reeves, no Lance Armstrongs. No pink boas or bracelets or ribbons or T-shirts. Silence and humiliation rule our playing fields. While others down performance-enhancing drugs and play on grass or Astroturf, we down antipsychotics and play on quicksand.

I wasn't diagnosed with bipolar disorder, also known as manic depression or manic-depressive illness, until years after leaving Stillbrook. Failing to recognize my propensity for mania, the folks at Stillbrook, like so many before and after them, misdiagnosed me with standard major "unipolar" depression. I never questioned them.

With bipolar disorder, it's mildly common to jump from depression to mania after a suicide attempt. I vaulted. My garrulousness, impulsivity, rapid speech and elevated mood, combined with my obsession with instructing the other patients in all matters imaginable, should have set off some serious bipolar alarm bells, but they didn't—at least not for any of my health care providers. Conversely, a few of my fellow bipolar patients lacking any formal mental health training or education quickly caught on. When they approached me, suggesting I seemed more manic than depressed, I immediately dismissed them. Telling someone who is manic that she's manic is like telling a dictator that he's a dick.

Neither is going to admit it, and both are willing to torture you to prove their points.

Never having been one for denailing or waterboarding, I tortured my accusers with pity: "I don't blame you for trying to recruit me. It's human nature. Misery loves company and all that. But as bad as I feel for y'all, I'm still nothing like you," I told them. And I believed it.

In my mind, I was a burgeoning guru, a mystic full of purpose and pristine judgment. In my mind, it had been a lifetime since I'd been on suicide watch. In my mind, I was put on that ward by God Himself to guide those broken women, my future disciples, toward the land of enlightenment: the Persian Dalai Lama of Stillbrook.

In reality, where time and the Divine aren't nearly as foolish or forgiving, I was just another floundering psych patient. Perhaps I would've taken my comrades' diagnosis more seriously had a doctor shared their concerns, but I doubt it. I've always been exceptionally gifted in the delusion department, and the idea of having bipolar disorder doesn't sit well with my classically bipolar delusions of grandeur. Still, by that point, I'd been living with the brilliant highs and debilitating lows of the illness for well over a decade. It was my normal.

At best, the marriage between mania and depression is a rocky one. At worst, it's lethal. It's just a matter of where your mind is when death approaches: so delusional and ecstatic that it tricks you into believing you can leap tall buildings in a single bound, or so depressed and hopeless that it has you begging gravity to work its morbid magic. This is what the land of manic depression looks like, though the terrain and mode of transport vary considerably from victim to victim. A disproportionately large number of us seek solace in words, art and music.[*] Others among us pursue more conventional professions, with positions ranging from CEO to media mogul to world leader to drug addict to ad executive to doctor to teacher to engineer to lawyer to invalid to some amalgamation thereof. Studies show that up to half of us attempt suicide at least once in our lives, and twenty percent of us succeed.[†]

No one arrives at or departs from insanity in quite the same way. The airports are plentiful and the gates are infinite. But whatever the route, given a certain history and genetic inclination, going crazy is cake. And for me, it's simpler still, for my bipolarity is more than a chronic clinical condition. It's a corollary of birth. A wide variety and combination of variables are responsible for my condition, but genes, history, a dysfunctional gut and perpetual displacement carry by far the most consequence. Though I don't know the exact weight of each variable, I do know that my bipolar identity was born long before any mental malady.

More than any others, three historical events provoked the byzantine geography of my body, brain and being. All transpired before I was born: the 1953 CIA- and MI6-sponsored coup that overthrew the democratically elected prime minister of Iran, Mohammad Mossadegh, who presumptuously tried to nationalize oil so that Iranians might benefit from their own natural resources; the American and British imperialism that defined my

---

[*] Kay Redfield Jamison, *Touched with Fire: Manic-Depressive Illness and the Artistic Temperament* (New York: Free Press, 1993).

[†] X. Gonda, M. Pompili, G. Serafini, F. Montebovi, S. Campi, P. Dome, T. Duleba, et al., "Suicidal Behavior in Bipolar Disorder: Epidemiology, Characteristics and Major Risk Factors," *Journal of Affective Disorders* 143, nos. 1–3 (2012): 16–26. doi:10.1016/j.jad. 2012.04.041.

parents' generation as a result; and the so-called Islamic Revolution that this imperialism ignited while I was still a fetus. Were it not for these events, I would have grown up, like my parents, inside Iran. Instead, born in Chicago in the spring of 1979, I was guaranteed a dual existence from the start.

As I grew in utero, a revolution brewed, one that would ultimately end more than twenty-five hundred years of Iranian monarchy. I was less than a month old when, on April 1, 1979, the Islamic Republic of Iran was born. Given the fact that April Fool's Day (or *Sizdeh Be-dar*) originated in Iran, it's only appropriate that it would also be the day that Ayatollah Khomeini pulled the biggest joke in modern history on the Iranian people—convincing them that Iran would never become an oppressive theocracy. Thus, Iranians traded monarchy, tyranny and imperialism for theocracy, tyranny and independence. A mild improvement, but pathetic nonetheless. Independence alone cannot bring about liberty.

Despite our closeness in age, the "Islamic" Republic and I are different signs. I'm a Pisces; she's an Aries. As a water sign, I should be able to put out a fire sign, but alas, no such luck. Regardless of my myriad efforts as a writer and activist, along with those of millions of other Iranians, we* have thus far failed to put out this duplicitous fire. Yet another reason to dismiss astrology as the stinking pile of crap it truly is.

So it was that I was born beside a nascent fire that I'd spend years trying to extinguish as an adult. At the time, of course, I had no idea. Nor did I have a clue that just by being born in the

---

* I use the terms "we" and "us" throughout the text in reference to both Iranians and Americans. Which correlation applies where should be clear from the context. As I consider myself a full-time member of both demographics, I see no alternative.

United States with distinctly Persian DNA, I was destined for a bipolar identity and propensity over which I'd have no control. In short, I was both Westoxified (in the Ayatollah's words) and highly inclined to lose my mind. Whether the former facilitated the latter is anyone's guess, but if it were calculable, I suspect there'd be a statistically significant association between the two.

Exactly eight months to the day I was born, several hundred Iranian students stormed the American Embassy in Tehran. Holding over fifty American hostages for 444 days, those students determined more than the fate of future Iranian-American relations. They determined the fate of my family, not to mention that of a generation of exiles, residents and political prisoners. To say that there were only several dozen hostages is about seventy-five million people off the mark, as that event affected the future of every Iranian alive today.

The hostage takers destroyed my parents' immigration documents (along with those of countless others), prompting their expulsion from the United States. As a result, like millions of other children of the Revolution, I spent my infancy as a nomad: from Greece to France to Iran to the United States and a bunch of countries in between. My first-ever photograph, taken in the hospital when I was less than a day old, doubled as my first passport pic.

When we returned to Tehran, the political situation was shit. The ideals of the Revolution (freedom and civil rights in particular) had fallen by the wayside. People were being imprisoned and forced into exile for being Baha'i, Jewish, Leftist, Communist or just opposing the increasingly fanatic regime in any way. The government had begun cracking down on women's rights— forcing ridiculous morality laws upon the entire adult female population, laws that had nothing to do with Islam and everything to do with politics and old-school, backward-ass patriarchy. Where the Shah had forbidden women from wearing headscarves (*roo-saris*), the Ayatollah was now forcing them to do so. Watching all of this, my parents quickly concluded that there was no way they'd allow their two daughters to grow up as second-class citizens, and they began searching for a new home.

One of their friends suggested Australia as a promising place for two young Iranian doctors to raise a family. They took a shot. My dad visited first, to sit for the Australian medical boards. While there, he garnered more than his fair share of nasty looks and was kicked out of a bar—not for being too drunk, but for being too "foreign." He quickly decided he wasn't going to bring his family to what he now calls "the bottom of the world." With that, like so many other Iranian professionals of their generation, my parents set their sights higher—on a place without monarchs or Ayatollahs on its money, where God is trusted but never a valid legal argument. On America.

But their final decision to cross the Atlantic, made even more pressing thanks to the start of the Iran-Iraq war, still wasn't easy. Today, when I ask my father about choosing to leave, he doesn't hesitate:

"After Australia, for about a year I used to sit down and put the pro and con on a piece of paper. This is a fact. I put on one line America. On another I wrote Iran. Then I wrote down what was the most important to me, and really truly it was the family. It was very difficult when people that you love, you want to decide between them. Between brother, sister, mother, father and all the memories that you have. Not only that, you will also leave all your friends and all those memory behind.

"Then on other side there was you, Romana [my older sister]

and Jazbi [my mom]. I thought you would have a better future in United State. And especially being a girl, I thought that you cannot have the full advantage of your abilities in Iran. And this is the main reason. I thought like woman lib, woman liberation, the way that a woman feels. I thought that you deserve more. So, between my feeling and your future, I decided to choose your future . . . I never thought about financial part. I thought I could live in mobile home if I couldn't find a job. But at least I know that the school that you go, it is a good school and they value you as a person, not as a girl or boy."*

When I ask my mother the same question, she pauses, then provides a far briefer, more practical and less overtly feminist response: "Iraq had bomb and keep dropping them. I didn't want for us to die."

---

* While, for the most part, I don't reconstruct my parents' accent throughout the text lest it become a distraction, I do re-create most of their standard grammatical errors (dropping or adding articles, confusing gender because there is no "he" or "she" in Farsi, mixing up singular and plural, et cetera). That said, I *do* re-create some of the most prominent features of their distinctly Persian accent from time to time throughout (where doing so proves more enlightening than distracting). Some such features include a tendency to replace some *w*'s with *v*'s and *th*'s with *t*'s, as well as to put an "*eh*" in front of most words beginning with "s." I should also note that they still speak English quite well, certainly a hell of a lot better than I speak Farsi.

two

absent patterns

I can't say whether I still would've tried to kill myself had we stayed in Iran and endured the war, but I suspect it wouldn't have made a huge difference. It seems stupid to off yourself after surviving a war, but then again, people do it all the time. My guess is that had we stuck around, I'd have a healthy dose of post-traumatic stress on top of the bipolar to show for it. Who knows, I might have tried to kill myself sooner and perhaps have succeeded. I highly doubt I would ever have received an accurate diagnosis in Iran, let alone proper treatment. There isn't even an agreed-upon label for bipolar disorder in Farsi. If anything, people just steal from English or French, saying *bi-polar* or *maniaco-dépression* with a Persian accent. And that's only if they're especially well educated.

The stigma surrounding mental illness in the States is bad, but it's beyond measure in Iran. People are about as likely to discuss their psychological issues as they are to discuss their bowel movements. That's not to say Iranians have no mental health concerns. Far from it. We just prefer to sweep them under our prettiest Persian rugs, hoping the intricate patterns sufficiently obscure the truth.

When I was first admitted to Stillbrook, the intake counselor asked me if there was any history of mental illness or suicide in my extended family, most of whom still live in Iran. Even in my miserable condition, I about died laughing before producing my most honest and thorough response: "Hell if I know."

The first things people want to know when they find out you've tried to kill yourself are how and why—generally in that order. As a rule, most of them suppress the urge and refrain from asking, at least initially. Unless, that is, they're in the same sinking boat.

I met Angela only a few hours after being admitted. We were about the same age, but she looked way younger on account of her petite frame, braces, the giant purple pillow in her arms and some extra melanin courtesy of her West Indian roots. One look at her and I knew she was another suicide attempt. Her hair was a hot mess, most of her turquoise nail polish had been chipped off and her eyes had about as much life in them as a turnip. She looked more than drugged. She looked defeated.

Everyone comes into these places looking doped up on something—generally because they are, but not always. That's not to say they're all drug addicts. In fact, most of the time, they're high on something they got in the hospital—something a caring health care professional prescribed and happily provided.

I still don't know what Angela was on, if anything, but if she was on any of the fun stuff, it didn't show. After finishing my tentative diagnosis, I set out to confirm. Since I was on suicide watch at the time, my movements were limited to the three-yard radius around the nurses' station that the patients dubbed "the observation deck." Until Angela arrived, all I had to entertain me was a random assortment of items you'd expect to find in most kindergarten classrooms: crayons, puzzles, construction paper, Play-Doh, glue, even glitter. But no scissors. Never any scissors. Not even the dull safety kind.

After hours of unsuccessfully trying to engage the nurses in conversation, I was happy to see Angela. I knew she'd have to stay on the observation deck long enough to check in, and perhaps longer if they decided to put her on suicide watch too.

"Hi, I'm Melody," I said as she approached the round table where I was sitting. "What's your name?" I asked, kneading a chunk of stale blue Play-Doh.

"Angela," she said, taking a seat and setting down her pillow.

"You look like crap," I said. "Couldn't go through with it, eh? How'd you fuck up?" The standard rules of polite society and social comportment don't apply on locked psych wards. Besides, I was conducting more of a test than a genuine interrogation. If she couldn't appreciate the humor in a query like that, or at least overlook the insolence, then she wasn't worth engaging anyway.

Without a hint of hesitation or annoyance, Angela confessed: "Pills. You?"

"Slit my wrist."

"A pair of traditionalists, I guess. You been here before?" Angela asked.

"Hell, no!" I replied. "What, *you* have?"

"Yeah," she said, looking at the floor. I could tell I'd offended her, and I felt bad for it.

"I'm sorry. I didn't know," I offered, hoping she wouldn't move to an empty table.

"It's okay," she said, looking back up at me. "I've tried a few times, and I keep screwing up. I throw up the pills or someone stops by the house or something. It's not like I have this horrible life or something. It's not like my husband beats me or I have some deadly disease. I'm just sick of waking up every day. So this is your first try, then?"

"First and last," I replied.

"That's what I said. But here I am. Again." She rolled her eyes and shrugged her shoulders. "Why'd *you* do it?"

"Well, my husband beats me, and I have a deadly disease," I said. Angela laughed. "Honestly, I have no good reason. I want to believe all the 'chemical imbalance' shit, but none of the meds have worked for me. If anything, they've made things worse. It doesn't matter now, though. I know it sounds weird—I'm not even a day out, but somehow, I feel fine now. I mean, as fine as you can feel in a place like this. Whatever the case, I don't want to die anymore. Just a few hours ago, I did, I *really* did, but not now. How does that happen?"

"Scared straight, I guess," Angela replied. "Happened to me the first time."

"Not this time?"

"Not yet at least," Angela sighed. "But who knows, it could happen again. It could even work for good in your case. I hope it does. It's just never lasted for me. Obviously."

"It *has to* last for me," I said. "Suicide just can't be an option

anymore. I don't care that it's a 'permanent solution to a temporary problem.' I'm *all for* permanent solutions. But I just can't do
it. I've got a fucking family. This is so my most dumbass move to
date. So selfish. Seriously, never again."

B ut after you've tried to kill yourself once, you've proven that
your "never again" can't be trusted. You've proven that you're
capable of abandoning the strongest and most basic human instinct, that even your reflexes can't be trusted. You can't reason-
ably expect anyone to believe your claims of "never again" ever
again after that, not even you.

Still, I was desperate to believe it. More than that, I was desperate to get Matthew to believe it. We'd been married for only
four years at the time. He didn't deserve to lose his wife at twenty-
seven—and certainly not at her own hands. He would have been
by far the most fucked had I succeeded, and I would have felt by
far the most guilty for leaving him. More than anyone else, he's
the one who has tried the hardest to help me, to *fix* me. He truly
believes that every problem has a solution, that all you have to do
is stick with it long enough to discern a pattern. I can't think of
anything more absurd, but I envy his confidence.

Matthew started keeping notes roughly a month before I slit
my wrist. He's done it before and since. He never tells me about
them until I make it back to sanity, and I've never had the slightest urge to see them. Not even now. Without them, however, my
story would be more than incomplete; it would be a lie.

Ultimately, I'm grateful for his diligent notes, not just because
they represent his relentless resolve to find a solution but also

because those pages remind me that my disease is real. They remind me that it isn't just "all in my head"; it's also all in my brain. They remind me that bipolar disorder is a legitimate and lethal illness that has nearly killed me on several occasions. And they remind me that my malady doesn't belong to me: it weighs on all of those who love and depend on me.

All illnesses leave collateral damage, but mental illnesses are particularly brutal on innocent bystanders. Matthew's records are my proof: my souvenirs from hell. They force me to continue using whatever weapons I have at my disposal to keep the demons and delusions at bay, not just for me, but for all of those I'm capable of taking down with me.

Matthew finds hope and solace in data, mathematical models, logic, proofs. When I first asked him to read this book and give me his thoughts, he came back with a chart and an intricate Venn diagram with themes and chapter headings. The man can't make any major (and many minor) life decisions without creating an Excel file full of folders and formulas; he adores charts and graphs and he's always hunting for patterns.

While he has yet to find anything close to a pattern in my madness, he refuses to quit trying. Some might distinguish this refusal as a type of madness unto itself, and I've accused him of as much. But he insists that having a consistent method to his madness makes it more pathology than chemistry, more personality than anatomy. Whatever the case, it's not the type of thing that would ever land him in a mental hospital, and for that, I thank God. One crazy person per family is more than enough, and if nothing else, Matthew's testimony serves as decidedly compelling evidence to that effect.

10/19 [2005, a few weeks before my admission to Stillbrook]

Morning (10:30): "Feels like ants crawling inside me"; "building a colony." Super restless; shaking and wanting to jump out of skin. Can't sit still. Pacing. Doesn't want to go outside for a walk. Just pacing for hours at a time.

Lessor [my psychiatrist at the time] *says avoid "death" conversation.*

Afternoon (1pm): Goes to gym after some coaxing. Used elliptical for ten minutes while confessing problems to Jesus [our building's super] *in Spanish. More of the same. Tightness, tense, very restless. Ant colony.*

Ask Lessor why he thinks it would help to admit her. Won't take benzos—rarely. Long-term plan?

→DR. LESSOR APPTMT:

She's behind on everything, but insists she has to finish the semester.

I can't see how she can. Won't go to class. Fine for law school [I rarely went before]; *not ok for MPH* [I was in a joint degree program, studying concurrently for a J.D. and a Master's in Public Health]. *She has homework there.*

Super anxious about school, but can't sit still to do work.
Talk to her profs. Disability services.

→Lessor Dx: Major depression; really bad; Recurrent type;
"3 options." She refuses all of them.

–Luxury treatment: $30,000/month

–Hospital treatment: $1,500-$2,000 [per day]. 3 days-
3 weeks. Overnight stays

–Middle ground: day treatment.

→Suggests Cymbalta . . . thinking about it

→Insurance: 70-80%? Call UHC [United Healthcare],
e-mail list of in/out of network to Lessor.

Evening (7-2): a lot worse; always worse at night; lots of
crying, shaking and pacing. Eventually cries herself to
sleep. Call Lessor, get another appointment alone.

The notes go on like this for over a month—meticulously documenting times, moods, behaviors and statements for nearly every day until my hospitalization. Only three days are unaccounted for. Matthew took over fifty pages of handwritten notes during that month, the only observable pattern being his consistent, visible frustration on the margins of nearly every page: "NO PATTERN."

three

white phosphorus

I've fantasized about suicide off and on since I was fourteen, but the floor of Dr. Lessor's waiting room was the closest I've ever come to execution. Such was not the plan.

My plan was a hell of a lot more original, not to mention way cleaner. Go far away: somewhere I can be sure no one I love would ever have to pass or revisit. Leave a note full of love and apologies, identifying my exact location to avoid a womanhunt. Do it outside, so no one would have to clean up the mess. No drugs—best to be conscious and in control at a time like that. Take a sharp chef's knife to a femoral artery (not a blunt Swiss Army knockoff to a radial one); be quick about it, and by all means, *don't do it in a psychiatrist's waiting room.*

Beyond that, the details vary, but overall, my suicidal fantasies have always run along these lines. Attempting suicide is like getting married. If you do it right, you only do it once, and to do it right, it's best to construct a solid plan and follow through. It's not enough to just sign a contract, you've also got to live up to the terms, and that's where I fell pathetically short.

So there I sat, still in Atlanta, a few miles away from home, across the street from the fucking CDC, directly upstairs from Dr. Lessor's office, surrounded by strangers, slicing my wrist with a dismally dull pocketknife. No note, no solitude, no fresh air, no chef's knife—no elegance or redemption. Only disgrace. After my abhorrent deviation from the ideal, all bets were off.

I was over an hour early for my appointment and kept my back to the receptionist as I waited. Nevertheless, my name was called quickly after the blood started dripping. I'm pretty sure another patient snitched. I got up and made my way to Dr. Lessor's office as if this were no different from any other appointment, as if I weren't leaving a faint trail of blood behind me along the way. But once I walked in and got a good look at my wrist as I shut the door behind me, I was immediately struck by the fact that he couldn't just let me go. There would have to be consequences. The liability alone was enough to call for an immediate response.

I'd been seeing Dr. Lessor for several months by that point, and he was well aware of my depression. That's why I first came to him, and that's why he first started prescribing me Zoloft. A couple weeks before my embarrassing theatrics in his waiting room, after increasing my dosage and realizing it still wasn't working, he'd latched onto a newer, supposedly smarter, drug. At that point, I would have tried battery acid had he suggested it might help. Enter Cymbalta.

Perhaps you've seen the ads: "Depression Hurts. Cymbalta can help." Apparently, psychiatrists are just as vulnerable to the lure of slick advertising as the rest of us. The drug had only been on the market for a year when Dr. Lessor first prescribed it to me, and it already boasted a black-box suicide warning. Two years after my misadventures with said wonder drug, the FDA sent Eli Lilly a warning letter maintaining that some of the company's promotional "claims and presentations [were] false or misleading."*

The most common danger in treating bipolar patients with antidepressants alone, and the reason that doing so can easily constitute medical malpractice, is the fact that antidepressants have been shown to turn depressed bipolar patients into manic ones at lightning speeds. In my case, I didn't go fully manic, but I did start a dangerous climb, growing increasingly impulsive after a couple weeks on the new drug.

Dr. Lessor—one of many psychiatrists who failed to catch my bipolar disorder, confusing it with unipolar depression—seemed convinced that Cymbalta was the solution to all my ills. Desperate to believe him, I tried my best. As both an added cause and consequence of my depression, my gastrointestinal pain (the result of a major abdominal surgery some years earlier) had grown increasingly irritating, and Dr. Lessor gave me a lot of false hope that Cymbalta would help with both my physical and mental anguish. Like killing two obnoxious vultures with one neatly encapsulated, chemical stone. It sounded brilliant, but combined with my pre-existing wiring and chemistry, it proved anything but.

Turns out, for me, depression hurts, but Cymbalta hurts worse. When I first came to Dr. Lessor, my chief complaint wasn't just "depression." It was a new and overwhelming sense that I harbored a real, albeit invisible, demon inside my body, squishing

---

* From a 2007 FDA Warning Letter. The complete letter is available on the FDA's website at www.fda.gov/downloads/Drugs/GuidanceComplianceRegulatoryInformation/ EnforcementActivitiesbyFDA/WarningLettersandNoticeofViolationLettersto PharmaceuticalCompanies/ucm054170.pdf.

and twisting my heart, guts and throat as though it were juicing an orange. My aim was simple: stop the squishing and avoid becoming a dried-up rind of a human being. But Cymbalta didn't help. Instead of ending or even lessening the torture, it turned me into a willing participant, an unwitting masochist, inviting a new companion along for the ride: unqualified motivation. Not to leap out of bed to face the day or write or read or do anything remotely productive. But to finally act upon my fantasies.

By far the most frustrating feature of bipolar disorder for me is the fact that my "poles" often fail to stay put, lacking even the basic courtesy to remain in their respective manic or depressive compartments. Even with the best medical treatment, they're painfully unpredictable. I can never tell when a color on one end of the spectrum will begin to bleed into one on the other, when the aims of my classically "goal-directed" manic propensities will direct themselves toward the morbid obsessions of my depressive vulnerabilities. And therein lies my most terrifying neurological deficit: a devil that I know exists, one that I've met before and never wish to meet again; one for which my own mind is unavoidably responsible, and one with the worst timing imaginable.

At twenty-six, I was less than six months away from completing an extensive formal education that had cost my parents well over two hundred thousand dollars. In addition to finishing up my last year as a law and public health graduate student, I was also making the last edits on my first book, for which I had finally procured a respectable publisher. But in order to collect my degrees and see my book in print, I would have to battle my own mutinous mind.

Things grew continually worse during the autumn before I was admitted to Stillbrook. Despite seeing Dr. Lessor at least once a week, despite taking my medications religiously and despite trying to will myself out of it, I was still caught up in an excruciating cycle of depression. I was still spending every waking moment wishing I were asleep or dead, still avoiding people, still skipping classes and still making up excuses for missing events where my presence actually mattered. Anyone paying attention would have concluded that I was cursed on account of all my lies. Instead of just telling people I was sick, I made up all of these more "acceptable" excuses: flat tire, stuck in an elevator, imaginary funerals for imaginary friends, someone *else* is in crisis, someone *else* is sick, someone *else* needs me. Anything but the truth. Eventually though, I lost the will and energy to come up with new pretexts, and I gave up. I made it a point to either forget or lie about forgetting any deadlines, meetings or appointments.

I wasn't sad. I was suffocating. In my case, depression can be mildly intoxicating at first, luring me toward an old frenemy— always loyal despite its vicious knack for distortion. It starts off like gasoline, paint or permanent marker. I know the fumes aren't exactly good for me, but I still enjoy them on the rare occasions when they come around. Such is Level 1: slightly toxic, but relatively innocuous in moderation.

Left unchecked, however, this mild, seductive melancholy can quickly transform. Level 2 is more like tear gas. It'll irritate your eyes, nose and throat; it'll hurt like hell; it'll make you cry; it'll make it hard to breathe, and it might even blind you temporarily. Still, it's generally not going to kill you.

Level 3, on the other hand, isn't nearly as forgiving. Think white phosphorus. Blisters, burns, smoke inhalation, death. This isn't just some clinical disorder. It's chemical warfare. And it's what I was fighting that fall—an insidious weapon of mass destruction that gets under your skin and into your lungs.

(Saddam Hussein used it on, among others, Iranians during the Iran-Iraq war. It's something Iranians have yet to forget, and I doubt we ever will. I don't know how old I was when I first saw pictures of people burned beyond recognition by the stuff, but it wasn't old enough. I've had periodic white phosphorus nightmares ever since. Sometimes I get away before the burns turn to blisters and I start gasping for air. Sometimes I don't.)

I've visited Level 3 only a few times. I pray never to return, but that's unlikely. The more you travel there, the more you clear the path, making it ever easier to circle back.

After a week on Cymbalta, I felt like I was waking from my nightmare (granted oblivious to the more treacherous one ahead). I started making appointments and keeping them. I got out of bed before noon, took showers, even showed up to class. I morphed into this mobile, *functional* depressive—hands down, the most dangerous kind. I wasn't just motivated to renew my daily routines. I was motivated to act on the emptiness I found in those routines. And I wasn't just *contemplating* suicide, either. I was actively planning for it. I had a goal, a purpose, and until I got there, I was determined to do whatever I wanted, consequences be damned. I began donating a lot more money than we could afford to our standard monthly *zakat* charities, eating a lot of cake and M&M's and openly telling classmates whom I barely knew how best to go about improving their lives. I even advised a handful of kids to drop out of law school because I, in my infinite wisdom, was certain they'd make incompetent, not to mention miserable, lawyers. I felt zero need or desire to censor or protect myself.

By then, I was neither manic nor depressed. I was in the midst of a so-called mixed state, one in which depression and mania exist simultaneously—like a parasite within a parasite. This rocky marriage between ostensibly incongruous symptoms (the restlessness and recklessness of mania and the despair and dysphoria of depression) is just as unbearable as it is counterintuitive.

I hung in this unsteady balance—consumed by a fog of liberating apathy, as real and all-consuming as the unremitting wind of desolation that had driven it into my life and mind in the first place. Floating on cloud nine under the giant shadow of an ever-expanding tornado, I finally felt free to surrender, free to strategize specifics for my far-away femoral plan. I had the perfect Santoku knife, and I'd narrowed down "far away" to a small town in the north Georgia mountains, hours away from home. Hicksville. Nowhere anyone I knew would ever want to go.

The plan was as reliable and comforting as it was demented. But as with most matters involving life and death, things didn't go according to plan. My new sense of purpose and motivation had given birth to a manic impulsivity, one that ultimately crashed head-on into my selfish and indifferent desperation, shattering all my fantasies of a clean, controlled and speedy departure.

M elody, you have to be admitted. We have to call Matthew." I hadn't seen that look on Dr. Lessor's face before. It wasn't concern. It was fear. He'd recommended hospitalization at prior sessions, and I'd laughed him off. I imagine he wished he'd been a little more insistent. Still, it wouldn't have mattered. I'd never have agreed, and he had no legitimate legal grounds for committing me involuntarily. I wasn't an apparent threat to myself or anyone else up until that point, as I never made any mention of my plan.

When it comes to getting what I want, what I think is fair, for me or for anyone else, I can be insanely persuasive. It's partly why I went to law school in the first place, why I'm sure Dr. Lessor didn't want to engage me in an argument, and why he had to have known I'd pitch a fit if he tried to report any of this to the administration. I was receiving his services as part of my university health care package, so the standard protocol would be to keep me at Emory and immediately report the incident to the university.

Dr. Lessor may have been a bad psychiatrist, but he wasn't a bad person. He made it a point to ensure that none of the details made it into my record by tossing the standard protocol and calling Matthew instead of an ambulance. Dr. Lessor let Matthew transport me: First, to the Emory psych ward, where I stayed for a couple hours before being "stabilized." Then, straight to Stillbrook. His only instructions: "No pit stops."

Of course, we stopped. Matthew didn't want to, but again, crazy or not, I'm highly convincing. Plus, my requests were neither absurd nor unreasonable. So he ultimately gave in, driving me home to pack a small bag of necessities, half of which were confiscated as "contraband" within a few hours of checking in.

Matthew kept quiet for the first half of the ride. Though at the time I construed his silence as anger, he tells me now that it was trepidation: "I didn't know what to say, and I didn't want to say the wrong thing. I was afraid of what Stillbrook would be like; maybe you would hate it and they couldn't help you. I felt like I was abandoning you, but I didn't know what else to do. I was afraid you'd try again, and I didn't know how to stop you."

Matthew is the least confrontational person I know. When presented with the option of fight or flight, his hypothalamus will trigger flight at least ninety percent of the time. In the fifteen years I've known him, I've heard him raise his voice once: the first and last time I tried the silent treatment on him. But now I was on the other side. He was giving *me* the silent treatment, and I didn't like it.

"Go ahead," I said eventually. "Say what you want. You're more than entitled."

"I don't know. I mean, what were you thinking? I want to be understanding, but I'll kill you if you try this shit again."

"With any luck, I'll beat you to it," I replied, hoping for a laugh that never came.

"How original. Seriously, what were you *thinking?*"

"I wasn't. I'll never do it again. Can we just not make a big deal out of it? I'll go to this Killbrook place, and I'll get better. Then we can forget any of this ever happened."

"Stillbrook."

"Whatever. Point being, I'll get better. Something will work. Oh shit!"

"What is it?" Matthew asked. "Did you forget something?"

"No. But what am I going to do about school? I have to finish. How long do you think they'll keep me? And what are we going to *tell* people? Just say I went on vacation or something. We can't tell anyone." Panic set in.

"Don't worry about it. I'll deal with it. You just focus on not killing yourself. You can't just leave me like that. I won't *let* you."

Matthew's voice cracked (his version of sobbing hysterically), and I cried for the first time in weeks. The deeper I fall into Level 3, the harder it becomes to cry—activating my tear ducts just takes too much energy. So crying could have been a good sign, an indication that perhaps my demon was loosening his grip. Still, I had neither the time nor presence of mind to notice. I was too busy focusing on Matthew.

I'd done more than let him down. I'd wounded him. Seeing how much made me think he truly might be better off without me. Maybe I *wasn't* being selfish. Maybe I was just protecting the ones I loved. White phosphorus is a gas after all. It's not like a pill that affects only the person who swallows it. It takes down everyone in the vicinity.

"I'm sorry," I offered between sobs. "I didn't mean to hurt you. I wasn't thinking. Just please don't tell anyone. I mean, you can tell my parents, I guess, but just not everything. I don't know. This is so fucking embarrassing! I feel like such a failure. No one's going to believe I just up and took a vacation right before exams. We've got to come up with something better. It's just really important that none of the Iranians find out." I opened the glove compartment and pulled out a stack of napkins to soak up my snot.

"Wait, so that means don't call Auntie Yasi and send her your medical records?" Matthew asked. I laughed. "Seriously, don't worry. Just get better. I'll deal with the rest."

My concern for secrecy may seem silly to some, but in my defense, gossip in the Iranian community spreads like kudzu on crack. There's no stopping it, and stories mutate with each successive busybody. While I was in high school, one of the Iranian moms caught one of us kids smoking a cigarette outside a restaurant. By the next day, rumor had it he was a hard-core drug addict, snorting and shooting up whatever he could get his hands on.

So there was no way I was about to insert the details of my psychiatric condition into the Persian gossip wheel. Who knows, by the time news made it from Atlanta to Tehran, the story might easily have been that I was locked in a back ward somewhere, playing with my own feces.

As we drove farther out into the boondocks, reality began to set in.

"I don't belong in a loony bin," I said. "If it's anything like the movies, it'll be useless. It'll just be a bunch of crazy people. *Really* crazy people. How am I supposed to get better surrounded by a bunch of lunatics? I'm not nuts. I'm just depressed. How is this going to make me *not* want to kill myself? Crazy people don't make sense. I'm totally making sense."

"Says the woman who just slit her wrist in her shrink's waiting room."

"I get it. I know I was wrong. I know you must be angry. I mean, I would be pissed if you pulled something like this on me. But I really think I can get better at home."

"If you could, you already would have. And I'm not angry. Anyway, it might even be fun hanging out with all those other crazy people. You can take notes. Write something about them."

"*Other* crazy people? So now I'm one of them? Whatever. I don't know, maybe you're right. I'm sure this place isn't that bad. Lessor said it was better than Emory."

"He said it was one of the *best*, and look, it's surrounded by all these woods. It's actually sort of pretty. Kind of Walden-esque," Matthew said as we pulled in.

"Yeah, more like Sing Sing."

T he first sign I noticed, driving into the "Stillbrook Institute,"
scared the hell out of me:

> **CAMPUS UNDER**
>
> **24-HOUR**
>
> **SURVEILLANCE**

"Oh, that's nice," I said. "It's a *campus*. The *institute* has a *campus*. Fanciness. You think they teach interpretive dance?"

Matthew laughed.

"I'm sure they do," I continued, desperate for distraction. "And what the fuck constitutes twenty-four-hour surveillance anyway? Cameras? Armed guards? Good thing I'm not schizophrenic because that sign is a fucking recipe for paranoia. Oh, and look over there—'Woodridge Assisted Living.' There's a nursing home right in the middle of the *campus*. It's a fucking *retirement* community. Where are you sending me?" I asked, laughing to hide terror.

Stillbrook wasn't a campus by any stretch of the imagination. It was a bona fide compound: a dream come true for any aspiring cult leader. All the units were long, sprawling, single-story gray wooden structures—perfect for collecting lost souls and senior citizens to brainwash.

four

the quiet room

If only the ATF had arrived before us, they might have had the good sense to burn the place down. But this not being Waco or Ruby Ridge, they didn't show. You can never count on federal agencies to be there when you need them, let alone to pick the right targets. They always have the most fucked-up priorities—oil over human life, corporations over citizens, countless portraits and busts of old, dead white men over bona fide art, wannabe "institutes" over mental patients. No, you can't count on them any more than you can count on a pair of drugstore pantyhose.

Once we got out of the car, I was overcome by a sudden instinct to run, but there was nowhere to go. We were surrounded on all sides by woods and "campus facilities." So, I resisted the impulse and followed Matthew. We were immediately greeted by a statue of ELLIE the Elephant and the gilded dedication placard planted in the grass in front of her like a gravestone:

Dedicated in 2001, the devoted staff of
Stillbrook Institute proudly named this elephant
"ELLIE"—
which stands for Every Lesson Learned Is Essential.
For each of us, every lesson learned has made us who
we are today. There is something to be
learned from every life experience—
positive or negative.
Ellie's presence reminds us of this each day.

Ignoring ELLIE, Matthew pulled me toward the door. I pulled back.

"You *have* to read this. You're totally going to throw up. Seriously, ELLIE? They couldn't come up with a better acronym?" I was actually talking *to* the elephant. Matthew was laughing. I was laughing. For a brief moment, things were okay.

Walking in, we were immediately met by yet another sign, instructing us to register at the lobby and declaring a prohibition on alcohol, weapons, solicitors and pets. We checked in at the front desk and were quickly led to a small nondescript room for an "assessment." As we waited for the intake counselor, I stared at the ground, unable to look Matthew in the eye. My wrist was bandaged; my eyes were red from crying, and the rest of me didn't look much better. A sloppy collection of ancient, mismatched sweats: an oversized gray Wesleyan sweatshirt over an Emory Law

T-shirt and red Ohio State sweatpants, all topped off with a faded Cleveland Indians baseball cap, the straps in the back tightly secured with black electrical tape. It killed me that Matthew had to see me like this.

The assessment went horribly. Initially, I tried to make as many jokes as possible in response to the counselor's questions, but he refused to let me get away with it.

"I realize that humor is a coping mechanism for you. It can be helpful sometimes, but it can also be distracting and destructive. You need to answer these questions honestly. Otherwise, we'll be here forever." The counselor looked exhausted. It was late in the afternoon, and I figured he just wanted to get home for dinner. My selfishness lifted momentarily, and I told him the truth: that I wanted to die and that to my great chagrin, I had made a go of it.

At the end of the assessment, the counselor asked if I minded if he spoke with Matthew alone, outside of the room for a minute. I said it was fine. Once they left, I scoured the room for something sharp. But there was only furniture. An empty desk, some chairs, an end table and me. Then I took a sip of my Diet Coke and saw a glimmer of hope in the aluminum. I started messing with the top and eventually managed to break off the sharp circular flap that pops into the can when you open it. Forgetting all of my apologies and promises, I tried again, digging the aluminum into my wrist, drawing just enough blood to elicit hope. Then Matthew and the counselor returned. Neither one of them noticed, as I pulled the sleeves of my sweatshirt down to hide my handiwork. Guilt set in after one look at Matthew, and I dropped the tab into the empty can. It wasn't working anyway.

The most immediate and practical aim of the assessment was to determine where I would be placed. The staff referred to the different units as "cottages." Yes, cottages. Each one had its own unique specialty and/or patient cohort. There was a cottage for addicts, one for adolescents, one for women, one for adults of both sexes, another for "older adults," et cetera.

I wasn't allowed to pick my cottage. That was up to the intake counselor. Still, he asked me where I wanted to go, and I imagine he would have respected my preference had I not expressed such supreme indifference.

In the end, I was unceremoniously and quite arbitrarily assigned to Cottage E: the women's unit. The other patients quickly informed me how lucky I was to be there. Cottage E was apparently the cushiest of the lot. Rumor had it that the staff at Cottage C, the coed adult unit, had a much stronger penchant for restraints, injections and isolation. Unsurprisingly, rumor also had it that the patients in Cottage C had a much stronger penchant for screaming. As a result, Cottage C was both legend and threat for those of us on the women's unit. The patients who'd been there confirmed the legend, and our caregivers threatened transfers to keep us in line.

Under the circumstances and given the alternatives, I was in fact fortunate to be where I was. The first night, I slept on a mattress in the hall, in front of the nurses' station. But after meeting with the psychiatrist the next day, he took me off suicide watch and assigned me to an actual room. I lucked out again and got Angela as a roommate.

I remember almost nothing about that psychiatrist. Not his name, his face, his voice, ninety-nine percent of his words. In fact, I can only distinctly recall our first session—and just a few seconds of it at that.

"So, when did you start cutting?" he asked.

"Um, never," I responded, offended. "I wasn't *cutting* myself. I was trying to *kill* myself."

"So, you've never cut before this?" he asked.

"I wasn't *cutting*! So no, never before. Never at all. I'm too vain for that. I would never."

After that first one-on-one session with Dr. Forgettable, I immediately asked one of the nurses if I could call Matthew.

"Just remember," she replied, "ten minutes. That's all you get."

Our only lifeline to the outside world was a drab beige rotary phone hanging on a wall in the middle of the main corridor. The cord was so short you had to stand up to use it. We couldn't take or make calls when we were in group or eating, or after nine p.m., or if someone else was using the phone. Still, Matthew would call every day, two or three times a day, and ask for me—or rather, for Number 5899008. Any chance to use the phone was a rare blessing, so once I got permission, I bolted to the hall.

"Thank God you picked up. Get me *out* of here! My psychiatrist is a moron. Plus, the food sucks. They put pig on fucking everything. And there's nothing but crazy people here."

"Well, you *sound* pretty good," Matthew said. "I'll be there to see you soon if that's any consolation."

"I know, but what's with these damn visiting hours? I want to see you *now*. Normal hospitals don't enforce visiting hours."

"Is it really that bad?"

"No, not really," I lied. I wanted to tell him just how bad it was, to spend my whole ten minutes bitching, but I wanted him to forgive me more. "I'm so sorry. I really don't know what the hell I was thinking. I promise I won't do it again. Honestly, I feel a lot better already. When are you coming?"

"Your parents fly in from Dayton tomorrow morning. We'll all be there at three thirty."

"Oh shit. What did you tell them? Were they okay?"

"I didn't make a big deal about it. I told them the truth. They're fine."

"Are they mad?" I asked. "They must be mad."

"Yes, they're pissed. They're going to seriously fuck you up when they get there. Jesus, Melody, no one's *mad*. We just want you to get better."

"I will. I think I already have. The whole thing was like a wake-up call, and I'm waking up."

"I know it'll take time, but you do sound a lot better."

"I am. I so am," I said, truly believing it for the first time since being admitted. "And I don't think it'll take that long, either. It's happening. Seriously, so many of these chicks have been through so much shit. You have no idea. I know it sounds bad, but seeing how fucked up they are makes me realize how good I have it. It's like I had a bucket of ice water thrown on me or something. I'm awake. I'm cool."

The phrase "visiting hours" was a lie. In fact, we had only a visiting hour and a half. Every Sunday and Monday, and twice on Saturdays, the doors of Cottage E swung open just long enough to remind us we were trapped. Matthew and my parents never missed a visit.

By the time our first family visit came around, I'd already

been at Stillbrook for three days, and the switch had been turned. No longer suicidally depressed, I was now (unbeknownst to me) happily under the spell of mild mania. All I cared about at the time was that I felt better and was able to convince my family of it.

Before that first meeting, I made it a point to dress up, put on makeup (which I was permitted to "check out" from my collection of contraband behind the nurses' desk for fifteen minutes), and put up my hair. When the gates of heaven opened at exactly 3:30 p.m., I was standing in front of my family, looking my best and lunging toward them like a lost puppy.

They were all surprised and relieved to find me in such high spirits. My parents immediately concluded that it was the drugs that brought on my momentary brush with madness. I hadn't told either of them about switching to Cymbalta before because I didn't want to worry them. But when I told them about it at Stillbrook, they took it as my reprieve. They were thrilled to hear that there was some chemical compound we could blame, and quickly agreed that going off of it would fix everything. After some pleasantries and my sincere reassurances that things were looking up, my mom asked to see my wrist. I showed her.

"Gooooood! Der von't be eh-scar," she said after grabbing my hand for a closer look. My mom doesn't like scars or wrinkles or blemishes of any kind. She is gorgeous and pale, the latter being a decided advantage in terms of typical Persian standards of beauty. Still, like many affluent Persian women, my mother hasn't settled for her God-given beauty. She has enhanced it via the miracles of modern medicine, and in doing so, she has defied aging, or at least the look of it.

Apart from my darker skin (inherited from Ahmad) and my

less pointy, European-looking nose (inherited from Jazbi 1.0), people say I look like my mom—some of our friends even call me Jazbi *koochooloo* (little Jazbi), which I've always taken as a compliment. All this focus on the outside may sound excessive to some because it is. Still, for us it's the norm.

As much as it sucks and as much as I hate to admit it, looks matter in our community. And lucky for my parents, even without the nose jobs they offered me and Romana as "gifts" throughout the years, we've both managed to live up to most modern standards of physical beauty—though in my case, I've collected quite a few scars along the way. Most visibly, a giant one across my stomach, a smaller one across my left hand and a tiny one across my forehead. The latter wound, the faintest, was the result of converting an ironing board into a fort when I was a kid. I expect it's entirely possible that the iron burned deeper into my head than we thought. Today, I steam my clothes, and when I build forts, I use only pillows, sheets and couch cushions.

O h, and you did it deh right vay," my mom continued, meaning I had cut vertically instead of horizontally.

"You taught me well." I beamed. There are some advantages to having a pathologist for a mom—not the least of which being the extra anatomy lessons while watching her do autopsies and brain cuttings on Take Your Daughter to Work Day.

"Of course," I continued. "Cut across, you clot. Cut up and down, you bleed. Everyone knows that."

"Not every-vone. Eh-so many people do it wrong vay. But it's good. Don't tell any-vone here."

"Jazbi, e-stop!" Ahmad scolded her, laughing. (Romana and I

have always called my father by his first name. None of us remembers how or why this started.)

As an ob/gyn, Ahmad has always preferred to discuss babies and life over corpses and death, so it made sense that the source of this conversation, not to mention the conversation itself, made him uncomfortable. I, for one, can think of nothing grosser than childbirth and nothing more fascinating than autopsies.

Whatever the disparities in their chosen professions, however, my parents share a radical worldview in common, one characterized first and foremost by delirious optimism. They're the kind of people who leave behind everything they know and love, traveling thousands of miles away in the hope of creating a better life for themselves, or at least for their children. They left Iran with two kids and a few thousand dollars to settle smack-dab in the American heartland. Today, they're happily retired, living atop a San Diego high-rise, traveling as they please—hopping between Romana in Denver, me in North Carolina, the family in Iran, and their friends everywhere else. They've done more than achieve the American dream for the next generation. They've achieved it for their own—with accents and decidedly more foreign-sounding names to deal with. So not only do they *believe* in rapid turn-arounds, they *expect* them. Add to that the fact that my parents had no idea what the past few months had been like for me, and they were more than happy to chalk up my regrettable whereabouts to an unfortunate drug reaction.

The whole time I was at Stillbrook, my parents brought flowers in glass vases, knowing full well that I wasn't allowed to have them in my room. Then, they'd praise me for being kind enough to "give" the flowers to staff, who placed them on the counter in front of the nurses' station. They stopped bringing food once I told them the nurses wouldn't let me eat it, but they always brought flowers.

I wanted Matthew, Ahmad, Jazbi and their yellow roses to stay forever. I couldn't have asked for a more supportive or entertaining crew, and I've never known an hour and a half to go by so fast. Before they left that first day, Matthew pulled me aside and whispered in my ear: "I put some Klonopin in your deodorant stick. You know, in case you get anxious or something. Just pull out the deodorant part, and it's under that."

"Ha!" I blurted, laughing. "Are you kidding? You're hilarious. You know they have drugs here, right?"

"Shut up," he whispered, annoyed. "I thought in case you couldn't sleep or got really nervous and couldn't stop pacing or something. You know. Anyway, it's there if you need it."

"No worries, they love doling that shit out here. They offer me Ambien every night and Valium every time I so much as start shaking my foot. It's nuts. I can't *believe* you!"

"Like I said, just in case."

Right after they left, I ran to my room and grabbed the deodorant. A bunch of the girls and a couple nurses were sitting in the "community room" watching television. When I got there, I hopped in front of them, blocking the screen and taking the stage, confident that my story would beat whatever painfully G-rated flick they had running. I held up my blue bar of Secret and went for the kill.

"Okay, you *have* to hear this. You're going to *die*! It's so sweet and hilarious. So, Matthew—my husband—just told me that he was worried that you guys"—I looked at one of the nurses—"didn't have enough stock or wouldn't treat me if I had a panic attack or something, so he filled my deodorant stick with pills. Look!" I pulled off the top of the deodorant and lo and behold there was a stockpile of Klonopin underneath.

All I can say in my defense here is that sometimes really smart people seriously lack common sense and sometimes even mild mania can make you supremely (if only temporarily) stupid. I thought the story was too funny not to share, so like an idiot, I did, not thinking that the nurses would be pissed or even find anything remotely wrong with this scenario. I clearly wasn't a drug addict. A drug addict would have just been grateful and kept mum. I, on the other hand, readily gave up all the pills, dumping them into one of the nurses' hands before she could even ask.

"Melody!" Nurse Judy exclaimed. "To the quiet room. Now!"

The "quiet room" wasn't a yoga studio or a prayer hall. No. It was a cold, sterile box, code for solitary confinement.

"I thought it was funny," I replied. "It's not like I'm a drug addict. You offer me these same pills all the time, and I always say no. He just didn't know what it was like here."

"He's an enabler," the other nurse insisted. "Come with us." She grabbed my arm. I jerked it back.

"Fine, I'm coming," I submitted.

They had no intention of using the "quiet room" for its primary purpose. Instead of throwing me into isolation—which, looking back, might have been preferable—they sat in there with me, lecturing me for at least a half hour, telling me that this would definitely keep me from earning further privileges and demanding that I submit to a full-body search.

"We don't have to touch you. You just have to stand in front of us and remove every article of clothing and hand it to us. You don't have to take off your underwear. You can just shake it at the bottom so we can be sure there's nothing in there."

"What, no full-on cavity search? Where's the fun in that?" I asked. Yet another dumbass move on my part, but one that thankfully wasn't used against me.

"Don't worry, from now on, we'll be closely monitoring your visits. You'll have to sit directly in front of the nurses' station, just like suicide watch, and we'll be pulling you in here early next time. You've just lost ten minutes off your visits. We have to search you following every visit now. Immediately."

"I get it. I'm sorry." I removed my sweater. "I didn't mean anything by it. I gave you the pills. I didn't even *want* them." Tank top. "I don't mind the strip searches, just please don't pull me out early." Shoes. "There's always fifteen minutes between group and visiting hours anyway." Socks. "We can just do it then." Pants.

"Melody, this is *not* a negotiation," Nurse Judy snapped.

I wanted to tell her she was a dense, judgmental cunt. I wanted to tell her that she didn't know me *or* Matthew. I wanted to tell her to go fuck herself. But there's something about standing before a hostile stranger in your underwear (in my case, a pink leopard-print bra and blue cotton panties with Cartman on the front, "Respect my Authority" emblazoned across the butt, and the elastic shot to hell) that makes it hard to construct coherent sentences, even for me.

As I undid the clasp at the back of my bra, I noticed one of the nurses avert her eyes. She told me I could turn around and hand her the bra with my back to them. As her pale, pockmarked cheeks morphed into bruised persimmons, I immediately realized that she was far more embarrassed than I—at which point, I exchanged whatever modesty I had left for delightful derision. I didn't turn around. Instead, I took a step toward the panel of nurses, making sure they got a full-frontal view. From that point forward, my strip searches were quick and painless, apart from having to leave my family ten minutes early.

I ultimately made a game of it, trying to see how quickly I could get my clothes off, often starting before we even got into the room. I never shook my underwear. I always took it off, flung it around my index finger, did a little dance and offered it to them. They never accepted. Eventually, it got harder to embarrass them. Still, I was always the least uncomfortable person in the quiet room.

five

treading water

By far the toughest part of living on a psych ward is the utter lack of freedom. Before Stillbrook, I had no idea how free I was. Growing up, I was allowed to do pretty much whatever I wanted as long as I got A's, which I nearly always did. I was used to winning liberties with my smarts, and I naïvely expected it would always be that way. I was wrong. No matter how smart you are, freedom is never guaranteed.

Still, I'm an instinctive and intractable activist—founding my high school Amnesty International chapter and frequenting protests and demonstrations since I was fourteen; making a living writing and speaking out against all kinds of injustices, from racism to sexism to Islamophobia to homophobia; and more recently, fighting the stigma associated with mental illness by "coming out" publicly while supporting greater research, improved facilities and increased mental health funding on all fronts.

Ever since I was a kid, petitioning the ice-cream man to add our neighborhood to his regular route (I won) and sending letters to ruthless dictators around the world, asking them to respect the basic human rights of their citizens (I lost), I've been dead set on fighting for what I believe is fair, even if I know I'm destined for defeat. Inspired by great lawyers before me (from Gandhi to Mandela to Atticus Finch), I entered law school as a crazy idealist, determined to become the best human rights activist I could be. I saw (and continue to see) the law as an invaluable weapon against injustice, so I devoted myself wholeheartedly to learning it.

Honoring that devotion, I set about studying all the edicts of the Stillbrook Institute. I received a stack of papers when I was first admitted, and shortly after the Secret fiasco, I pulled them all out. Scouring every page, I quickly found what was akin to the Cottage E Constitution.

Some of the "Women's Unit Policies" made sense, some didn't, and others were downright absurd. Using several highlighters, I color-coded the three-and-a-half-page list of regulations as though it were a legal case summary. All the while, Angela looked on, insisting my new undertaking was an exercise in futility ("Maybe you'd rather take up knitting like all the other crazy people here?"). I knew she was right (about the futility, not the knitting), but I didn't care. I sat for at least an hour, glued to my bed, going nuts with the highlighters.

Green for sensible: "Be respectful of our facility, your fellow peers, and staff members"; "Stay in group and use group time efficiently"; "No smoking, phone calls, or individual therapy time during group time"; "Refrain from disturbing any religious paraphernalia on the unit"; "Attend to your personal hygiene while in treatment"; "Do not leave your cigarettes on the unit unattended"; and "Dispose of butts in the proper receptacles."

Blue for understandable: no "low-cut shirts, low-hanging

pants, or high-cut skirts or shorts" and "no clothing . . . that promotes drug or alcohol use"; "No visitors in patient rooms"; "Never give a cigarette to an adolescent." Then there was the sole blue rule I felt a constant need to disregard, as it grew into a vital part of my recovery and escape plan: "Be careful not to focus on others' treatment."

Pink for ridiculous: "Do not touch one another" and "Practice giving 'verbal' hugs"; "No gum chewing on the unit"; "Refrain from profanity" and "Practice healthy ways to express anger and frustration"; "No outside food of any kind"; "Cell phones are prohibited on the unit (this includes visitors)." By the end of my highlighting session, nearly two-thirds of my copy of the Cottage E Constitution was pink.

Given my frequent disregard for many of the blue rules and my concerted efforts to violate the pink ones, I became notorious for "triggering." That is, doing or saying anything that might induce discomfort, pain or anxiety in the other patients. The thing is, though, it was almost always staff members accusing me of triggering, not the other patients, who seemed totally fine with my obscenities, unsolicited advice and tactile hugs. Then again, as the Constitution so clearly pointed out, many patients have "difficulty with assertiveness and boundary setting."

While the solutions to this assessment (verbal hugs and the like) were clearly in the pink, the rest was fact. Given I've never had the slightest difficulty with assertiveness or boundary setting, I admit that I likely stepped on more than my fair share of toes in my efforts to recover. But I was desperate to get well, and in my case, the best medicine had nothing to do with me and everything to do with my fellow patients.

Most mental health professionals would insist that this is a misapprehension, and maybe it is. Still, it's my experience. Given no two crazies are built alike, it only stands to reason that what would make some of us snowflakes melt on contact might very well make others among us crystallize, sparkle and thrive. Realizing how good I had it, how much more pulled together I was than so many of the other women there and, most important, how much I could help them—no matter how delusional these "realizations" were—helped *me*. Focusing on guiding my fellow inmates (however misguidedly) made me happy. So I kept at it, testing nearly every other patient on the ward.

The only ones wholly immune to these efforts were also my only friends: Angela and Marie. With them, it was a back-and-forth. No advice, no pleasantries, no bullshit. They had both tried to kill themselves too, but unlike most of the other unsuccessful suicides on the unit, they had a sense of humor about their circumstances.

Apart from sharing a common coping mechanism, the three of us were also all "foreigners": Angela was from Trinidad, and Marie was French. But we were all fully American as well. Together we formed a trio of recalcitrant hybrids: one part stunning, disaffected, painfully thin, porcelain-white redhead; one part cute, petite, wickedly sarcastic black West Indian; one part naïve, delusional, mocha Iranian. Stir vigorously, then bake. French Trinidadian Persian bipolar tart. A little too sour for most palates, but edible nonetheless.

Both Marie and Angela had been to Stillbrook before; both had tried to overdose on a random pharmaceutical cocktail, and both were bipolar. Angela hadn't been raped, at least not to my

knowledge, but Marie had. Marie was also anorexic and bulimic—
I frequently "bathroom-buddied" her to the restroom, waiting
outside the cracked door to make sure she didn't misbehave. All
eating-disordered patients were required to have a non-eating-
disordered "bathroom buddy" join them whenever they visited
the restroom. Marie couldn't take a shit with any other bathroom
buddy, and I took great pride in that.

As if being a bipolar, suicidal bulimarexic weren't enough to
deal with, Marie also couldn't move her right arm. She used to be
a pretty fancy-pants gymnast, but following a disastrous vault,
her dominant right arm gave out and never gave in again. After
that, she learned to do everything with her left hand (and on occasion, her teeth). She was good at it. I never once saw her ask for
help. Marie was also crazy smart—a med student at the University
of Pennsylvania who'd just written a book with a psychiatrist
about anorexia.

While Angela hadn't finished college, she was just as bright.
School just wasn't her thing. And even if it were, her depressive
episodes were so frequent and all-consuming that she simply
didn't have time for anything else. I've known Angela for over five
years now, and in all that time, as ridiculously smart as the girl is,
she's always been on disability. She has a loving family, a gorgeous
daughter and a caring husband, but even with all that, I know
she's worlds away from meeting her full potential. She has yet to
find a drug cocktail that keeps her moods fully in check and, as a
result, despite all the joy she brings to others through her wit,
wisdom and compassion, she still suffers from brutal psychological paralysis. According to the World Health Organization, bipolar disorder is the sixth leading cause of disability in the world. I

doubt Angela is aware of this statistic, but no matter.* It's the first leading cause of disability in her world.

Angela and Marie were the only individuals I considered intellectual equals at Stillbrook. But despite my snobbery, I continued to take interest in the other patients as well, ever confident that if I could help them, I could help myself. While I highly doubt I actually helped any of them recover, the simple act of *trying* to do so made a huge difference for me. It gave me purpose and hope, however unwarranted. It worked.

United by helplessness, fear, fragility and common enemies, the Cottage E residents of November 2005 weren't much different from those in myriad other residential psychiatric facilities across the country. We were, however, quite extraordinary as compared to our "normal" counterparts on the outside.

There was Compass (I never learned her real name), a middle-aged schizophrenic teacher who'd stabbed herself in the jugular with, you guessed it, a compass. To her, I recommended dickies, turtlenecks and antipsychotics.

Then there was Ellie (not the elephant, but a teenaged girl), short for Elham. She was Iranian too and had a wicked case of bulimia. She came to Stillbrook after nearly dying from a ruptured esophagus. Subsequent to her statement that she'd do nothing more than buy a boatload of shoes if she won the lottery, I gave up on Ellie. Plus, she didn't speak Farsi, so we couldn't talk behind people's backs together.

---

* Ursula D'Souza, "New Developments in Bipolar Disorders," *BioMed Central*, 30 March 2012, blogs.biomedcentral.com/bmcblog/2012/03/30/new-developments-in-bipolar-disorders.

Eating disorders were painfully common within Cottage E. Besides Ellie, there was a thirteen-year-old cheerleader who refused to sit still, terrified she might burn one less calorie (She said she'd start a cheerleading camp if she won the lottery. I told her to eat and trade in cheerleading for debate or a sport with longer skirts and shirts. She declined.); a teenaged binge eater who was always eyeing the anorexics with envy (She said she'd give half her winnings to the Humane Society and spend the other half on a personal chef and trainer. I advised her to eat less and exercise. Being way too polite for her own good, the poor girl thanked me.); and a pregnant bulimic who was trying to stop vomiting to save her baby—forget herself (She'd have socked away her prize money for said baby's college fund. In an attempt to scare her straight, I suggested she give up her antics, as she could be prosecuted for child endangerment if her baby was born retarded or even manslaughter if it died. She told me not to use the word "retarded.").

There were a few cutters—most of whom were frequent flyers, refugees who took trips to psych wards the way most people take vacations. I counseled all of them to stop.

Most of the drug addicts boasted a dual diagnosis, as they were often self-medicating an underlying mood disorder: coke, meth or Ritalin for depression; heroin, Vicodin or Percocet for mania. Apparently the drugs work quite well before they rot your teeth, rob you of your life savings, chisel holes in your brain and/or stop your heart. Besides brilliantly advising the addicts to stop as well, I also suggested they refuse to accept there was anything they couldn't change.

Overall, I couldn't have given shittier advice had I tried. Still, most of my victims were patient with me, as I wasn't deliberately nasty, just misguided and delusional.

Of all the other patients at Stillbrook, Rachel troubled me the most. She was always smiling and showering people with compliments, but visibly uncomfortable when any were returned. A lot of the other patients *ooh*ed and *ahh*ed at Rachel's missing eyebrows and eyelashes, not to mention her nearly bald head when it peeked out from under the pink bandanna she wore to conceal it. I expect what distressed me most about Rachel, the reason I didn't *ooh* or *ahh* at the consequences of her compulsion, had to do with the fact that I was intimately acquainted with it. I understood Rachel's disorder, trichotillomania or "trich," because I'd dabbled in it as well. While I managed to avoid such extremes, I recognized what it was like to have a bizarre and embarrassing habit that baffled and revolted the general population. My mom, on the other hand, didn't. Her first response upon meeting Rachel: "*Vai*, tanks God that never happens to you."

At thirteen, I began pulling out my eyelashes. I had no idea why I started, and I certainly didn't expect that it was a real "disorder" with its own name and patient cohort. As far as I was concerned, I was the first person on the planet to pick up this strange and disgusting habit. I tried to hide it, but eventually I couldn't. When I came to the dinner table one evening looking like an early-stage cancer patient, my parents were appalled. Their solution was no different from the one I'd suggested to so many of my companions at Stillbrook: "Stop." They threatened to send me to a psychiatrist if I kept it up—an empty threat by all accounts, but effective nonetheless. Undoubtedly repulsed by the unsightly consequences of my new habit, they nevertheless failed to view it as anything more than an unfortunate alternative to nail-biting or hair-twisting.

Thoroughly petrified at the prospect of seeing a psychiatrist at thirteen, I stopped. This is rare with trich, but given the mild nature of my case and my mounting vanity, I managed to beat the odds—sort of. I still attack my lashes on occasion, usually when I'm particularly nervous. But it's never been as bad as it was back then, when every day seemed full of new and ever more excruciating humiliations.

There is little in life more anxiety inducing at that age (fuck it, at *any* age) than being subjected to a shirtless scoliosis test in the girls' locker room when you're the only girl in the class who doesn't wear or need a bra; or wearing shorts in gym class when you're the only girl in the class not allowed to shave her legs—and bonus, the hairiest of the lot; or being asked if your dad regularly beats you thanks to the untimely release of *Not Without My Daughter*; or being told to go back to IraQ thanks to Desert Storm. I mean, who *wouldn't* start pulling out her eyelashes when faced with such daily degradation? Don't answer that.

Sure, there are far more devastating fates, but at the time, I was certain there was nothing worse than enduring the seventh grade as a staggeringly skinny, flat-chested brown girl in Ohio, with a budding unibrow and a faint mustache—not to mention a seemingly endless array of unusual lunches intended to fatten me up.

My mom was obsessed with getting me to a more "normal" weight, dragging me to countless specialists, all of whom told her that I was fine despite missing most of my physical "milestones." Still, she continued stuffing me with kabob, rice, steak, potatoes, various stews, casseroles and sweets. On the weekends, she fed me *haleem* (a mixture of barley, wheat, onions, sugar, lamb, butter and God knows what else) or, worse yet, *kalleh pacheh* (a soup containing an entire lamb's head, including the tongue, brain, and eyes, feet and a whole series of other segments of the godforsaken creature). Nothing helped. I remained an increasingly hairy, pencil-sized mutant who was force-fed lamb's brain on the weekends. Again, who *wouldn't* start pulling out her eyelashes? Again, don't answer that.

Still, if only I'd felt compelled to pull out my leg, arm or a few eyebrow hairs instead, I might have saved myself a lot of grief. Thankfully, though, my lashes grew back, and by high school, I'd dropped the habit for the most part, gained a few pounds and picked up a razor.

I considered sharing my struggles with Rachel, but they seemed so lame and distant by comparison. She was almost completely bald, for God's sake. Counseling her without admitting my personal experience just seemed hypocritical. So miraculously, in an astonishing feat of self-restraint given my growing delusions of grandeur, I held my tongue. Her strain of madness simply struck too close to home.

As much as there exists a sense of hierarchy, scorn and competition among psychiatric patients (Who's the most or least fucked up? Who's worse or better off than you?), there also exists a strong camaraderie. When someone arrives on the ward, you try to make her feel welcome, remembering how scared you were when you first got there. You teach her the ropes—which nurses to avoid, which doctors to disregard, which puzzles are missing pieces. When someone leaves the ward, you wish her the best and, in most cases, you really mean it. You pray she stops pulling out all of her hair or vomiting till her throat explodes or stabbing her neck with drafting instruments. After all, if Rachel, Ellie and Compass can come around, then there must be hope for you.

No doubt much of our empathy comes from a shared respect for suffering. But there's more to it than that. We share mutations. Most doctors agree that mental illness is the result of a combination of our genes and experiences. Some of us are born with a predisposition toward it, and for us, certain emotional and/or physical traumas trigger our minds to revolt in the most pesky and peculiar ways. As such, we often don't fit into the same spaces as "normal" people. Our hearts, heads and helixes won't allow it. Herein lies our bond and our unique ability to rescue each other when others can't.

From the moment I first met ELLIE the elephant, I was desperate to get the hell out of Stillbrook. I hated most of the staff, the food, the rules, the routines. I hated the six-inch-thick sagging mattresses, the distorted glassless funhouse mirrors, the premature plastic Christmas decorations, the furniture, the quiet room, *all* the rooms. But as much as I despised and disdained Stillbrook's aesthetic, treatment, culinary and architectural styles, there remained a new and distinctive saving grace for me there: my fellow patients.

Their horror stories did more than remind me to count my blessings. They reminded me how to give a shit. When I got to Stillbrook, I was drowning in an ocean of despair. All the people I loved—all the sane, strong and sturdy people who wanted to save me—were stuck on a steady shore. Once at Stillbrook, I noticed a bunch of other people drowning around me, all within reach. It wasn't just me in the abyss anymore, and now that I knew I wasn't alone, I had a reason to tread water. Killing myself meant I couldn't save them. Killing myself meant killing them. Suddenly, I had no choice. I *had* to swim. So, I swam to save the others, only to find, upon reaching shore, that they had saved me.

part
two

six

fat-free hell

You never fully appreciate an organ until it turns on you. I first learned this lesson at eighteen, and have been regularly reminded of it ever since.

The doctors explained pancreatitis to me as a condition in which the pancreas decides to eat itself with its own enzymes and becomes inflamed as a result. As if that weren't gross enough, they then told me that it occurred mostly in overweight, middle-aged, alcoholic men. Having no part in this delightful demographic made me, as they put it, "lucky."

For some reason, people love telling you how lucky you are when misfortune strikes: "You're lucky the cancer hasn't spread to your liver." "You're lucky you were wearing a seatbelt [never mind that you're now paraplegic]." "You're lucky you weren't conscious when he raped you." Call me presumptuous, but my guess is that most people would feel a hell of a lot luckier cancer-free, peripatetic and unraped.

Following my first attack of acute pancreatitis, X rays revealed a mass in the middle of my pancreas, which doctors presumed to be a cyst. The "cyst" was blocking vital digestive enzymes from entering my intestines, rerouting them into my blood, rendering them useless.

As a result and to my great dismay, I was no longer allowed to eat ice cream, peanut butter or anything too heavy or fatty for my pitifully deficient digestive enzymes to process. Doing so could easily trigger another attack, and eventually, after several separate attacks, I was warned that another one could wipe out my pancreas, cause organ failure and kill me.

Upon learning about this mass and experiencing the excruciating pain it was capable of producing, I begged the doctors to cut it out. They refused, and my parents backed them up. It was me against half a dozen M.D.s. I lost.

"Who knows," they told me, "maybe the mass will just shrink on its own." And with that, my life became a waiting game.

At the time, I'd just graduated from high school and was dying to get the hell out of Dayton. I was *finally* going to college. And not just *any* college—the *perfect* college.

I'd been accepted most everywhere I'd bothered to apply. My parents pushed hard for either Duke or the University of Pennsylvania, but I ultimately decided on Wesleyan University. Romana had gone to Duke, so it was out for lack of originality—plus, it was way too conservative for my liking. Penn was out too. I visited and hated it—a lot of drinking, fraternity parties and vomiting (both on the part of drunk frat brothers and the skinny sorority sisters they had a reputation for date-raping).

Then I visited Wesleyan. Officially, it was one of my "safety" schools, but the second I set foot on the campus, I knew it was reach material. The sidewalks were littered with colorful chalkings, and within moments, my eyes were drawn to one in particular: "Keep your LAWS off my CUNT!" A school where you can write "cunt" on the sidewalk, and no one bats an eye? Now, that's where I belong, I thought. And it was.

But I never imagined I'd be headed there with this ticking time bomb inside of me. The whole reason I'd picked Wesleyan in the first place was that it was the freest place I'd ever been—a place where you could do, say or be whatever you wanted, without even a hint of judgment. And now I'd be arriving on campus in this prison of a body. I mean, what's the point of being able to write "cunt" on the sidewalk if you can't eat cake or pizza?

Becoming a girl who worries about the fat content of anything was a colossal mind-fuck. My only weight-related concerns growing up revolved around how I might be able to gain some. I never fretted over fat grams or calories. I knew girls who did, and they baffled me. But now, I would have to turn into one of them—not because I was trying to lose weight, but because I was trying to avoid organ failure.

Such was my fate, stuck on a ridiculous diet, waiting for this treacherous trespasser to shrink—all during what were supposed to be the most liberating years of my life. Despite all my attempts to stick to the diet, I still often found myself in pain. During the summer after my freshman year (or first year as most students and professors preferred to call it, all in a self-righteous effort to subvert patriarchy and hegemony), I got a stent placed in my pancreas. It was supposed to help me digest, and therefore *live*, easier. It was supposed to stop the pain. It didn't.

When I returned to Wesleyan the next year, I'd lost a good fifteen pounds thanks to the useless stent and another bout of pancreatitis. The only "treatment" for pancreatitis is starvation (to give the tiny organ a rest from digestion) and narcotics (to give the human harboring it a rest from excruciating pain). Thus, my weight loss (from about a hundred thirty to a hundred fifteen pounds) was largely thanks to this "treatment." When my friends saw me on campus, however, they didn't say, "Wow, what happened to you? Have you been in the hospital?" Rather, they said, "Damn, Mel, you look amazing! What did you *do*?"

When I told them I'd gone to the hospital, women would often say things like, "Yeah, I *wish* I could get sick." Or "How do I get what you have?" For the first time, I recognized that I belonged to an entire generation of smart, articulate, misdirected women who *wanted* to be sick or, worse yet, who were actually *making* themselves sick.

From all the positive reinforcement I got for this relatively minor weight loss, you'd think I'd won a Nobel Prize or cured cancer or something. But I hadn't won or done *anything*. So I concluded that I must have looked like some hideous beast beforehand. And just like that, I was duped into the ranks of countless other misguided women of my generation.

Where I'd never thought about my weight before, now it seemed to be *all* I could think about. I figured if losing a few pounds could get me that much positive feedback, then keeping it up could earn me even more. Plus, I had a decided advantage over all the other starving girls. They said it themselves: I really *was* sick. In my case, eating often hurt like hell anyway. Thus, by starving myself, I could give my pancreas a *serious* rest and win whatever prize it was that all those other "healthy" starving girls were competing for. (This, of course, was before I learned that the prize is just deeper and ever more self-loathing.)

Over the first few months of my sophomore year, my weight plummeted. By the time I left school to finally get the surgery I'd wanted two years earlier, I (at five foot six) weighed roughly ninety pounds. But my clinical anorexia was quickly written off because of my pancreatic problems. This, by the way, is any anorexic's dream—to have a "real" excuse.

The consensus was that I'd lost all the weight merely because it hurt when I ate. I know that was part of it, but I'd also lost the weight because, as much as I hate to say it, it feels good when people call you pretty. And the more weight I lost, the prettier people seemed to think I'd become. Until I lost *too* much. Then I went straight from "pretty" to "scary." I'm not sure exactly where that line is, but I do know that in twenty-first-century America at least, there's no more than a five-pound difference between the two.

During that fall semester, I started running. To me, running is not a sport. It's something you do when someone is chasing you. Perhaps you know somebody who runs "for fun." I'm telling you now, that person is a liar. Nobody runs for fun. People *dance* for fun. People run because there's a predator nearby. I am no exception.

I took up running in an attempt to outrun my mind, to prevent it from completely betraying and devouring me. I had a lot of trouble thinking straight, and I found that when my body was moving, my thoughts slowed down. When I sat still, they raced far too fast for me to connect, let alone tolerate. So I just kept moving. I ran somewhere between one to five hours daily, figuring that if I moved my body quickly enough, for long enough, then I'd eventually get tired. I figured wrong. Even with all that running, I could barely sleep. I was lucky to get a couple hours a night, if that. I spent the hours I wasn't sleeping deliberating my new existence. I was a shell of my former self, and worse yet, I was cracking.

I left school just before the end of the semester, after having a "panic attack," which I now know was my first full-blown hallucination. Lying in bed, sleeping over at my friend Roxana's place with her fast asleep at my side, I noticed a large green spider on the ceiling. It was glowing. Most bugs creep me out, but not spiders. It was a spider who saved the Prophet Muhammad's life during his famous flight from Mecca to Medina. With the Quraish on his heels, the Prophet sought refuge in the Cave of Thawr. His enemies quickly reached the cave by following his footsteps in the sand. They then noticed a large spiderweb at the entrance of the cave. Convinced that no spider could weave such an elaborate web in such a short period of time and that no human could have gotten past that web without destroying it, the Prophet's would-be assassins left without entering. So it was that one of the greatest prophets the world has ever known was rescued by an arachnid.

So I felt no fear, only admiration for this glowing creature capable of spinning silk miracles out of its butt. Still, as it descended toward me, I quickly realized that it wasn't hanging on silk. Its web was made of grape bubble gum. One whiff, and I knew it was poison. And not the patient-carcinogenic-kill-you-in-decades variety, but rather, the voracious-merciless-kill-you-in-minutes kind. Less Marie Curie, more Socrates.

This couldn't be a real spider, I thought, now terrified. Spiders don't glow. At least not in Connecticut. And they definitely don't shoot grape chewing gum out their asses. This was no miracle. This was a nightmare. But I wasn't dreaming. I was wide awake, and there it was, clear as day, this incandescent spider ready to trap me in his violet web, wrap me up like a mummy and suck out every last drop of blood.

Then it started whispering. Though I couldn't make out the words, his message was clear. He wasn't Muhammad's spider. He was Cleopatra's asp. I slowly crawled out from under the covers, keeping my eyes on the trespasser, making sure not to get caught in his web. I walked around the bed and shook Roxana.

"Rox, I'm going to die. This spider. It's going to kill me. It may have already leaked some venom onto my arm. I swear I felt it. We need to get out of here. It'll kill you too."

"Melody," she said, her eyes still closed, "it's a dream. Just drink some water and go back to sleep."

"I don't need water. I'm serious. I'm going to *die*. *We're* going to die." I said nothing more about the venom or the spider or the gum. I just cried, grabbed my chest and proceeded to hyperventilate. Assuming I was having a panic attack, Rox walked me to the bathroom and grabbed a Klonopin out of the medicine cabinet. When that didn't work, we went to the emergency room. I didn't say another word about what I'd seen. I just told her, and anyone else who would listen, that I was going to die. When I finally realized I'd live, some five hours after arriving at the hospital, I quickly accepted the panic disorder diagnosis. It was certainly a much preferable explanation than the one I suspected, namely "batshit crazy disorder." So, I ignored my suspicions and treated the incident as a fluke—even though it wasn't the last Technicolor "panic attack" I experienced that year.

I don't remember much after that. Roxana apparently called my mom, and the next thing I knew, she and I were meeting with my professors, asking them to be lenient with me because I would be leaving right before finals. I could barely take a deep breath, let alone a Medieval Philosophy final. My professors were all very understanding, likely because I looked like a decaying carcass of the girl they'd met at the start of the semester.

After that, my mom took all ninety pounds of me back to Ohio.

I quickly sank into a deep and restless depression—sleeping well past noon, listening to way too much Morrissey and reading lots of Plath, Styron and Kafka. I started seeing this thin, blond, blue-eyed therapist for my "eating disorder." Think Barbie, ten years past her plastic prime. If this was a disease of white, upper-middle-class American women, then who better to treat me for it. Still, like most everyone else, she came to the conclusion that my disordered eating was largely the result of my disordered pancreas, about which she was partly correct, and my depression, about which she was dead-on, sort of. She never tried to rule out mania and certainly never asked about delusions or hallucinations. I mean, that was the territory of *really* crazy people, and I was the overachieving daughter of rich doctors. I was a National Merit scholar with a Phi Beta Kappa future. Shit like that just doesn't happen to people like *me*. Or that was Barbie Ph.D.'s take on it. Again, I was more than happy to agree, to believe the professional and take all the antidepressants she suggested. Not that they helped. After realizing she had no cure, I decided to humor her into thinking she did. I started eating and walking into her office with fabricated smiles and phony stories about my mood in an effort to get rid of her. It worked.

Within a few months, I'd gained thirty pounds and dropped the therapist, as well as the drugs she'd suggested. I was still as depressed as ever, fantasizing about suicide the same way most of my friends were fantasizing about Leonardo DiCaprio. But at least now I could be miserable in peace. I wouldn't have to check in with some clueless American lady, pretending to understand what it was like to be me. Still, I should give credit where credit is due. In my desire to ditch therapy, I also managed to ditch most of my eating-disordered behaviors, though it would take years to even begin to address the fucked-up philosophies, let alone the principal mood disorder, driving them.

My ship was way off course, and looking back, I now realize that entire year was a big bright blinking warning light with a Day-Glo spider on top. Thankfully, having a previous engagement, Celine Dion wasn't available to write the soundtrack. Even without her though, it was clear that something was off—way off—and as much as I tried to convince myself otherwise, it sure as hell wasn't purely gastrointestinal.

seven

don't fuck with the pancreas

The intruder in my pancreas never shrank on its own, so the doctors finally agreed to cut the damn thing out. Not long before the cutting began, I learned the first three rules of surgical residency: (1) Eat when you can; (2) Sleep when you can; and (3) Don't fuck with the pancreas. Apparently, it's one of the most sensitive and unpredictable organs in the human body, and as such, it doesn't take well to manipulation. Having always been a stubborn, don't-fuck-with-me kind of person myself, I found it highly fitting that my most damaged and pain-provoking organ would share the same attributes. I knew what I was up against, and I was willing to take my chances.

Less than an hour before surgery, lying in a sterile hospital bed complete with wheels on the bottom and metal bars on the sides, I could no longer disregard the pressing demands of my relentlessly contracting and expanding bowels. The term "evacuation" once conjured images of large masses fleeing fires or hurricanes or nuclear disasters, blocking exits and major roadways. No longer. Now, images of the messiest and most unavoidable consequences of human life came to replace them. Images of excretion, humiliation and death.

I was intensely aware of the pathetic nature of my new existence, marked by a constant preoccupation with what were previously "normal" life functions—ones that ideally took place in a bathroom, a kitchen, a living room, a bedroom. Now they all took place in a single bed courtesy of bedpans, nurses, needles, IV drips, catheters and a seemingly endless variety of other plastic tubes hell-bent on tangling around one another whenever the opportunity presented itself.

My instinctive biological obligations overcame the spiteful silence that had become my choice response to humiliation. Dreading my impending dissection and partial evisceration, I had already proclaimed that a bedpan would not be necessary, and regrettably, my request had been respected. Having consumed three bottles of cherry-flavored magnesium hydroxide the night before in order to achieve the thoroughly barren gastrointestinal tract that the surgeons insisted was essential for my "intimate" surgery, I had been "evacuating" all night, and the intestinal acrobatics continued well into the morning. I was bracing myself for a final emergency landing, but I couldn't get out of that godforsaken bed.

I sat up, pulling harder and harder on the metal bars that the nurse had so easily pulled up and clicked into place after transporting me. My palms were sweating and my heart had adopted an unremitting crescendo, pounding at a preternatural tempo *fortissimo prestissimo*. My dreaded fate was fast approaching, and panic was the only rational resort. The other patients in the room looked so serene, catatonic by comparison.

I took my first real look around in desperation. What kind of room was this anyway? Did it have an official name? For some reason, I felt that if it did, if there were a sign above it reading "Pre-op Prep Room" or "Gastro-Intestinal Care Unit," then I'd be okay. Then I'd be able to break free from that wretched gurney and take a shit without someone else's help or permission; then I'd be able to swallow my pride and ask for a fucking bedpan; then I'd be able to get one of those white coats to hold still long enough to notice me.

My mind was racing, every neuron firing interrogatives: Who would notice if I contaminated my crisp, sterile bedsheets? Would they laugh at me? Pity me? Would they do it to my face or behind my back? Or would they think nothing of my fecal incontinence, brushing it off as business as usual? And how would it actually *feel* to poop my pants? How much would there be? Is it common for pre-op patients to poop their pants? Does it still qualify as pooping your pants if you're not wearing any?

Most important, how could I be certain that the profound indignity of lying in my own feces, no matter how briefly, wouldn't kill me? I'd never heard of anyone actually dying from embarrassment, but part of me was sure that I'd be the first. As weak and delusional as I was at the time, I was absolutely positive that even the slightest trauma could kill me and that shitting my pants was just as likely to do it as having my stomach sliced open and my organs dissected, removed and rearranged.

No one seemed to perceive how badly I wanted, *needed* to get out of that bed. Even if my IV tubes weren't tangled to all high hell, making it impossible to climb over, I was still far too weak from the evening's tribulations to climb out by myself. Defeated, I called for help: "Um, hello?" Nothing.

Everyone was flying around the room, pulling out charts from the bottoms of beds, running with them, then replacing them. I had decided to catch the attention of the next person to pull out or replace mine. A tall, thin resident with gold wire-framed glasses, curly raven hair and translucent skin.

"Um, hi. I really need—"

"The anesthesiologist should be here shortly," she told the chart.

I've found that when people think you might die and they don't know you in the first place and don't absolutely *need* to look at you, they do their best to look elsewhere. And if they have to look at you, they generally focus on the part that is presumably the most damaged. In my case—that is, the twenty-year-old, five-foot-six, hundred-twenty-pound, nonsmoking, nondrinking, otherwise healthy female with a badly situated pancreatic mass—the majority of my beloved health care providers tended to look at my pancreas (directly below the ribs, slightly to the left, some three inches above my belly button) when addressing me.

I used to move my head down toward my abdomen to catch their eyes, but ultimately I just gave in and started talking to their pancreases too, as though it were a conversation between organs and not sentient human beings.

More recently, however, as my case has transformed into that of a twenty-nine-year-old, five-foot-six, hundred-twenty-pound, nonsmoking, nondrinking, relatively healthy female *mental* patient with a significantly less dysfunctional pancreas, I've finally gotten my wish: the doctors have started talking to my head. Not necessarily looking me in the eye, but a decided improvement. With my brain being the focus of this newer bipolar diagnosis, they can't exactly look elsewhere without arousing suspicion and disdain. Also, I expect they are often on guard—

making sure to step back should I decide to attack or something. I have yet to attack a stranger, let alone a doctor, and judging from my personal history, any physical violence I'd pursue promises to be weak, if not laughable.

Thus far, I've only seriously assaulted three people in my life: Matthew, Joe Yensil and Gary Osser. My attack on Matthew was pathetic and harmless, in a fit of psychosis and in response to his gracious efforts to subdue me. More on this later.

The Joe Yensil incident was a playful schoolroom spat that ended with a pencil in his arm and a tetanus shot. I had to write "I'm sorry for stabbing Joe Yensil with a pencil" a hundred times. I was genuinely contrite, told Joe as much, and he graciously forgave me.

Gary Osser, however, was a different story. He deserved it. By calling my best friend, Nobar Elmi (a sister really; we grew up together; the Elmis were our closest family friends in Dayton), a bitch on the playground in the second grade, he marked himself as a worthy and legitimate target. So, fully sane and with great pride, I succeeded in kicking his ass and defending Nobar's honor. Apart from the fact that he clearly had it coming, my secondary defense is that I was seven. Furthermore, since the Gary Osser and Joe Yensil incidents, I've consistently grown intellectually stronger and physically weaker, which has forced me to express my hostility through words, not fistfights.

In keeping with this approach, I feel compelled to set the record straight regarding the relationship between violence and mental illness, not just in my personal experience, but in general. Despite what you'd expect from watching *Law & Order*, research has shown that the mentally ill are, in fact, no more likely to commit violent crimes than their otherwise "sane" counterparts. Furthermore, we're much more likely to be victims of violent crime than we are to be perpetrators.*

Still, once people see you as crazy, unprovoked violence suddenly seems a possibility and therefore tends to provoke a genuine fear. And no matter how irrational those fears may be, they're intense and pervasive, even among some of the most well-informed mental health professionals. Open wounds and catheters are much less threatening, a relief by comparison.

It took nearly ten years after my surgery for doctors to recognize that in many ways my pancreas was the least of my problems. When you have a serious physical illness, even if you're suicidal as a result, it's quite common for any potential mental health issues to go unnoticed. And mine did.

Given that basic human functions like digestion are necessary for survival, I can't say I'm surprised. No matter how crazy you are, if you haven't killed yourself yet, you still need to eat and excrete. I rank the loss of bowel function right up there with the loss of sanity. Both tend to stink and need to be addressed immediately. And often, in the effort to address one, the other goes unnoticed, and in either case, pride and dignity generally end up taking a backseat.

I knew that my surgery was high risk and potentially lethal, but while I was entirely ready to die, even a little hopeful, I was *not* ready to poop my pants. My time was running out.

To add insult to injury, the pallid brunette had just replaced

---

* Mark Ragins, "The Fear Factor," *Los Angeles Times*, 24 July 2012; articles.latimes.com/2012/jul/24/opinion/la-oe-ragins-colorado-shootings-mental-illness-20120724.

my chart and run away again. I pulled at the bars until I was finally shaking the entire bed, rocking it back and forth, leaving marks on the gleaming white linoleum floor, forcing a nurse to notice me. She looked around, then at me: "Can I help you?" My angel in lilac hospital scrubs. I wanted to kiss her, but there was no time.

"Yes," I conceded, "I have to go to the bathroom, and I can't get this thing down." She pulled down the bars, and I thanked her as I hobbled toward the bathroom, dragging my IV behind.

For the first time in my life, I sat on a public toilet without having my ass and the seat separated by at least three layers of toilet paper. I figured the breach in hygiene was acceptable, though, as I was facing much more serious risks upon my return from the lavatory.

I wiped, used my IV pole to hoist myself up and made my way back to the cage, where a handsome young man was awaiting me. He was tall and well built, and his white coat contrasted beautifully with his skin, just a shade or two darker than my own. At first glance, he could easily have been Iranian too.

I imagined for a moment that he was my devoted lover and had come to steal me away from the sterility. We would move to a small Mediterranean island and he would take care of me. We would live off his massive inheritance and accept and await my death. He would paint and sing to me. He would copy down my every word. My each expression, movement, utterance would drip with remarkable insight, and he would listen, finding me terribly wise. I would die in his arms, and he would spend the rest of his life honoring my legacy: dedicating hospital wards, orphanages, libraries and schools in my name; building cancer, AIDS and Alzheimer's research centers around the world; and ensuring that nearly every

PBS and NPR program ended with "brought to you by the Melody Moezzi Foundation." I would become outrageously famous in death thanks to him.

"Hi, I'm Dr. Slorion, and I'm the anesthesiologist. Have they explained the operation to you?"

The fantasy was shattered. I noticed his nose was inordinately large and he was in fact mildly overweight. He was an attractive still life, but once he started moving and talking, his beauty faded almost immediately.

"Yes, several times," I responded.

When my condition was initially explained to me, the doctor couldn't help grinning like a child discovering his first long-awaited bicycle under the tree on Christmas morning. "One in a million," he kept repeating, referring to the odds of this happening to me. He and his colleagues made it quite clear that my case was exceptional, and accordingly, I felt anything but. Still, I seemed to intrigue every doctor who met my recalcitrant pancreas. That is, with the exception of my immediate family. Understandably, they were a bit less impressed by the baffling statistics.

"So if you could just start counting backward from a hundred now. Carrie is injecting the Versed," Dr. Slorion directed.

"One hundred, ninety-nine, ninety-eight, ninety-seven, ninety-six, ninety—" I stopped counting. What if I fell asleep for good? Did I really want my last words to be "eighty-two" or "seventy-seven"?

"Melody?"

"Oh, I'm awake. I just don't like counting much. Maybe I'll just talk to you, and you'll know I'm out when I stop talking, or what—"

"Let's just count, Melody. Okay?"

"Fine. Where was I?"

"It doesn't matter. Just count."

"If it doesn't matter, I can talk. If it doesn't matter . . ."

Those were the last words I remember speaking before passing out.

On the day of my surgery, my family was joined by about ten of our closest family friends, mostly doctors as well. The ultimate accomplishment for most any Iranian is becoming a doctor, and as the only member of my immediate family who hasn't taken that route, I've always felt like somewhat of a failure. There's this joke about an Iranian mom watching her son being sworn in as President of the United States: during the ceremony, a woman next to her says, "You must be so proud." The soon-to-be First Mother replies, "This is nothing. His brother is a doctor." That pretty much sums up the Persian perspective on medicine.

To their credit, however, my parents never doubted or discouraged my childhood dream of becoming a lawyer. At six, I announced my ambitions, and by sixteen, after my first encounter with Atticus Finch, I was certain. Despite never having read *To Kill a Mockingbird*, my parents were relentlessly supportive and proud of my aspirations. To them, the law was just as respectable as medicine. And later, after some convincing and the publication of my first book, they ultimately came to accept that writing was right up there as well.

Still, once I got sick, they couldn't have cared less about what profession I pursued or my reasoning for doing so. All they wanted was to keep me breathing. Meanwhile, all *I* wanted was to figure out what the hell was wrong with me before I died. They tried to keep me from reading medical journals because nearly all the statistics were based on outcomes for fat, middle-aged alcoholics and, therefore, pretty grim. Still, I was desperate to know what was happening to me.

The whole ordeal began right after my high school graduation. One night I was living it up, rockin' out to the Black Cats (bad, catchy Persian pop band) and Puff Daddy (bad, shallow American sampling whiz) at the party I shared with a few other Persian kids who'd graduated that year as well. The next, I felt like I was going to die, and I wasn't far off. My insides were mutinying, and I couldn't eat a thing. Ahmad and Jazbi insisted it was just gas, but by the time they finally took me to the hospital, my blood was swimming with pancreatic enzymes. My numbers were off the charts, and despite not having eaten anything for nearly two days, I was vomiting uncontrollably. I threw up more in that single night than I expect your average bulimic does in a month.

Within a few hours, there was a priest standing over me (Muslim or not, I wasn't about to decline anyone's prayers at that point) and a helicopter waiting to fly me to Indianapolis. There was some fancy pancreatic specialist there. I was hurling enough as it was, and I knew a helicopter ride wouldn't help matters, so I convinced my parents to drive me instead. Ahmad got us to Indiana in record time. I doubt the helicopter would have been much faster.

I spent the next week recovering as my parents freaked out more than I ever thought possible. Ahmad spent the whole time cursing himself for not taking me to the hospital sooner—that is, when he wasn't cursing the nurses for turning me into a pincushion. Apparently, I have terrible veins—ridiculously small and slippery by all accounts. I quickly learned to request pediatric needles, but even so, my veins ran out in no time.

At one point, Ahmad woke up to find a nurse searching for a vein in my foot. I was afraid he might kill her. He grabbed the needle himself, cursing her in Farsi the whole time: "*Pedar sageh beesharaf* [Your dad is a dog, dishonorable one]," "*Goh too saret* [Shit on your head]," "*Lamazhabeh khar* [Religionless ass]" et cetera. Miraculously, between expletives, he managed to find a vein in my arm and get it on the first try.

On the whole, my mom was much more composed, though she spent every waking moment either brushing up on her pancreatology or petting my head as though I were an abused one-eyed kitten on one of those ASPCA commercials with Sarah McLachlan or Natalie Merchant crooning in the background.

It was May 1997. Google wasn't even a registered domain name, and I was still using a Smith Corona word processor. In short, I was pitifully helpless in the research department. When I first figured out that my pancreas was to blame, I immediately asked if I needed it.

"Can't you just take it out? Isn't it like the appendix? You know, vestigial?" I asked a nurse, proud to have used the word "vestigial" in conversation for the first time.

"No, honey. It's not like the appendix."

She was as nice as she could be about it. Didn't laugh or anything. Still, I was more embarrassed by my stupidity than I was crushed by the fact that I couldn't easily get rid of the offending organ. In contrast, when I was first diagnosed with bipolar disorder over a decade later, I knew right away that there was no getting rid of my offending organ. You don't have to be a neurosurgeon to know that you need your brain. Still, this time I was exponentially more embarrassed. Not by my ignorance, but rather by my inability to singlehandedly cure myself without the aid of modern medicine. I was embarrassed by my perceived spiritual weakness, my sickness of the soul, my diseased moral character.

Bipolar disorder has some relatively classic signs, and though I like to consider myself unique and extraordinary in every way, my symptoms were pretty damn textbook. Apart from the severe vacillations in mood for which manic depression gets its name, I was also particularly prone to a handful of typically manic symptoms, even in some of my most depressed states. Racing thoughts, flights of ideas, rapid speech and delusions of grandeur have been frequent visitors in my mind's landscapes as far back as I can remember. I'm pretty sure they own their own time-share.

Had I become a medical instead of a juris doctor, I expect I might very well have recognized some of these symptoms sometime during the ten years I was misdiagnosed with unipolar depression. Had I followed the light and pursued the family business, maybe I could have even come up with a cure by now, or at least prevented it somehow. Admittedly unlikely, but possible.

It's well established that bipolar disorder is highly heritable: children with a parent or sibling with the disease, for example, are four to six times more likely to have it than those without one.* Still, while genes plainly appear to predispose a person to manic depression, they are far from the entire story. Environmental factors also play a part, and in my case, I suspect they played a pretty big one.

---

* J. I. Nurnberger, Jr., and T. Foroud, "Genetics of Bipolar Affective Disorder," *Current Psychiatry Reports* 2, no. 2 (April 2000): 147–157; see also National Institute of Mental Health website: http://www.nimh.nih.gov/health/publications/bipolar-disorder/complete-index.shtml.

The stress of dealing with a serious physical illness and facing death at an early age may well have pushed me over the edge, from predisposition to presentation. Though I can't imagine that growing up in Ohio as an Iranian-American Muslim in the immediate post-revolutionary era has helped much either. And then there's that time I tried to slide front-first down our banister when I was eight—"Look, just like Dennis the Menace!"—and fell face-first onto our marble foyer floor. Or all the times I sneaked into the medicine cabinet to feed my out-of-control Flintstones vitamin habit. (They taste like Smarties, for God's sake, and all my friends were doing it.) Whatever the precise formula of precipitating factors, however, the fact remains that I'm not normal. A lot of people can go through similar traumas and experiences without losing their minds. Most people, in fact. But not me.

Still, denial is a powerful force to which I have never been immune. Accepting or believing anything less than the best about myself or my own private universe has never been easy for me. I believe in miracles, signs, ghosts, angels, God—all of it. And I've always had this incurable conviction that I can do most things better than most people, most of the time.

Part of the reason it's so hard for me to shake my delusions of grandeur lies in the fact that on occasion they actually come true. Whatever the case, they're always there—dancing in the back of my mind like strawberry Pop Rocks, eschewing the possibility of the impossible and making it hard as hell to believe that I'm even slightly damaged.

Though my delusions have nearly killed me on several occasions, they've saved me on countless others. For whatever reason, sometimes I simply need to abandon reason for the sake of mere self-preservation.

eight

vital signs

Anesthesia is perhaps the ultimate reversal of reason. You
don't just lose memory and consciousness; you lose time.
Having never been good with time or space, I imagined that the
amnesia associated with general anesthesia wouldn't affect me. I
was wrong.

I woke up feeling as though someone had hit Control-Alt-
Delete in my brain, bringing me back from months of ruthless
melancholy that neither Dr. Barbie nor her elixirs nor any of the
Dr. Moezzis could cure, a hollowness more excruciating than any
of the post-operative pain that required round-the-clock IV narcotics. It was the beginning of my steady climb up and out.

The spark that resulted in this reversal of mood and consciousness took only eight hours to set off, and I can't say I
wouldn't have had the surgery just to cure my depression had I
known it would. While I've never undergone electroconvulsive
therapy (ECT), I've heard it can have similar effects—not that I'm
dying to find out.*

---

* Aaron Beck and Brad A. Alford, *Depression: Causes and Treatment*, 2nd ed. (Philadelphia:
University of Pennsylvania Press, 2009).

During those eight hours, as my family and friends sat in a large waiting room, I underwent a partial mid-pancreatectomy with a repositioning of the remnants of the pancreatic duct into the small intestine, which by itself, before any mention of cancer, had a good ten percent chance of killing me. Or at least that's the number I'd heard being thrown around.

Once they'd sewed me back up, my surgeon, Dr. Stryker, came out and informed everyone that the cutting and stitching had gone well. He also informed them that my "cyst" was in fact a tumor, which the pathologist had declared "highly suspicious for malignancy." After further examination, the pathologist reported that the tumor was indeed malignant, about the size of a small plum with radiating cancerous growths orbiting it like little moons. Pancreatic cancer has one of the lowest survival rates of any other cancer; less than five percent of patients survive more than five years after diagnosis. In short, this was not good news.

When I began to regain consciousness, I noticed Romana standing over me, rubbing giant gobs of Vaseline on my lips. The taste and consistency of the petroleum jelly was thoroughly nauseating, but I couldn't tell her to stop. No matter how hard I tried, the words only came out in my head.

All the while, I could tell that something was wrong. I just couldn't maintain consciousness long enough to find out. Without the privilege of narcotics, however, my family was forced to deal with the news, and they did so exactly as I'd have expected.

While my mother refused to accept the diagnosis and used every last bit of her medical knowledge to disprove it, my father seemed to forget that he'd ever gone to medical school or that his daughter, and not he, had just received the death sentence. This was completely in character for him. I always tried hardest to hide my pain from Ahmad more than anyone else during the two years before my surgery, as he couldn't help but mimic me. When I stopped eating, he stopped eating; when I lost weight, he lost weight; when I was put on antidepressants, he was put on a higher dose. And so, understandably, when my allegedly cancerous growth was first discovered, his was already in its final stages.

Thus, as my mom stayed and fought the verdict, studying slides and journals, ignoring those who kept telling her that her emotions were tainting her medical opinion, my dad bought a pack of cigarettes and, in a daze, took a late-night stroll through the less-than-glamorous streets of the South Side of Chicago that ran alongside the hospital. So it was that as I fell in and out of consciousness, my family began to cope with the prospect of my impending death: my mother with her books and slides, my sister with her Vaseline and my father with his Marlboro Lights.

I, on the other hand, wasn't nearly as distraught. My distress would come later, when the narcotics had worn off and my mother had won her case. I wasn't present when my family was informed about my terminal cancer, nor was I told personally until it was no longer a reality. But, in my ever-vacillating state of consciousness, reality itself was playing tricks on me, and I was growing highly skeptical. It was at that point—when my veins were being routinely injected with narcotics, when my mind was still unable to fully distinguish dream from reality, and when my family had not yet chosen to share my terminal status with me—that the faithful medical staff working on my case had some elementary revisions to make regarding their original diagnosis.

The phone rang. My mother answered. Within five seconds, the room was singing: "It's benign, it's benign . . ." This, I thought, was real. Do phones ever ring that loudly in dreams? Apparently, some dye on a slide hadn't picked up where it should have, and as a result, I'd been diagnosed with terminal cancer for seventy-two hours. "A fluke, so sorry, never happens, one in a million," the pathologist explained to my mother. "It isn't cancer after all. A mistake: it's benign." Somehow, I'd managed to grow a truly exceptional tumor—one that apparently affects only a few hundred people in the world at any given time, most of whom happen to be adolescent Japanese girls. Having already made her own diagnosis, my mom wasn't surprised by the reversal. The doctor on the other end of the phone, however, was. He kept repeating "one in a million," in what I suspect was an attempt to both marvel at the odds and cover his own ass. Whatever the case, if I never hear the phrase "one in a million" again in my life, it'll be too soon.

My souped-up private hospital room (only the best for Ahmad and Jazbi's youngest) boasted a large adjoining sitting area. It was nearly always full of friends and family members, most of whom had flown or driven up from Dayton to Chicago just to see us. The only time I spent alone was on the toilet, and my room was so full of flowers that my parents eventually started giving them away to other patients on the floor. I was loved, and I felt it.

When the doctors called in my reprieve, the room had my entire immediate family and nearly a dozen of my closest aunties, uncles and cousins in it. The way they were cheering and hugging each other, you'd think Iran had just won the World Cup. Watching them, I too rejoiced—not just for my new lease on life, but for the ridiculously large and loud family with which I'd been blessed.

Just then, a nurse walked in to inform us that we were being

too rowdy. Only one of my aunties even acknowledged her existence, and that was simply to say: "*Boro gooreh pedaret.*" Translation: Go to your father's grave. Meaning: piss off. The nurse then
turned to me, refusing to relent: "I need you to control these people or we'll have to start getting much more strict with your visiting hours. I have to take your vitals." She lifted my arm to take my
blood pressure, and I yanked it back.

"We just found out that I'm plenty vital, and I need *you* to
control *your* people," I responded. "*These people* are part of my
treatment. They're family, and most of them are doctors. I need
them here way more than I need you taking my blood pressure." I
suspect the nurse never went to visit her father's grave, but she did
leave the room after that, and the celebration continued without
pause. That wasn't the last time I was asked to control my "people"
in a hospital, but it was the last time in *that* hospital.

Still, I couldn't join in wholeheartedly on the celebration. I
mean, how could I be sure there wasn't some other mistake that I
would discover in a week or a month or a year, some other "one in
a million"? How could I be sure there wasn't something else the
doctors weren't telling me? How could I be sure that I wasn't still
in surgery dreaming this?

I found out all too soon that this was no dream, as my early
experiences recovering made me almost wish I'd had cancer after
all, just so everyone would leave me alone. There's a certain amount
of relief that comes with being a lost cause. It's not so important to
do the routine blood pressure/blood sugar/temperature/heart rate/
breathing tests as often, and it's not the end of the world if you
don't go for walks. But once everyone found out I wasn't dying, I
was forced to move and function when all I wanted to do was sleep
to escape the pain.

More than anyone else, Romana insisted on walks, pulling me out of bed and up and down the halls whenever she got the chance, holding me up only when I absolutely needed it and making sure I didn't trip over any of my tubes. More than six years my senior, Romana has always scared the hell out of me, though I can't say exactly why. She's never been overtly abusive in any way, but she's never been especially warm, either. My dad used to call her "The Untouchable" on account of her strong distaste for physical contact, particularly hugs and kisses. (Her husband, Robert, and her three kids have largely cured her of this, but a few quirks remain.) Now, in a twist of fate, I had become "The Untouchable," begging Romana to get her hands off me and stop dragging me on those ruthless walks. She refused to let me win.

From time to time, Dr. Stryker and his gaggle of residents, nurses and med students dropped by for a visit. Dr. Stryker was a world-renowned surgeon, and as a result, his entourage was scared to death of him. In fact, they were always so busy being terrified and answering his questions that not a single one of them ever addressed me directly.

My first such visit took place less than a week after surgery, when I was still a weak and wasted collection of tubes—one in my nose to stop me from gagging, one in my urethra to stop me from wetting the bed and two coming out of small holes they'd cut in my sides directly above my hip bones to stop blood and other fluid from accumulating in my abdomen. On this particular gathering, I was wearing only a loose green hospital gown. The tubes and my swollen belly made it impossible to wear anything else.

"Good morning, Melody. How are you feeling?" Dr. Stryker asked my belly.

"Um, okay. When do you think I can eat?"

"I'll have the nurse bring you some ice chips," he answered, and started explaining my case to his disciples.

They proceeded to focus in on my left upper quadrant, one of them pulling the sheet off me at Dr. Stryker's request. I almost fell off the bed in an attempt to get it back. My gown had ridden up, exposing my entirely naked lower half. I would have said something, but I was too drained and anesthetized to protest. Besides, the spectators had already turned their attentions to the large throbbing scar running from one side of my torso to the other, closely following the curvature of my lower ribs. (Today, if I suck in far enough, I can hide the entire scar under my rib cage, a grotesque sight by all accounts and thus one of my favorite party tricks: "Now you see it; now you don't!")

"Wow! You did a great job with the patient's stitches here," one of the students noted, poking me. I felt like a rare parasite under a microscope, my observer calling everyone over to see, the others getting all keyed up over the extraordinary specimen and wishing they'd been the ones to first discover it.

Disgrace comes in many guises, especially in a hospital. Shortly before I was released, it came in the form of a late-night visit from a first-year resident. He entered my room without knocking and proudly proclaimed his intent: "I came to take out your drainage tubes." He looked twelve.

All the other doctors in the room—Romana (an endocrinologist), her husband, Robert (a pathologist), and my parents—were glad that this was finally being done. But I had grown somewhat attached to the twin tubes coming out of my sides and was worried about what would happen to the small holes constructed solely for their inhabitance once they were removed. They seemed too big and deep to just heal on their own, and I expected they'd bleed.

"Do I get any pain meds?" I inquired, hoping I wouldn't have to be fully conscious for this.

"Oh no, this shouldn't hurt at all," he told me. Again, my clan agreed. "You see, you have no nerve endings to sense pain inside your intestines, and it shouldn't pull the skin too much. It'll just be a little bit uncomfortable, okay?"

"Whatever you say."

Ten years later, I still remember that he began with my right side. He tried to pull the tube out quickly and entirely. He failed. I screamed.

"Oh, I'm sorry. I wasn't at the surgery. I didn't know the tube was so long," the resident said, frantically trying to explain himself.

Not only was the tube longer than he'd expected, but the part of the tube inside of my body was twice the width of the part on the outside. As a result, pulling the tube out stretched my skin considerably. And given his confident assurances that there were no nerve endings inside my intestines and that I wouldn't feel anything more than slight discomfort, I was sure he'd never experienced the procedure himself. It felt like a live power wire whipping through my newly rerouted entrails. But it was difficult to decipher which was worse—the pain from the serpent flailing about my viscera or the agony from the stretching skin of the open wound at my waist.

"What the hell are you doing? Are you trying to *kill* me? Do you have any idea what this *feels* like?" I cried.

He was out the door and quickly reappeared with a nurse and

some Demerol. She injected it, and he pulled out the rest of the tube as I bawled and screamed. By the time he got to the second tube, I'd already passed out.

Four days later, I was discharged. Initially, Dr. Stryker insisted he wouldn't release me until I had a bowel movement, but the Demerol had left me constipated, so he settled for a fart. I'd lost a good deal of weight but couldn't leave the hospital in my jeans because my stomach was so swollen. That, the docs told me, would take up to a year to completely return to normal. I looked like a starving child. All skinny arms and legs, with a big distended belly. But I didn't care. My sanity, my exuberance, my *self* was returning. Plus, I was finally allowed to eat. They told me I was completely healed. No excessive scarring, no bleeding, no diabetes, no leaks, no tumors, no cancer. They were particularly proud of the cancer part, which surprised me, considering I'd never had it in the first place.

Since then, I've had a few more bouts of pancreatitis resulting in hospitalization and many more bouts of chronic pain lasting anywhere from a few days to months. The unpredictability, more than the pain itself, is the most maddening part, but there's an upside: My pancreas is famous now.

Thanks to the fact that my benign pseudopapillary tumor was so rare and the surgery wasn't particularly common, the surgeons ultimately managed to publish an article about me and a few other "lucky" patients in an elite medical journal. I was Case #1, which I admit made me happy. Always best to be first. And understandably, my surgery was deemed a triumph because it saved my life. There was nothing else they could fix with a knife, so from their perspective, I was all better: another case study to add to their list of accomplishments.

Despite the fact that my recovery is ongoing and has been marked by perpetual degradation thanks to the American health care system and its often inhuman training methods and protocols, all the doctors who documented my surgery still consider it a categorical success, *their* categorical success.

Sure, I still experience some pain from time to time, but on the whole, I'm "cured," at least as far as my surgeons are concerned. They got the mass out; they sewed me up, and they even published their promising conclusions: "Post-operatively, the patient recovered without event . . ." What happened next, the "events" the authors failed to observe, were neither their concern nor their responsibility. They were, however, mine.

nine

glaciers in july

Facing mortality, especially at twenty, changes a person. In my case, it lit a fire under my ass and set off sparklers in my brain. Convinced I'd survived for some reason, I resolved to seek it out. Enter the Beloved.

Many an atheist has told me that my belief in God and the hereafter is based on a delusion meant to make me "feel better." To that, I say duh, and so what? Having had my fair share of decidedly unpleasant delusions, I figure I deserve a few that actually make me feel *good* once in a while. What's more, there's always been some grain of truth behind *all* of my delusions, no matter how infinitesimal.

So, as irrational and unfashionable as it may seem, I continue to believe in the presence of a Divine force that both informs and exceeds human understanding. And despite the obvious epistemological limitations, I have long sought and continue seeking to understand. However impossible, this search, this love for knowledge, has time and time again introduced me to and rescued me from madness. I refuse to give it up.

When I announced I'd be majoring in philosophy, at the start of my first semester at Wesleyan, Ahmad's immediate response was, "Vat the hell are all these eh-secretary classes?"

I wasn't surprised, but I *was* annoyed—particularly because Ahmad is one of the most philosophically oriented people I know. In all likelihood, *he* was the one who most inspired my interest in the topic.

Still, he has a ridiculously common immigrant mentality (one that has waned significantly, though not entirely, over the years), which includes a strong conviction that good boys and girls become doctors, lawyers or engineers, and that neither Kant nor Confucius could pave the way toward any of the aforementioned professions. There isn't much room or respect for intellectual curiosity for its own sake. That's the domain of "hobbies"—not formal schooling. The idea that college is a time for personal exploration is ludicrous as far as most Iranians are concerned, Ahmad included.

Failing to remember this fact, I explained to him that college was my chance to ask the big questions and "find myself." "*Vaghan* [Really]?" he said. "You are lost? College is your chance to get *education*. You tink I pay this much for you to *find yourself.* I see you in front of me. You are not lost. I found you. You are in Dayton, Ohio. Congratulation. *Tamoom shod* [It's over/solved.]. You are welcome."

These days I partly agree with him on this point—in fact, more than I ever thought possible. From my experience, I've found that the best way to "find yourself" is to find people who have less than you and help them—not to study Plato or backpack through Europe or drop acid. Still, I never bought into Ahmad's dismissal of metaphysical inquiry as preparation for secretarial work. Accordingly, I was a bit of a brat about it.

"Didn't you know," I told him, "the whole reason I went to college was to become a secretary—because everyone knows philosophers make the best secretaries. I mean, look at all of *your* secretaries." Running the largest ob/gyn practice in Dayton meant that Ahmad had a lot of experience with this demographic.

"You can do this and it's okay for law school? They are okay with this?" he asked, unamused.

"Sure," I responded. "Supposedly philosophy and music majors do the *best* in law school." Perhaps I made this up, but I was sure that I'd heard it somewhere. Whatever the case, he believed me and continued paying my tuition.

Following my release from the hospital, three semesters of secretary classes behind me, I focused squarely on the scariest and most personal of all my philosophical pursuits: frantically rummaging for God. The game was on. Eyes closed. One, two, three, four, five, six, seven, eight, nine, ten. Eyes open. Ready or not, here I come. First stop: Big Sky Country. I'd never been, but I'd seen photos, and I was sure that if God lived anywhere, it had to be Montana. Now, all I had to do was convince my parents to let me go.

"Montana?" my dad replied when I revealed my plans. "What are you going to do *there?* Probably it's no better than Dayton."

"I got a job working at a resort, and when I'm not working, I can go hiking. It's beautiful there. They have mountains and glaciers and lakes, and in the summer, the days are super long. It stays light until ten or something. Actually, it sounds a lot like Shiraz. I mean, just as beautiful." Besides being naturally stunning, Glacier National Park has little in common with the gardens of Shiraz. Still, I thought appealing to Ahmad's Shirazi roots might help. Not so much.

"*Nothing* is as beautiful as Shiraz," he replied. "*Mageh kholeey?* [What are you, a fool?]"

"Hiking?" my mom chimed in. "You don't even like to *walk*. Now you want to *hike?* In *Montana?* I don't even know where *is* Montana. Not even are you healed yet. You can't climb mountains. You can't even get up from bed properly."

For about a year after my surgery, I literally *rolled* out of bed every morning. It hurt like hell when I tried to sit up, so I just took to rolling. My doctors suggested I do crunches to rebuild the abdominal muscles they'd cut through, but it hurt, so I stopped.

For weeks, I persisted in my Glacier campaign, which unexpectedly required far more convincing than even my secretarial major. I showed them pictures; I made them watch *A River Runs Through It*; I explained that the resort would provide food and lodging, and as part of my killer closing argument, I told them that now that I was out of the hospital and supposedly cured, now that I wasn't dying, I had the right to start *living*. I'm not above appealing to pity. It worked. Ahmad ultimately even agreed to drive out with me.

After four days of driving, we finally made it to the park. Looking at the mountains as we drove in, I began bawling uncontrollably. This wasn't at all in character for me (especially in front of my dad), but then again, it's hard to stay in character when you're confronted with that much natural beauty for the first time. Montana put my imagination to shame. It was more striking than I'd pictured heaven itself. Ahmad didn't cry (at least not that I could tell), but he was just as awestruck.

"*Shiraz keh neest, amah vaghan zeebast* [It's not Shiraz, but it's truly beautiful]," he said.

Ahmad stayed for a few days, and we hiked together. The highlight of our adventures was stumbling upon a lone purple orchid growing beside a pile of melting snow.

Ahmad has always loved gardening. Shortly after the Revolution, he planted two hundred small trees on an empty lot near my grandmother's house in Tehran, all in an effort to prevent the government from developing it. Miraculously, he succeeded. The government didn't develop the land, and several years later, they erected a fence around it, declaring it a public park.

Since moving to America, Ahmad hasn't saved any large swaths of public land, but he has always taken great pride in doing our landscaping—to the point where one of our neighbors once asked how much he charged, not realizing the gardener owned the house. (True to form, Ahmad took the inquiry as a great compliment, entirely missing any potentially racist undertones.) When I was thirteen, he fell madly in love with orchids and built a greenhouse beside the garage to raise and pamper them. So, to see one growing in such a seemingly inhospitable environment astounded him.

"Imagine how it grows here. *Vasateh barf, bedooneh heecheey, tanhayeh tanha* [In the middle of the snow, without anything, all alone]." Then he began reciting Rumi, as he is wont to do several times a day. In terms of a pastime, such recitations are right up there with orchid cultivation for him. His car is always full of Post-its with poems on them. His office has ten times as many books of poetry as it has medical ones, and his homepage is devoted entirely to Rumi.

As usual, I understood only about half of the poem Ahmad recited that day. Something about never being alone when you're enamored with God. I don't think it mattered to him, though, as he didn't even bother to translate into more modern Persian for me the way he usually does. It was as though he was reciting it purely for the benefit of the orchid. I was irrelevant.

Ahmad has never been particularly religious, especially compared with the rest of his family. But he gets God more than a lot of "religious" people I know. I remember him once coming home from this Qur'an class taught by Dr. Motekallem, one of the more devout Dayton Iranians and a cardiologist by trade. Apparently, one of the moms in the class asked about why Muslims have to pray so frequently. Though supremely annoyed, Ahmad managed to keep quiet—a serious feat for him. He wasn't so quiet, however, when he got home.

"No one says you need to pray at all. Pray as much as you vant. Who cares! You have to be in love first. She's not in *love*."

To Ahmad (and to a ton of other Iranians including myself, thanks to Rumi, Hafiz, Saadi and all the other Sufi poets), you can't be a true believer without being in love—not only with God, but with all of His creation. Thus, God is more than some distant, removed "Almighty." He is as the poets and mystics refer to him: the Lover and the Beloved. It's tough not to feel in love when you're face-to-face with a bright purple orchid brazenly rising out of the snow—especially when you've spent years raising orchids in a temperature-controlled greenhouse, convinced that such a specimen was impossible.

After Ahmad left, I scribbled this down in a sparkly orange journal that Nobar gave me before I set out on my journey.

5/3/99

INCREDIBLE! I've never seen anything this beautiful in my life. I dropped Ahmad off at the airport in Kalispell around 11:00, and I got back around 2 pm. First thing, I had to fill out a fucking W-2. I was totally lost. It was like having to fill out tax forms at the gates of heaven—seeing it in the background but stuck inside doing fucking paperwork. Then I had to go on this "tour" of the resort. I could so give a shit. All I wanted to do was run around the park like a ten-year-old. Once they showed me to my cabin, I just threw my shit down and got back in the car to drive around . . . I saw elk for the first time today. Fucking elk! Amazing.

My pen just exploded. I'm so going to love it here.

And I did. I worked at the gift shop and espresso bar of St. Mary Lodge and Resort, which stood at the east entrance of the park, right at the foot of Going-to-the-Sun Road—the only road that runs through the park. I folded T-shirts and made espressos, americanos, lattes, café mochas, as well as every flavor of fudge known to man, with an emphasis on huckleberry chocolate, by far our best seller. I also tore off more "Made in China" stickers from more knickknacks than I could count. Wouldn't want to disappoint the tourists with the truth.

Upon arriving, I knew no one. Nevertheless, I easily made friends with both locals and seasonal imports, mostly college students as well. At St. Mary, I was the only brown girl who wasn't Blackfoot, the only nondrinker who wasn't Mormon and the only Muslim, full stop. Still, I felt right at home. I was loud, gregarious and eager to share all the lessons I'd learned over the past year with anyone who'd listen.

I packed a ridiculous amount of life into those four months. Atop a mountain on the Canadian side of the park, I had my first and only mystical experience to date, which felt sort of like being eaten by the sun. I had a boyfriend for the first time in my life— and for a short period, two at once. I went to the Calgary Stampede, my first rodeo. I ate bison, huckleberries, venison and more huckleberries. And I saw more stars, wildlife, mountains, lakes, glaciers and Wranglers than ever before.

It may as well be a different country up there, and in a way, it is. The park itself is officially known as "Waterton-Glacier International Peace Park," as it spans the U.S.-Canadian border. You can use Canadian and American money everywhere, and crossing the border is quick, easy and painless. I once crossed through in a Jeep full of white guys who had, unbeknownst to me, racked up nearly half a dozen DUIs among them and hidden a sandwich bag full of pot under the driver's seat. Though we were stopped, nothing came of it, and after twenty minutes of polite questioning, we crossed into The True North, Strong and Free. I yelled at them, told them to thank God this wasn't Mexico and made them smoke all the pot before we headed back. I drove.

Fewer than fifty people live in St. Mary year-round, and they're all crazy. Apart from the fact that they've chosen to live beside glaciers and freeze their asses off for at least nine months out of the year, they're just unabashedly peculiar on the whole. Shortly after arriving, I drove to the nearby town of East Glacier for groceries and ran into a man casually walking up and down the aisles with a rifle slung over his shoulder. No one else seemed alarmed. I gathered the nerve to ask him what the deal was, hoping he was just an avid hunter. His reply: "Ya never know when the gov-ment's comin' 'round." I wished him a good day and left without my groceries.

My only encounter with the "gov-ment" in Glacier came in the form of Officer Kim Peach. Yes, that really was his name, and yes, he really was a *he*. Officer Peach pulled me over for speeding. My immediate response was emphatic: "There's no speed limit in Montana."

"There is inside the *park*, ma'am."

"Seriously?"

"Seriously."

Apparently, I was going 60 in a 25.

"I'm so sorry, officer," I responded, batting my eyelashes. "I had no idea."

"You know I could arrest you, but consider this your lucky day. I've seen you around with Moses, and he says you're good people."

Yes, he really used the phrase "good people." I'd just started seeing Moses, a local who worked for the park service, and given the tiny population, Kim knew him well. I was released with a stern warning, after which I spent several minutes laughing. I even wrote down his name on the back of a receipt for a milk shake from Pie in the Sky, lest I achieve the impossible and forget a name like Kim-fucking-Peach.

Moses was a white, Catholic mountain man who lived in a trailer provided by the park and spent most of his days clearing trails. He grew up right outside of Glacier, so he was a terrific tour guide. He took me all around to places only locals seemed to know existed. One day, we were driving up to the North Fork over these crazy dirt roads in the middle of nowhere. You can't get to the North Fork without a truck. My Camry would have kicked it within the first five minutes. But his park-issued flatbed was pretty rugged, and we were doing fine—until he stopped and said, "Oh shit. We're out of gas." I looked at the fuel gauge. It was on "E" and blinking. The nearest gas station was about twenty miles away.

"Are you fucking kidding me?"

"Nope," he said, in a tone as deadpan as he could manage.

"What are we going to do? We're totally going to *die* out here!"

Then he flipped a switch next to the steering wheel, and the indicator flew to "F." Apparently a lot of park vehicles, his included, have two separate gas tanks. I wasn't amused. Even less amusing was the fact that once we got up to the end of this dirt road, which might as well have been in Calcutta, and finally started hiking, we ran into a grizzly within the first half hour. A lot of tourists get excited at the prospect of seeing a grizzly. A lot of tourists are dumb-fucks. Grizzlies are gigantic and way faster than you'd expect. Supposedly they prefer fish and berries to humans, but knowing this isn't at all reassuring when you're face-to-face with one.

The bear was only a few yards away. I froze, terrified, thinking how useless our stupid bear-bells were. Moses was totally calm. He grabbed my shoulder and pushed me toward the ground, whispering, "Don't look at it." We crouched there, looking away from the bear, for what seemed like hours. Moses insisted it was less than a minute. Eventually, the bear slowly wandered off, and the second it turned its back to us, I turned around and booked it. Moses was pissed.

"You can't *do* that," he told me. "You've just got to be calm and relaxed in a situation like that."

This is the kind of shit Montanans are capable of. But if you grew up in Dayton, amid squirrels, house cats and a few deer, it's hard not to run like hell when you see a bear. Despite the fact that the owners of the resort made us sit through this whole seminar on what to do when faced with bears, moose, mountain lions and pretty much any other species of wildlife in the park, I responded roughly the same way in every scenario. Moose? Run. Black bear? Run. Grizzly? Run. Mountain goat? Okay, I never ran from a mountain goat, but that was largely because the goats generally had the courtesy to keep their distance.

I knew from the start that Moses and I were from two faraway planets. Apart from the fact that he was unnaturally calm around bears, there was also his being a white all-American boy who lived in a double-wide and cleared trails for a living. Not exactly the obvious fit for a spoiled, brown Iranian Muslim girl who took prayer breaks in the middle of the day and was never going to sleep with him. To his credit, he never pressured me, but I expect that was partly because much of my allure lay in the fact that I was unlike any other American girls he'd dated.

He took me to his parents' house one afternoon, and his mom

had a single issue of *National Geographic* on the coffee table. I knew the issue well. "IRAN" appeared prominently on the cover, and there was this girl (definitely from some remote village where I'd never been and had absolutely no intention of ever going) wearing a weird, colorful, traditional garb that covered pretty much everything except her eyes, which (of course) were swimming in eyeliner. It was the only magazine in the room as far as I could tell. How sweet, I thought to myself. Now get me the hell out of here.

I learned how to pray in Montana. Before Ahmad left, I asked him to pray into a tape recorder, and I played it back a hundred times until I learned how.

Once I got the words and motions down, I was hooked. I began doing all my prayers—on time and no matter what. I prayed in the middle of a Native American powwow, inside and outside of several restaurants, at the bases and peaks of any number of mountains, in my cabin, beside a couple of glaciers and a ton of lakes, on the continental divide, and many times on the side of Going-to-the-Sun Road. I've never been as spiritually disciplined as I was that summer. Perhaps it was the inescapable natural beauty, or perhaps it was the fact that there were no other Muslims around to tell me what I was doing "wrong." Whatever the case, the only time I was able to clear my head and stand relatively still was in prayer.

When I wasn't praying, I was living it up with my new friends— hiking, swimming, sliding down glaciers, visiting weird places like the House of Mystery (Montana's only "natural vortex"). But my newfound friends were constantly asking me to slow down. My speech, my movements and my thoughts were running at astonishing speeds. Every last one of my senses was on high. Food tasted better. The sun shone brighter—likely the cause and/or result of the aforementioned sun-swallowing incident. Music seemed louder—I could even *see* it sometimes. And then there were the stars and the northern lights, which required no mind tricks to dazzle and delight. The combination of this natural splendor and my mild mania that summer felt much like how drug addicts describe their first hit—but it lasted an entire summer, with no apparent side effects. No track marks, no nausea, no constipation, no nightmares. Just joy.

Thus began my grand entrance into the world of clinical bipolarity, though I wouldn't know it for years. My experiences at Wesleyan—hallucinations and all—could have easily been written off as a byproduct of starvation or sleeplessness. Montana, however, served as confirmation. It was my formal debut.

This was the kind of euphoric mania that inspires mystics, poets and composers. Not to say that I was writing music or poetry or anything. I was too busy *being*. This was worlds away from what I'd endured at Wesleyan. *This* was fun.

Unfortunately, however, it was also the type of mania that I later learned becomes less and less common throughout the progression of the disease. Years later, I would also discover how quickly this breed of euphoria can turn on you—how it can inspire the kind of mania that leads to incoherence, irrationality and, ultimately, psychosis. I don't expect I'll ever again experience the same kind of bliss I did in Montana, at least not without paying for it later, with ever-increasing units of suffering.

5/?/99

I absolutely LOVE it here! I love the place, the people, the whole feel of it. I can't explain it. I can't write it. If I were a musician, maybe I could capture it. But alas, such is the curse of my name—sucking at all things musical. I saw the northern lights tonight for the first time. . . . AMAZING! Light whitish, bluish, greenish, purplish. They weren't dancing or anything, but apparently they start doing that later in the summer. I was sitting in the living room talking with Pete and Alfred after all the others had gone to Kip's [Beer Garden], and we decided to go sit out on the bridge where Going-to-the-Sun starts. It was freezing, but I toughed it out, and it was worth it. Alfred was telling a story about how he was in this bicycle race and peed all over himself. Apparently to save time during races, men pull over to the side of the road and piss without getting off their bikes. So yeah, Alfred was sort of an amateur trying this for the first time, and he fell off his bike into a puddle of his own pee. So we're all laughing hysterically at his story, and then we see them. Pete looks up, and he's like, "Shit, are those the northern lights?" I guess he hadn't seen them before either. Seriously, they were incredible. I talked to Nobar today. She's working in Dr. Hamidinia's office [one of the Dayton Iranians, a urologist]. Apparently she's watching a penile implant tomorrow. I'm so happy I'm not

spending the summer in Dayton. Did I say I love, love, love,
love [there are about two dozen more "love's" after this]
it here.

I think it happened right after seeing the northern lights that first time—right after writing all those loves. Feeling as though there was just way too much to do and see, I pretty much stopped sleeping. I started going to Canada nearly every day. The border was only about fifteen minutes away, and I loved the idea of being able to jump from country to country so easily. I saw lots of bald eagles on the Canadian side of the park and, oddly enough, not a single one on the American side. For some reason, beyond the eagles, I was convinced that the Canadian side was more beautiful. Looking back, both sides were pretty much on par, but I guess it was just the allure of the unfamiliar. Or it may well have been the Dairy Queen that gave Canada its edge.

It was right near the border, and I went several times a week. I always ordered a large chocolate M&M Blizzard, and I never ate more than a few bites. You'd think after the tenth Blizzard or so, I'd start ordering a small, but no. I had to have more than I could eat. That's what mania is all about. Too much. Of everything.

I spent most of my time at the Dairy Queen checking voice mails and returning calls, as the reception in St. Mary was shit. I talked with Matthew most of all. We'd met and become friends two years earlier, and while he was in England at the time, he still called at least once a week. We hadn't started dating, but I was now privately toying with the idea.

Our Dairy Queen chats were almost entirely one-sided. I

talked and talked and talked. He listened, said "uh-huh" and "yeah" a lot, occasionally speaking about his life in London before I inevitably interrupted him. I don't know how he tolerated my soliloquies, let alone stayed on the line for hours at a time, but he did.

What I remember most about those conversations is Matthew's patience and quickness. Unlike everyone else with whom I spoke that summer, he never asked me to slow down. Rather, he kept up, my only match. I took note, preparing to practice my latest lessons on him, fully equipped to fall in love, and not entirely aware of it.

In the end, my great Montanan search for the Divine was a categorical success, for it was there—on the land the Blackfeet call the Backbone of the World, where the sky refuses to contain itself and the glaciers struggle to survive humanity's greed—where I learned that God cannot be found, only sought. It was there where I learned how such seeking trains us to love without restraint. And it was there where I learned that to be unreservedly mad for another human being who neither bore nor raised you is to unite with the Beloved.

ten

sleeping with the enemy

I'm not one of those girls who fantasized about her wedding day as a kid. My biggest fantasy, fueled by steady delusions of grandeur, consisted of winning a Nobel Peace Prize. The second I found out such a prize existed (thank you, Aung San Suu Kyi), I wanted one. As far as I was concerned, any mate of mine would have to understand and accept lower priority to this ambition.

I met Matthew less than two months after freshman orientation. He was a sophomore, and at the time, I was about as interested in a romantic relationship as I was in dentistry. But he had a serious edge over the other boys, and it had nothing to do with who he was. Rather, it was all about who he *knew*.

Matthew first approached me as I was walking home from the library one afternoon. I'd just spent hours researching the tobacco lawsuits of the early '90s, and I was looking forward to a nap. As I pondered how long it would be until I could sue thieving, lying corporations of my own choosing, Matthew materialized beside me as though he'd just fallen from the sky. Attempting to casually fall into my stride, he succeeded only in scaring the hell out of me. As far as I was concerned, every male on campus was a potential rapist, and from my informal research (speaking with several women who'd been raped on campus and watching too many crappy Lifetime movies), I'd come to the swift conclusion that pretty much all rapists were attractive, young white men. Matthew fit the stereotype. I discreetly fiddled with my keys, making sure my pepper spray was close at hand.

Apparently, the boy had been at the library as well, and like a lunatic, he'd followed me home. I was a few steps away from my dorm when he approached me.

"I never do this," he began. I rolled my eyes and tightened my grip on the pepper spray. "I've just seen you around and noticed you. And I've noticed you noticing me." Bullshit, I thought to myself. I've never seen you before in my life. Still, I kept quiet, all the while clinging to my trusty pepper spray.

"So, I was just wondering if you might want to go out sometime."

"Yeah, I don't know," I responded, thinking, Fat chance, weirdo.

"Just one date," he pleaded before quickly changing the subject. Perhaps he'd realized that getting to know me a little might increase his chances.

"What's your name?"

"Melody."

"I'm Matt," he offered without my asking. "Is that your *real* name? I mean, where are you from?"

"Yeah, it's my *real* name," I retorted, offended, though it was a question I faced frequently. My mom, eschewing the urge to give me a more traditional Persian name, chose to name me after a

Bobby Vinton song called "My Melody of Love." It's beyond bad. "I'm from Ohio."

"I mean originally," he added, pissing me off even more. But I wasn't about to have anyone thinking I was ashamed of my heritage.

"Iran."

"Really? I thought you were Puerto Rican or something." He wasn't the first. "My best friend here is Iranian. Her name's Roxana. She's great. You should meet her."

I feigned ignorance, despite knowing exactly who he was talking about. As far as I knew at the time, she was the only other Iranian girl on campus. We'd never met, but I knew of her, and I found out later that she knew of me too. She'd even seen me in the library a couple weeks earlier when she was with Matt. Legend has it she pointed me out to him, saying she thought I was beautiful. Apparently Matthew agreed enough to ask me out later without knowing a single thing about me.

"Yeah, I'd love to meet her," I responded, suddenly changing my tone.

"Well, I can introduce you." He knew he had his in. "You know, if you agree to go out with me," he said, smiling.

"Fine," I replied, "but I can't eat fat. It might kill me. My pancreas is fucked up."

"Um, okay," he said. "What about Friday?"

"I'm going to a Morrissey concert on Friday. How about I get back to you."

"Why don't we go together?" he asked. "I've never really heard his music, but I've heard *of* him. You can school me." This guy had some serious nerve. Plus, he'd never listened to Morrissey. That was at least twenty points off, I thought. Within less than five minutes, he was down to a B-minus at best.

"Sacrilege," I said, not joking in the least. "Morrissey is like my god. I can't go with just anyone. It's too personal. I'm actually going alone." I was, and I did.

"So how about Saturday or sometime next week?"

"Sure, we'll figure it out," I replied, releasing my pepper spray.

"Can you write down your number for me?" he asked.

"I don't have a pen," I lied. He rummaged through his backpack clumsily and couldn't find one.

"Yeah, just tell me. I'll remember it," he said.

So I told him, and he remembered. He called that Saturday to ask about the concert and to press me more about our date.

"I'll cook for you. I live in Russian House. Right across the street from the Butts." (I lived in the Butterfield dorms— affectionately known by the student body as "the Butts.")

"I know where it is. What are you, Russian or something?"

"No, I just speak Russian and love the culture. I'll tell you more about it when you come over. How about tomorrow night at seven?"

"Okay," I said, "but remember, I can't eat fat. Oh, and I don't eat pork either."

"Sure, no worries."

"Why don't you invite Roxana, too," I suggested, trying to sound nonchalant.

"Yeah, maybe another time. This time I just want to get to know *you*."

Ackhh, I thought, how many times would I have to go out with this dude before he introduced me to Roxana?

During our first "date" (as we were sitting in Matthew's room, uncomfortably watching the scene from *Deconstructing Harry* where this guy is fucking Elaine from *Seinfeld* from behind as her nearly blind grandmother walks in on them), I told Matthew that I would never sleep with him and that I was going home.

"Wait," he said, "I had no idea this movie was so porno-graphic."

"It's not the movie. I just don't feel like dating right now. Why don't we just be friends?"

While he was clearly let down, Matthew agreed and walked me out. I figured that would be the last I'd hear from him, but it wasn't. He kept calling. He didn't *actually* want to be just friends, but being the most persistent human being I've ever met, he settled for it, all the while expecting that one day I'd change my mind.

That is, until he stopped expecting it and started seriously dating Lera, a Ukrainian girl he met during a junior-year study-abroad program. When he returned to campus, Matthew and I were living in the same house. It wasn't planned. I was supposed to be living next door to our mutual friend Meeth, but last minute, she decided to spend that year in London. So Matt and Meeth switched places. Our rooms were separated by a set of sliding wooden doors.

By that time, Roxana and I were best friends, thanks to Matt's introduction. Rox was always trying to convince me to date Matt, and I was always telling her he wasn't my type.

"I mean, for one, he's white and Christian," I explained. "He can claim bullshit 'agnosticism' all he wants, but his parents are Christian; *he's* Christian. As if that's not bad enough, he's half-American and half-British, for God's sake. Did you know his mom is *British*? Seriously, think about it. He's the fucking *enemy*! What two countries screwed Iran more than any others on the planet? England and America. Everyone knows it. *You* know it!"

"Duh, but I'm also pretty sure that Matt had nothing to do with a CIA coup that happened before he was *born*. And I doubt his mom or dad had anything to do with it, either."

"How can you be so sure?" I asked, only half kidding.

"Matt's not the enemy. *You* are. You're totally sabotaging yourself. It's obvious that you guys are meant to be together. *Az khar-eh shaytoon beyah pa-een* [Come down from the devil's donkey]! You know you love him." (The above is a strange idiom that Roxana loves to use. I'd never heard it before meeting her. Her family is from some small village in northern Iran where people talk funny and say weird things like this. Basically, it means "Stop doing whatever crazy shit you're doing.")

"I do not. Serious *estefragh* [vomit] alert!" (This is a strange Fanglish idiom I made up. It means "You're grossing me out.")

"You're an idiot," Roxana said.

This is how many of our conversations about Matthew ended— with my *estefragh* alerts and Roxana's statements of the obvious.

I didn't fully realize just how much I'd grown to like Matt until I saw his pictures from his year abroad. Lera was in nearly all of them, and she was gorgeous. I hated her immediately, and Matthew's stock skyrocketed. I wanted him for myself.

So I did what any crazy girl would do. I sent myself flowers and invented a fake boyfriend. He even called the house a couple times, and by that, I mean Roxana called, pretending to be him. I made sure that he called only when Matthew was around of course, and I did my best impression of a girl trying to dump a guy who was desperately in love with her.

Matthew insists my absurd tactics had nothing to do with his dumping Lera. Regardless, their long-distance relationship began to fall apart over the first few months of the school year, and I was happy for it.

The night before he broke it off—and it kills me to admit this—I kissed Matthew. Yes, it's true. *I* kissed *him*. Not that he protested. The next day, he called Lera to break up with her. I eavesdropped, of course. She was clearly heartbroken, and as much as Matthew tried to comfort her by saying it was more about circumstance than it was about love, he seemed much less distraught than she. I'd like to say I didn't relish this as a victory, but I did.

Still, I owe Lera a lot. Even with all of Roxana's coaxing, I'm not sure I would have realized how interested I was in Matthew, how much I was missing by not being with him, if she'd never come into the picture. Unlike Matthew, I'm ridiculously jealous.

Thus, a day after breaking up with the Ukrainian, two years after accosting me in front of the Butts, Matthew was in bed with an Iranian. Not *literally*. I'm not *that* easy, but it was literal soon enough. Before long, we stopped closing the wooden doors between our rooms; we were sleeping on the same futon every night, and we made an appointment at Planned Parenthood.

Since Matthew had slept with three other girls before me, I made him get every last test they offered. Initially he asked me to get tested too, but when he saw me light up and say, "Sure, of course!" he just told me to forget about it. From day one, I made no secret of the fact that I was a virgin, and he believed me.

Nevertheless, I wasn't exactly polite about my request. He didn't even mildly object to getting tested, but I still felt the need to explain my appeal: "AIDS is totally on the rise in Eastern Europe. I don't know anything about all your Natashas." I had taken to calling all of his previous girlfriends Natasha. His first serious girlfriend in high school was named Natasha and all the rest since were Eastern European as well, so I just called them all Natasha. I still do. I think it's funny. He thinks it's mildly racist. I don't see why it can't be both.

Matthew came up clean, and I quickly became the biggest fan the Pill and Planned Parenthood have ever known. For some reason, despite the fact that they'd never officially expressed any such expectation, I was sure that my parents were vehemently against premarital sex—particularly as it related to me.

By the time Matthew and I started dating, my parents knew him well. The first time they met (over a dinner my parents treated a few of my friends to while they were visiting me at school), Matthew sat next to Ahmad and managed to immediately impress him with his vast knowledge of current events, the stock market and Iranian history.

Matthew reads more than anyone I know. He's always trying to get me to include more facts and stats in my commentaries, while I'm always more concerned with thoroughly expressing my opinions, just assuming people know the facts or expecting them to learn the entire backstory elsewhere if they don't. Unlike me (and I'd guess most people on the planet), Matthew *loves* fact checking. Once, after I submitted a commentary to NPR, the producer made it a point to praise my thorough fact-checking. When I told her that my husband was behind it, she asked if he wanted a job. Probably a joke, but still telling.

Over the past decade, Matthew has worked as a sixth-grade social studies teacher, an education policy researcher and analyst, the cofounder of an education social media company that helps teachers share lesson plans and, most recently, a Harvard education fellow proposing district-based policy initiatives by running a bunch of statistical models I don't understand.

What makes Matthew a killer educator, among other things, is the fact that he's an insatiable learner. Nothing escapes his curiosity. While I'm easily bored by most things and more than happy to remain ignorant on a wide variety of topics, Matthew always wants to learn more about more. Some part of him truly *believes* he can learn everything there is to learn if he just reads enough. So he never stops trying. No matter how many times I tell him that his attempts are futile, he persists. It's equally inspiring and annoying.

B ack to sex. So, I wasn't about to tell my parents I'd lost my virginity. Besides the fact that I was sure they'd kill me, I thought it would make Matthew look bad, and they both really liked him. One afternoon, however, my parents decided to surprise me. They hopped a flight from Ohio to Connecticut and just showed up at the door. One of our housemates answered. Matthew and I were upstairs. Together. In no position to be disturbed by *anyone*, least of all my parents. They happily climbed the stairs to my room, which had now turned into *our* room given we hadn't used the doors between those rooms for months. The first thing they heard, over Morrissey's crooning, was a hammer.

Let me explain. I'm a fan of canopies and forts, so I was creating a makeshift tent out of sheets, under which I was planning on doing things no one would ever want their parents to think, let alone know, about.

So, that's when I heard them knock. Matthew got up to answer *my* door. He was wearing my teal terry-cloth robe with dolphins on it. It barely covered his butt. He opened the door a crack and peeked out. He immediately shut it.

"It's your parents."

"Shut the fuck up. Seriously, who is it?"

"Seriously. It's your parents." He ran for the bathroom, which, thank God, was attached to our room, and he proceeded to take a shower. There was nothing inconspicuous about any of this. I pulled on some pants and a T-shirt, too terrified to realize the shirt was Matthew's, and answered the door.

"Hi, Mom. Hi, Ahmad," I said awkwardly. "What are you doing here?"

"Ve came to surprise you. Are you okay? Vhere is Matt?"

"Oh, he's in the shower," I said. This wasn't looking good. But my parents didn't seem even remotely upset. Instead, they actually looked a little embarrassed. I told them to come in. They both sat on my neatly made bed, which I hadn't used since October. It was now March.

They didn't say a word. They just sat there looking everywhere but at me. Then Ahmad saw the open case of birth-control pills on my vanity. I wanted to die.

"Vait," he said, "you *pay* for bert control?"

Seriously, was this happening?

"You know I can get it free for you, right?" Ahmad offered. "I have million samples at vork. You should *never* pay for bert control." Was this really his only concern? Really? It appeared so.

"Yes, Melody," my mom agreed. "He can get you best bert control for free. The newest brand. Vhat is this?" She actually *picked up* the pack. "It is same von they had in sixties. Ahmad can get you newer von. They have much lower dose of hormone. They are much safer. You should have tell us this." She was more distressed that I wasn't using designer drugs than she was about my shameless fornication. Jazbi wears almost exclusively designer clothes: Ferragamo, Fendi, Chanel, St. John—these are her prophets; Saks and Neiman Marcus—these are her gods.

I was dumbstruck. At this exact moment, Matthew walked in. There weren't enough books on Persian culture or history in the world to prepare him for this absolute mind-fuck.

"Hi, Dr. Moezzi, Dr. Moezzi," he said, shaking each of their hands.

"Hi, Matt," my dad said cheerfully. "Let's go for lunch, huh?" We'd both already had lunch. Chicken pesto panini. I could taste the pesto rising in my throat.

Yes, that's how it went down. They didn't kill me. They didn't even get mad. They just wanted to make sure I didn't waste any money on birth control pills and that I took only the Prada variety.

They took us to Athenian, a popular Greek diner in Middletown. My mom ordered souvlaki and told stories about how I used to pick live snails off the walls of our garden in Greece and eat them.

"Ve tried to eh-stop her. Lucky the shells are soft. She only ate the baby ones. She never got eh-sick."

Matthew has never tired of making fun of me for this. He loves buying me snails. Stuffed snails, glass snails, plastic snails, crystal snails—even live snails once in Portugal. It's been over ten years now, and he still can't stop himself. Sadly, I expect this joke will never die.

After that day, Ahmad began regularly mailing me sample packets of hip new designer birth control pills, which admittedly weirded me out at first (a sentiment that quickly faded once I discovered that my friends were paying upward of fifty dollars for the same packets).

Thus began my love affair with Matthew and hormonal contraception. The former for being smarter, cooler and funnier than anyone I'd ever met, and the latter for giving me a sense that I could control my own body for the first time in years.

Having lived at the mercy of my fucked-up pancreas for so long, I wasn't used to feeling in charge of anything as far as my body was concerned. In fact, I was sure it was out to destroy me. But the ability to enjoy sex, to derive so much pleasure from a body I was sure hated me up until then, and the miracle of being able to do so while actively preventing the introduction of another foreign, unwelcome collection of cells into my being was a revelation.

My physical body and I had finally declared a truce. Sweeter still, at least in this round, I had won. And seeing as how there is nothing I've ever wanted less in life than children of my own, it was a big win.

part three

eleven

christmas in tehran

On July 7, 1999, Tehran erupted. In all, it lasted a week. But it marked an awakening—a once-presumed dormant volcano was now active.

The student demonstrations, which at the time were the most widespread since the Revolution, began in response to the judiciary's decision to shut down the reformist newspaper, *Salam*. Paramilitary forces raided a student dormitory after the first day of protests, killing one student. After that, it was on.

For six days, the protests continued. At least three others were killed, hundreds were injured and around seventy people just up and "disappeared." If anything, these demonstrations proved that young Iranians were willing to rise up, and ten years later, they did so in the millions.

Had we never left Iran, I expect I would have been part of the 1999 student protests, and were I not killed or arrested, I likely would have joined the ones in 2009 as well. Instead, I spent the summer of 1999 frolicking about the Montana wilderness, steering clear of newspapers, televisions and computers in my effort to commune with the Divine. As to global politics, I was fucking clueless. The same girl who spent her high school weekends protesting in front of Shell gas stations after being so moved by the plight of the Ogoni people in Nigeria, the same girl who acted as an official Amnesty International representative at the Dayton Accords, the same girl who sent weekly letters to President Carlos Menem inquiring about the up to thirty thousand "disappeared" after Argentina's Dirty War, was now MIA as her own country, her own generation, her own *people* rose up in the biggest way they ever had in her lifetime.

By the 2009 protests, I was keeping up with the events in Iran, writing about them and, in my public support for the opposition movement, ensuring I would never again be able to safely return to my homeland so long as the allegedly Islamic Republic remained intact. What a difference a decade makes.

I last visited Iran several months after the 1999 protests. It was just Ahmad and me. I had no idea it would be my final visit. I had no idea I'd soon become a "dissident" writer. And I had no idea how much I'd come to miss Iran.

We went to visit family and bring my grandmother back to America with us. By that time, the protests were history, but the sentiments that provoked them were still alive and well. My cousin Negin served as my primary guide. She was a few years younger than I, but a hell of a lot braver. Sick to death of living under such a ridiculously repressive regime, she staged her own private protest—one that tons of Iranian kids had taken up. She dressed as provocatively as she thought she could get away with. Tight jeans, tight *caption* (the minimum mandatory body covering that looks pretty much like a raincoat) above the knees, thin *roo-sari* that looked like more of a headband than a true head covering, and impeccable makeup. I, on the other hand, wore a full *roo-sari*, which I pulled up to my forehead, covering every strand of hair, a long, loose *caption* and no makeup. All this gained me the nickname *Khanoom-eh Hezbollaheey* [Lady Hezbollah]. I looked like shit, but I didn't care. I wasn't looking to pick up guys. I had Matthew at home, and I wasn't about to get thrown in jail for going on a date. So as much as possible, I tried to avoid going out to restaurants or teahouses with nonrelatives after dark, which wasn't hard given I preferred family house parties to public outings anyway.

I had a lot of trouble sleeping on that last trip, and I couldn't stop hiccuping for nearly two days after getting there. My grandmother insisted this meant someone was thinking fondly of me. I insisted it meant that I had the hiccups. Iranians can be crazy superstitious. One of their favorite pastimes involves interpreting minor annoyances and bad dreams as good omens. If your palm itches, it means either that someone is thinking or speaking highly of you or that you'll be coming into a lot of money in the near future—or perhaps both. If you have a dream about your best friend dying, then she should expect to live a long life. The reverse, however, doesn't apply: *good* dreams and experiences aren't at all interpreted as bad omens.

One day, after my grandma had gone to the bazaar to buy eggplants, Negin sat me down to do a *Fall-eh Hafiz*. It's a form of divination—sort of like reading someone's tarot cards—but instead of cards, you use a giant book of Hafiz's poems. Negin opened the book to a random poem and read it to me. As always, I barely understood a thing thanks to the old-school Persian, but she graciously translated it to modern-day Farsi and filled in any gaps, using whatever English she'd learned from watching way too many bad American movies. I don't remember the exact poem, but I do remember the divination. She told me the poem was positive (no surprise) and that there was a great love in my life (sure, there was Matthew; we'd just started dating and were still in the gaga phase of our relationship) and that he was a little too interested in money, so I should watch out for that. A year later Matthew took a job as an investment banker at Lehman Brothers. There was no indication that his future employer would contribute to one of the worst economic crises in American history less than a decade later, but given Hafiz is more master of poetry than global markets, I don't hold this against him.

Not being well versed in the art of divination, I couldn't return the favor and read Negin's *Fall* for her. Had I been able to, we might have discovered that she would soon join us in America, becoming yet another one of a growing number of Iranian émigrés. We spent the rest of the afternoon eating saffron and rosewater ice cream, getting our eyebrows threaded, watching my grandmother sauté what seemed like a thousand eggplants and watching *10 Things I Hate About You*. I did my fair share of mediocre translating for Negin, but mostly she understood. We agreed it was one of the worst movies ever made, and I assured her that there were still a lot of great American movies out there. It just so happened that the large majority of bootleg videos that made it to Iran sucked.

Yet another sucky thing I discovered on that trip: the Backstreet Boys. Negin's room was plastered with their posters. I'd never heard of them. I specifically remember telling her that these goons would never make it in America. Turns out they were *already* big in the States, and she was just more attuned to American pop culture than I (apparently the only one left on the planet who hadn't gotten the memo about the cruel comeback of the boy band). Negin was well on her way to becoming a bona fide American.

Today she's a pharmacist in Southern California without even a hint of a Persian accent. Her Facebook page shows "Other activities and interests" ranging from Dancing Shiva Yoga Studio to Orange County Affiliate of Susan G. Komen for the Cure to "American Navy, stop calling our Persian Gulf as Arab Gulf. DO NOT CHANGE HISTORY."

I kept a diary during my last visit—something I generally avoid. Reading it now reminds me why. Looking back, I have so many positive memories of my trip, but reading my entries shows me how much I've managed to romanticize without realizing it.

December 16

Don't know how much I belong here. My Farsi has turned to shit. . . . I miss the States. I know that sounds totally pathetic after being here just 2 days, but I think it's just not being able to do things on my own. . . . So, yeah, I'm having the expected identity crisis. . . .

December 17

Lately, for some reason, I find it comforting to fantasize about suicide. Of course I'd never do it or even consider it, but still I take comfort in the idea. [This was seven years before my first attempt.] *It reminds me that I exist and that I'm free.*

December 18
Not feeling so suicidal this evening, but that's not to say that all fantasies have perished. . . .

December 21
My scar itches like absolute hell, and I swear it's getting bigger. Can't sleep—haven't slept. Hiccups are gone, but sleeplessness persists.

December 22
So apparently the pollution here is 6x the World Health Organization's allowance. I nearly passed out praying. We're leaving a week early. You can see the shit in the air. My dad isn't doing well and can't take the pollution either. They even canceled school because of it.

People are really unhappy here. It's like they're in prison. They joke about how only 100,000 people out of a million pass the koncour *[a grueling university entrance* exam] *and how Khomeini took all that was good in this country with him when he died. They say things like:* Zendeh Neesteem. Ein che zendegeey-eh? Dast-o-payemoon rah bastan. Ma ra mesleh bachahayeh panj saleh

meedoonan. [We are not alive. What kind of life is this?
Our hands and feet are tied. They treat us like five-year-
olds.] *They're really not doing well as a nation. I feel like
I should document the despair that hangs over this country.
It's fucking suffocating. All this shit in the air has got to be
carcinogenic.*

December 23
*Tonight Negin and I went out with a bunch of her friends.
I was mad scared of getting caught by the Komiteh* [the
disciplinary patrol charged with enforcing compliance with
"Islamic ideals"] *with all those boys* [being caught out with
a man who isn't your spouse or relative can get you into
serious trouble, even arrested]. *Her friends took us home
and then asked if we wanted to go out for coffee. I refused
b/c I'm crazy tarsoo* [afraid]. *Besides, apparently the
Komiteh raided that same café recently. They were all—
"That's why it's safe; they won't come back so soon."
I wasn't convinced. I think Negin was mad at me.
Apparently, going out tomorrow isn't an option, as the
pollution is said to be getting worse. I'm not sure how that's
possible. I can stand it, but I can't stand all the bullshit
laws more. I'm sick of wearing my roo-sari and being
scared every time I go out with Negin. I really don't know if
I can ever come back here after this trip—not until the govt*

changes. As it is, everyone who can is fleeing. They're sick of the bullshit too.

I have no memory of thinking that I didn't *want* to go back to Iran after that. I can't imagine I was serious, but then again, I *do* remember this gross suffocating feeling that had nothing to do with air quality indices. Still, it was the literal air that cut our visit short, that made us leave a week early. Perhaps if it weren't for the pollution, I would have left with a better impression. Perhaps it was the combination of the heaviness in the sky and on the ground that made things so bad. Perhaps if the air were pure, if they'd bothered with emissions tests, I'd have enjoyed myself more. Or perhaps not. Whatever the case, not being used to it, the smog made us especially light-headed, and before I knew it, we were on a plane headed back to the States. My snot was still black throughout our ten-hour layover in Frankfurt.

The air quality is even poorer in Iran today—as are its people. Inflation is through the roof. Unemployment is rampant. The morality, civil and criminal laws are abominable. The crackdowns on the opposition are growing and ongoing. In short, everything's worse.

While this is something I know, it's not something I experience on a daily basis. Instead, I have only fantasy and longing. I'm free to say, write and do pretty much anything I want as an American, but I'm not free to feel fully at home anywhere. It's better than rotting in a prison cell, but it still stings. I'm glad my parents brought us to the United States, but I'm not glad we left Iran. Granted, the former would have been impossible without the latter, but that's how I feel. Our excuse has always been that we left

Iran because Iran left us, but I've forever been haunted by the belief that we could have fought harder to get her back.

A t a time when everyone else seemed to want to get the hell out of Iran, with America being the choice destination, my grandmother was intent on staying. Mamaan Koochooloo, which is what everyone called her, is a play on the phrase *Mamaan Bozorg*. Literally translated, *Mamaan Bozorg* means "big mother"—more specifically, grandmother. Mamaan Koochooloo, however, means "small mother." She earned the nickname on account of her diminutive stature, though her size belied a massive presence. She was a big deal in her neighborhood, a section of northeastern Tehran known as Gheytareeyeh. Owning several properties in the area, she was a landlady by profession, which gave her a lot of free time to pursue her true calling as the sage and guru of Gheytareeyeh. For decades, people came to her with their problems—from failing marriages to misbehaving children to unemployment to poverty. Unlike your standard Western therapist, she had no formal training in the art and she actually gave advice—as opposed to keeping quiet and occasionally asking how something made a person feel.

When we got to Iran on that last visit, Mamaan Koochooloo was experiencing the very early stages of Alzheimer's disease, an affliction that is terrifyingly common on my mom's side of the family. By the time we got Mamaan Koochooloo on the plane to America, she was visibly distraught. On the last leg of our flight, a few hundred miles from the Dayton International Airport, a flight attendant came by to ask if she would need any special assistance upon landing. "No, thanks. She's fine," I replied. Mamaan Koochooloo looked at her and said, "Tank you. Tank you." Then she turned to me and said in Farsi, "I will die in this country." She did.

Without much to do but cook and watch videos of Iranian movies and television shows, she deteriorated quickly. Soon, she couldn't even cook because she'd either burn the food or just forget to turn on the stove or oven. One night, she fell out of her bed and injured her back so badly that she had to get one of those giant halos drilled into her head. She'd hold on to it from time to time and ask why there was a chair on her head, then try to pull it off. The doctors said it was time to put her in a home, but none of us could bring ourselves to do it. She clearly wasn't safe in the house anymore, and with both my parents working, Romana over a thousand miles away in Denver and me at school in Connecticut, there was no one to watch her during the day. Still, my mom simply *couldn't* put Mamaan Koochooloo in a nursing home.

Being the most rational and practical one in the family, however, Romana stepped in. She flew to Dayton to do the thing that all of us were too weak and selfish to do. In a weekend, she found a beautiful nursing home up the street and checked Mamaan Koochooloo in. In doing so, Romana spared my mom and the rest of us a world of guilt.

Over the next couple years, we watched Mamaan Koochooloo disappear. She communicated with the staff at the nursing home through a pile of notecards with Farsi on one side and English on the other. It took us a while to come up with this system, but it seemed to work once we made enough cards. Eventually, however, it didn't matter. She was making little sense even in Farsi.

Most of the time, she thought she was back in Iran or on pilgrimage in Mecca. She repeatedly asked why there were so many Americans around, and after a while, not realizing her own age, she also started asking why there were so many old people around. But all of this was a minor blessing of sorts. By tricking her into believing that she was young and in a more familiar place, her mind was doing her a serious favor. She was happier, more care-free and less consumed with anxiety when she thought she was elsewhere. My mother, on the other hand, was consistently devastated. She had no fantasy world into which she could escape. She always knew exactly who and where she was. Watching your mom die hurts like hell, but watching her evaporate is excruciating.

For the agony that Mamaan Koochooloo endured in America and the terror and grief my mother endured watching her disintegrate, I am livid. Mamaan Koochooloo shouldn't have died in Ohio. She shouldn't have spent her final years communicating through notecards. She shouldn't have had to trick herself into believing she was somewhere else. She should have been guiding her disciples in Gheytareeyeh, drinking tea instead of juice and eating *zoolbia bamieh* instead of tapioca pudding.

While I still have lots of family in Iran, Mamaan Koochooloo was by far my strongest human connection to the place. Without her to guide and protect me through the streets of Tehran, I'm not sure I could ever fully gain my footing there again, even if I *could* go back.

My last diary entry before uprooting Mamaan Koochooloo is a poem, entirely in Spanish—perhaps because it's the most neutral language I could find, one that I chose instead of one that chose me. More likely, however, I expect it's on account of vanity, for I am no poet. And this being the only poem I've ever willingly written in my life, it's dreadful. Still, departing Iran and permanently displacing Mamaan Koochooloo, no matter how welcome the prospect of fresh air, unsettled me—mercilessly flinging me toward the most foreign and unnerving literary invention imagin-able. Reading these words now, like leaving Iran then, nauseates and embarrasses me beyond measure:

> *Arrancada de la tierra de mi madre, la tierra de mi*
>
> *padre, la tierra de mi sangre. Traída a la tierra que va*
>
> *destruyendo mi patria negada.*
>
> *La tierra que veo ahora pertenece a un sueño fantástico,*
>
> *imposible. Pertenece al cielo y al infierno.*
>
> *Este país no me toma como suya. Me toma por extranjera,*
>
> *traidora.**

---

* Uprooted from the land of my mother, the land of my father, the land of my blood. Brought to a land that continues destroying my denied homeland. The land I see now belongs to a fantastical, impossible dream. It belongs to heaven and hell. This land doesn't take me as her own. She takes me for a stranger/a foreigner, a traitor.

twelve

toward a post-9/11 world

Being Iranian and American is like being a child of divorced parents, both of whom have killed a bunch of your siblings on account of their disdain for each other and neither of whom has any interest in civility, for the sake of their children or anyone else. Throw Islam into the mix, and you now become the object of the worst in a seemingly endless series of bitter custody disputes, leaving you doggy paddling in a murky, mosquito-infested morass. When your ridiculously fertile parents have resorted to filicide on hundreds of thousands of occasions, you can't help but worry you might be next.

Thus far, apart from the delusions, hallucinations, melancholia, hair-pulling and nail-biting, I've been largely spared—though admittedly, since 9/11 these unfortunate side effects have grown significantly worse, leading to three separate psychiatric hospitalizations and an ever-expanding personal pharmacy. In many ways, that day and the climate it incited represented the hostage crisis of my generation. But this time, all of us were the hostages, and the crisis continues.

Just to clarify, I had nothing to do with 9/11, nor do I know anyone who did. I share this only because I've been asked if I was involved—once in a job interview by an overweight lawyer wearing a hideous Aloha-print button-down shirt with three too many buttons undone; once at a book signing by a proud, self-professed Christian fundamentalist; once in a gay bookstore while defending the right of a *hijabi* girl not to be run over by a truck while crossing the street; and several times under a variety of other circumstances. So yeah, I figure it's worth clarifying.

In September 2001, I was a recent college graduate sharing a first-floor apartment on West 105th Street with a middle-aged gay couple, their five cats and a pug. I moved to Manhattan right after graduation, and I loved it. Sure, my living quarters were smaller than my parents' master bathroom in Dayton. Sure, my sole window overlooked a rundown fallout shelter inhabited by a loud Dominican family, a Chihuahua and a rooster our elderly Italian neighbor insisted they used for voodoo rituals. Sure, I could never get all the dirt out from under my fingernails. And sure, the city was full of rats the size of housecats. Still, Wesleyan was a sort of training ground for what nearly all of the kids there called "the city," as though it were the only one on the planet. Plus, Matthew was already there.

He lived downtown, two blocks from the World Trade Center. At the time, he'd just finished his first miserable year in investment banking at Lehman, and I'd just scored a prestigious position as a hostess at Café Lalo—a hopping Upper West Side eatery famous for its kosher cakes and a brief appearance in the film *You've Got Mail*. The pay was crap, but I got free meals during breaks, it was only a short walk from my apartment, and the hours left me with more than enough time to study for the LSAT.

On the morning of September 11, neither Matthew nor I went to work, as we were visiting my parents in Ohio. Driving past Dorothy Lane Market on our way to Lincoln Park, we heard a radio report about the first plane hitting the North Tower. We turned around and headed back to the house. The park could wait.

By the time we arrived, the second plane had hit, and my mom was in full-blown panic mode. Having lived through the Islamic Revolution, she was convinced that this was all some twisted rerun. "This is just like the Revolution," she kept saying in Farsi, pacing around the house. She was obsessed with deciding where to go and how to pack for our imminent departure. "Maybe we can go to France? Or back to Greece? Montreal?"

"Mom, chill. We aren't going anywhere," I said. "Just relax."

She wasn't used to being home in the middle of the afternoon, but the security officers at the VA hospital (where she'd worked since I was eleven) had instructed her and most everyone else to leave. This alone was enough to terrify her. It didn't help, moreover, that there were rumors around the VA about a plane headed that way.

"Mom, you *really* think anyone cares about the Dayton VA? Maybe L.A. or Chicago. I promise you: Dayton is safe."

Matthew and I tried to calm her down. We told her all the ways in which this was *nothing* like the Revolution. But terror had already taken hold. For her, the reality of the situation was no match for the weight of memory.

Within a few days, she accepted the fact that we wouldn't have to flee. Still, all of us knew we *would* have to face some serious hatred and bigotry by staying. "It will be over soon," Ahmad insisted, even after one of our Jewish Iranian friends told him (only half kidding) that he might want to consider changing his name.

At the time, there was a genuine fear among Muslim Americans that we would soon learn what it was like to be Japanese American after the bombing of Pearl Harbor.

Quickly recognizing this possibility as well, countless Japanese Americans made it a point to stand in our defense. I was smitten by every last one of them. I'd always been a huge fan of sushi, Hello Kitty and those little origami cranes, but now, I suddenly became a fan of *all* things Japanese (short of anime porn, of course).

I have no doubt that the courage and backing of Japanese Americans had a huge impact in terms of preventing history from repeating itself. As did the massive outpouring of support from other minorities who knew what it was like to be targets. Blacks, Jews, Latinos, Catholics—they stood by us more than any other Americans. And they didn't wait for the smoke to clear; they didn't wait for the first *hijabi* girl to get stabbed; they didn't wait for the first mosque to be vandalized. They stood up right away, even faster than many Muslims. While everyone else was talking about putting a boot in our collective Islamic ass, they were pleading for reason and tolerance.

Still, it was suddenly a colossal bitch to be Muslim in America. Thanks to some mass murderers who single-handedly hijacked our faith and our country in one fell swoop, all American Muslims were now expected to prove not only that we were "real Americans," but also that we weren't terrorists. Overnight, we became suspect. Some went into hiding, some fled and others spoke out. I joined the latter contingent, not realizing that it would lead to a lifetime on the defensive, trying to achieve a seemingly impossible level of understanding. Nearly a decade later, I was invited to a

State Department *iftar* dinner as a member of Generation Change, a group of seventy-five young Muslim-American leaders who the Department expects will help change the country and, in doing so, the world. No pressure.

In the meantime, I'd spend the years in between fighting to convince my countrymen and -women west of the Atlantic that being an American Muslim was neither an oxymoron nor a predicament of circumstance. Or at least that's what it says in my first book. Still, I'm not sure even *I'm* fully convinced yet. At least not about the "predicament of circumstance" part. Certainly, it shouldn't be, but in a lot of ways, that's what it feels like, both for me and for countless other American Muslims since 9/11— constantly feeling the need to demonstrate our patriotism, only to be dismissed by "real" Anglo Americans as frauds and impostors.

Upon returning to New York shortly after the twin towers fell, Matthew and I were instantly assaulted by a stench so pungent and so nauseating that I fully expect some of it is still stuck in the recesses of my olfactory system. His apartment was uninhabitable, and soon after, he was informed that his new job, working for an international investment firm, no longer existed.

With each new report of anthrax, we grew increasingly nervous about breathing the air, which was already suffocating enough, full of hateful and offensive comments about my faith, my people, *me*, around every corner on a near-daily basis. I wanted out. I sensed no brother- or sisterhood. I sensed no unity after the storm. I sensed only hatred and isolation. We moved to New Haven a couple months later.

I got a job working at a jewelry store, and Matthew collected unemployment and a small FEMA payment. We stayed there a year, living together in sin in a two-bedroom apartment on Court Street with our fat black cat, Olyan. I continued studying for the LSAT and applied to law school.

As I pored over practice tests, Matthew took it upon himself to read all the classics in the Western canon. He devoured all my old philosophy books and then moved on to Homer, Dante and Cervantes. Though privileged enough not to have been forced to read it in high school, he even picked up what is hands down my least favorite book of all time: *Beowulf.* Unsurprisingly, he managed to find it worthwhile, even enjoyable.

That Christmas, we visited my parents in Ohio. They hadn't moved to Athens or Paris or Montreal, but they *were* planning a trip to Iran in January. After five years of friendship and two years of dating, I decided it was high time for Matthew and me to get engaged. He hadn't asked, so I figured it was up to me.

"I think we should get married," I told him one night in my childhood bedroom. "My mom is going to Iran, so it's a good time for you to ask her to pick up rings for us. I don't want any crap American jewelry."

"Okay," Matthew responded, unflustered, as though I'd just suggested going out for Chinese. "Should I ask your parents or something? How does this work? I don't want to mess up or say something offensive."

"You'll be fine," I replied. "We can talk to them after dinner."

"Good deal," Matthew said, reaching out his hand to shake on it. He smiled and pulled me toward him, then proceeded to hold my head in his hands, squish my cheeks together and force a fish face. He kissed my puckered lips until I started laughing. Then he grabbed my hand and we headed downstairs. The house reeked of fenugreek. Dinner was ready.

———————

W e'd like to get married," Matthew informed my parents after we'd only partially digested our *ghormeh sabsi*. My dad was cracking open a pistachio.

"Yes, we want to get married," I confirmed.

"Is that okay?" Matthew inquired, as if asking Ahmad to pass the pistachios.

"That's wonderful!" my mom exclaimed, then looked at Ahmad.

"You know," my dad said calmly, "if your parents were divorced, Matt, I would never allow it." My parents always call Matthew "Matt." Actually his parents and most everyone else who knew him growing up generally do as well. Anyone who knows him through me or met him in the twenty-first century, however, calls him Matthew—with the single exception of all the Iranians. There being no *th* sound in Farsi, it always comes out as a *t* anyway. So Matt it is.

"It's important your parents are married. You have good example. You know? I would love if you got married," Ahmad said.

I don't remember what else was said, but I do remember that, as is frequently the case, Ahmad spoke more than the rest of us combined. When we finally climbed upstairs to go to our separate bedrooms (me in my old room and Matthew in Romana's), we were both officially engaged and exhausted. But by the time I sneaked in to join Matthew in Romana's bed after I suspected my parents had fallen asleep, we were both alert and excited, reviewing possible locations for the wedding. Napa was top on our list.

"You want to bring everyone to California?" my mom responded when we brought it up the next morning over *noon-o-*

paneer (a quintessentially Persian breakfast: feta, walnuts, mint and radishes sandwiched between a special flatbread you can only find in Iranian stores). "No. Dayton is better. Or Cincinnati. Naapah *cheecheeyeh?* [What is Napa?] No one knows Naapah. What about you have one wedding in Dayton, one in Tehran?"

It was clear from the start that this wedding would be more for my mom than anyone else, and that was fine by us. Neither Matthew nor I had any interest in planning a wedding, and we knew my mom would make it classy and elegant. She loves throwing parties and has a preternatural knack for it. So after getting over Napa, we happily gave her free rein. Plus, she and Ahmad were paying for the affair, so we figured they deserved the final say.

Matthew called his parents to tell them the news that afternoon. They weren't pleased. Given I was the one who proposed, there was no way he could have told them sooner. Still, they were offended not to have been included in the process. I hadn't thought to ask for their blessing, and given how traditional they are, it's unlikely they would have found my asking for his hand appropriate at any rate. Besides, they undoubtedly would have tried to talk me out of it.

Matthew's dad, Tom, the vice president of their hometown Ellenville, New York, bank since Matthew was a kid, is from Brooklyn, the son of Catholic Slovenian immigrants. A fully assimilated American, he doesn't speak a word of Slovenian and carried none of his roots into adulthood. Matthew's mother, Jean, is from Ramsgate, England, and immigrated to the United States shortly after finishing high school. She met Tom in New York while they were both working at the same bank—she as a teller and he as a loan officer. Eventually they married and moved upstate to raise Matthew and his brother in the heart of the Catskills.

They're good people, down to earth and kind, but their initial failure to just shut up and be happy for us seriously pissed me off. So much so that I held it against them for a year, until we visited Ellenville the next Christmas and his mom had hung a stocking with my name embroidered on it above the fireplace. I'd always wanted a stocking (religious undertones be damned), and even though it was filled with practical gifts like socks and contact lens solution, I was overjoyed and overcome. So in the spirit of a season that holds zero spiritual significance for me, I gave up my grudge.

But that little miracle would be a few hundred days in the making. *This* Christmas left me cold and suspicious when it came to both Tom and Jean. Having heard some less-than-politically-correct language escape their mouths before, I suspected racism played a part in their early disapproval, though today I'm sure it didn't. Their main argument had to do with an outdated sexist notion that Matthew wasn't financially secure enough to take a wife. Never mind that I was headed to law school and he'd just finished over a year of saving and investment banking. Never mind that I fully intended to support myself. Never mind that my parents were paying for the wedding (accommodating American traditions, not theirs; typically the groom pays for the wedding in Iran). Never mind that by nearly all non-Western standards, Matthew was "marrying up," as my parents were significantly more educated and financially secure. Sure such sentiments sound snobby and elitist, and admittedly they are, but were we in Iran and were my parents less accepting, *they* would have been the ones advising against the marriage—not the Lenards. So the fact that my parents were so happy about our engagement just made Tom and Jean's unrestrained whining worse.

What's more, while Matthew's parents knew he'd converted to Islam, they didn't take his conversion seriously back then. They just blew it off as something he'd done to please me, which was anything but the case. Shortly after our engagement, Jean asked if we were having a church ceremony. When Matthew said no, reminding her that we were both Muslim, she again ignored him and asked, "What will the Church of England think about your marriage?"

I kept quiet, which was challenging to say the least, while Matthew told her that we couldn't care less what the Church of England thought. Looking back, I expect she saw Matthew's conversion as more of a defection than anything else, and as much as I resent her interpretation, I understand it nonetheless. Unlike Jean, Matthew saw his conversion as a homecoming. Explaining his sentiments today, he says, "It was like I'd always been Muslim. I just never knew it."

I didn't ask Matthew to convert. A few years after we met, he simply took it upon himself to read the Qur'an. He did so purely as an academic exercise, but it became more than that. When he told me he wanted to convert, I wasn't just surprised, I was scared. He couldn't have picked a more politically inconvenient time had he tried, and I told him so. I also assured him that he didn't need to convert for me. His reply: "Way to overestimate your influence."

As he explained how much the Qur'an spoke to him, his eyes lit up. I could tell his convictions were heartfelt, but the timing still troubled me. He didn't care. The way he saw it, his shitty timing was just another testament to his sincerity.

Matthew's formal conversion was far from ceremonious. He recited the *shahada*, or testament of faith ("There is no god but God, and Muhammad is his messenger") one afternoon in the privacy of his bedroom with me as his only witness. By that point, he knew a hell of a lot more about Islam than I (which, for me, was equal parts embarrassing and inspiring).

Then again, he knows a hell of a lot more about most things than I do. He reads more books and loves highlighting and writing in the margins. I watch more television and love ghastly, mindless reality shows. He prefers dreary, well-shot foreign films and documentaries. I prefer cartoons and comedies in English, Spanish or Farsi where I don't have to read subtitles (though generally not even in Farsi, given how damn depressing most Iranian films are). Our Netflix queue is absurd. We should have signed up for separate accounts, but it's too late now. Thus, we're left with recommendations that range from *Family Guy* to *Kagemusha*. Feel free to guess who watches what.

Despite our varied tastes and the conflicts we knew they'd cause when choosing which movie to watch on a Friday night, marrying Matthew was hands down the best decision I've ever made. I got up this morning, some ten years since our wedding day, and he grabbed my arm to pull me back to bed.

"Dude, I need to pee," I whined, pulling my arm back and heading to the bathroom, where we never close the door. Yes, we're one of *those* couples. As I relieved my bladder, I heard Matthew, still half asleep, from the bedroom: "I would give up everything just to have you—in a hut. Nothing else. That would be fine." Then he fell back asleep. If there's anything better to hear while taking a leak on a Saturday morning, I don't know what it is.

On August 17, 2002, Matthew and I were married in a packed ballroom at the Crowne Plaza Hotel in downtown Dayton. We took our vows before roughly two hundred and fifty Iranians (mostly in tuxes and fitted black Oscar-worthy evening gowns) and about fifty Americans (mostly in regular, occasionally mismatched suits and floral dresses fit for Easter Sunday).

It was a typical Persian, Muslim ceremony—heavy on old Zoroastrian traditions, sprinkled with a little Arabic and a few mentions of the Prophet Muhammad here and there. Amoo Ali (Nobar's dad and my godfather) conducted the ceremony, Nobar read a poem by Hafiz and my best friend from high school, Christina (an Egyptian-American Copt whom I've known since scrunchies and slap bracelets), entered in front of me and Ahmad, carrying a gilded bowl of burning incense that took forever to light.

Keeping with tradition, Matthew and I sat together on a small bench (piano, in our case) draped in white satin. We faced our guests, smiling and holding a large ornate Qur'an on our laps while happily married women stood around and behind us (most notably our moms and Romana), holding a large white scarf above our heads and taking turns rubbing two giant sugar cubes together over our heads in an effort to ensure a sweet union.

When it came Matthew's turn to say "*baleh*," the formal "yes" in Farsi, he was quick to respond. When it came my turn, however, I nearly missed my chance. While the groom traditionally says his "I do" right away in Persian ceremonies, the bride doesn't say it until the third time she's asked—this is so she can consider her prospect more seriously, as the cultural consensus is that the bride has more at stake. Every time she doesn't answer, the chorus of allegedly happily married women says, "She's gone to pick flowers"—or pears or herbs or something of that nature. Then everyone laughs.

The reason I hesitated in voicing my "*baleh*" had nothing to do with cold feet. Rather, I was waiting for Amoo Ali to ask me three times in both English *and* Farsi. He'd only asked twice in Farsi and once in English, but apparently what I considered the second time was the third to everyone else. Not realizing this, I remained silent. Then all the supposedly happily married women above us started loudly whispering in Farsi, "That was the third time, no?" I quickly responded: "Oh, sorry. *Baleh, baleh.*"

Everyone clapped. Then we kissed and licked honey off each other's pinkies (again to ensure a sweet union) as the ululating and traditional joyful music commenced. The standard wedding song translates to, "May you be, may you be blessed, may you be . . ." I used to think that the "may you be" part (*bada*) was actually "run" (*bodo*) because it really sounds more like *bodo*. But I guess "may you be blessed" makes a lot more sense than "run and be blessed."

The line repeats so many times you'd think it was a broken record, but no, that's just the song—painfully lacking in lyrical creativity, redeemed only by its jubilant tone. Amid all the ululating, Matthew stood up and took my hand to lead us out of the room toward the larger ballroom where the reception was to take place. I pulled him back.

"Wait. This is the best part," I whispered. I had forgotten to mention that Persian ceremonies tend to end with offerings of jewelry to the bride. Aunts, uncles, cousins and friends all swarmed around us, putting bracelets around my wrists, necklaces around my neck, rings on all my fingers, and earrings and gold coins in my hands to hold. By the end, I'd gained at least a few pounds in jewelry alone.

The reception was a blast. An auntie made a giant fruit sculpture that nearly hit the ceiling; a cousin brought mountains of Persian sweets from Toronto and a friend brought fireworks from Indiana. Our first dance was a lively merengue to Carlos Vives' "Fruta Fresca." After that, our Iranian DJ complied (for the most part) with our requests: half Persian music and half American/Arab/Indian/Latin. We danced all night, and still managed to save energy for our bridal suite. During a lull in the festivities, Matthew went upstairs to write "I Luv My Wife" in rose petals on our bed—an insurance policy of sorts.

The next day, shortly before we finished packing up the car to head to Atlanta, my parents gave us one of their Nain Persian rugs. Ahmad spent an hour lecturing us on its care and construction: "You have to flip it every six months—so sun hits it evenly. This is how you comb the edges. Look at the back. Look at all the knots. It takes a whole family months, even a *year*, to make a rug like this. You must *respect* the rug."

On a side note, in case you were wondering, children *do* play a vital role in these rug-weaving families. The best Persian rugs, the ones with the most intricate detail and the tiniest knots, are both stunning works of art and the products of countless hours of child labor. The activist in me wants to be appalled, but the Iranian in me knows that without those children and their teeny-tiny hands, a great art form would be lost—or at least permanently diminished. Plus, I can't see how this is any worse than what America does to its child actors. Far fewer child rug weavers grow up to become emotionally inept cokeheads. Not that I have any reliable data to that effect.

Ahmad folded up the rug and put it in the backseat of my car, warning us not to leave it alone. As if anyone would be able to steal a rug that heavy anyway, let alone realize its worth as we drove through Kentucky and Tennessee. Still, my mom packed us nearly a dozen potato cutlet sandwiches in a large Neiman Marcus shopping bag to ensure we didn't have to stop at McDonald's and, God forbid, abandon the rug for any extended period of time. She also managed to stuff an extra cooler full of cutlets in the trunk— enough to sustain us for at least a week after we got to Atlanta— just in case.

And by "cooler," I mean a Styrofoam box originally intended to transport organs. She brings them home from work. Once, while I was in college, she sent me one that had a biohazard sticker on it. My housemates were, like, "Melody, there's some toxic waste on the porch for you," and I was, like, "Oh, no worries, it's probably from my mom." Looking back, I now realize that perhaps that was an insufficient explanation.

Two days after the wedding, with the Nain, "cooler" and Olyan in tow, Matthew and I headed south. I started law school a week after we got there, and soon after, Matthew began training as a teacher through the Teach for America program. As he embraced his new calling, teaching sixth grade social studies to inner-city Atlanta public school students, I quickly realized how much I loathed law school. I was getting mostly B's and C's, but for the first time in my life, I didn't care. I adopted the Cookie Monster philosophy so popular among law students after the first semester: "C is for cookie, and that's good enough for me."

I'd spent my entire life getting good grades so that I could get into a good law school. Now that I was there, all I wanted to do was learn. Grades were an afterthought. I entered law school with a very specific aim in mind: Learn enough law to successfully defeat any injustices I might come across in life, paving the way toward a brilliant career as a kickass international human rights lawyer who'd eventually win a Nobel Peace Prize. Within my first few weeks at Emory, however, I quickly learned that international human rights laws are about as easy to enforce as teen virginity pledges.

Disenchanted by the diminished utility of my legal education and refusing to drop out after the first, notoriously grueling year, I decided to apply for Emory's joint J.D.–Master's in Public Health program. It would add only a semester to my schooling (a semester I didn't know at the time would drive me to attempt suicide a couple years later, but such is hindsight) and it meant I could spend a year at the School of Public Health instead of in the chamber of misery and torture known to my fellow inmates simply as "the law school."

Aside from realizing that the law was too inefficient, not to mention slow and painstaking, for me to endure, I also managed to make a total of two real friends in my entire time there—Amina, a Bosnian refugee who spent way too much time studying for me to play along, and Ilham, a Moroccan New Yorker who studied just as little as I did, only to do twice as well. The other law students failed to get me. On the first day, I noticed a table full of *desi* kids. Having a similar shade and immigrant background, I always had a lot of Indian and Pakistani friends growing up. So, I approached the table with what I thought was a killer joke that would undoubtedly win them all over at once: "So, none of you got into med school, eh?"

I guess there was more truth there than I'd anticipated, because instead of laughter, I garnered only scowls and silence. With that, I was summarily blacklisted from the South Asian crew. And I failed to fit in much better with any of the other cliques. So, I resigned myself to being a loner. I didn't join a study group, I didn't go to social events and I didn't go to class that often, either. The wonder of law school, the saving grace, is that there's no busy work. There's generally just a test at the end of each semester, and most of the professors don't care about attendance. Though I had only two true friends, other more dutiful students were always approaching me in the halls to let me know I'd been called on in class when I wasn't there. How these kids even knew my name was and remains a total fucking mystery to me.

The School of Public Health was a breath of fresh air by comparison. Although it involved way too much math and busywork for my taste, I still preferred it. The students there were genuinely interested in changing the world for the better, whereas most of my law school classmates seemed obsessed with nothing more than competing for the most insipid, high-paying corporate gigs upon graduation.

After the first year and a half of school, I was bored out of my mind, largely convinced that I wasn't cut out for either the statistical analysis involved in public health policy or the mind-numbing tedium involved in the law. I wanted to do nothing but cross-examinations and closing arguments, but turns out lawyers spend tons more time preparing for those arguments than they do presenting them. And while I was keen on feeding and vaccinating starving children around the world, I had zero interest in compiling data on them or anyone else, let alone translating that data into lifeless charts and graphs. There had to be something better for someone like me—someone with so little interest in numbers and contracts and so much facility with delusions and hallucinations.

thirteen

law school dropout

M.D., J.D., Ph.D. These are the altars upon which Iranians worship. In rough order from most to least esteemed, these are our gods. We have no Krishnas or Vishnus or Shivas, no Rockefellers or Carnegies or Vanderbilts. Instead, we have degrees. And just to clarify, a bachelor's doesn't count for shit. You must go higher or risk being a relative outcast. It may seem harsh, but when you consider the fact that the greatest dream of nearly all Iranian parents is to facilitate their children's educations (financially and otherwise), it seems a lot more like a gift than a demand. Though make no mistake, it is a Commandment. My parents take more pride in having financed and encouraged our educations than they do in any of their other life achievements. Together, Romana and I have earned more than an M.D. and a J.D. We've earned nobility, even a dash of divinity.

So, when I decided to take a semester off from law school, delaying my baptism and coronation, my parents went ballistic. They were terrified I wouldn't go back, that I would be damned to mere mortality, that I would get sick again. Because, as we all know, doctorates are the best defense against all disease and disaster. If more Pompeians had managed to get a higher education, they'd certainly never have been buried alive under the ash and lava of Mount Vesuvius. If more Europeans had earned doctoral degrees during the Middle Ages, no doubt the plague would have been avoided. If more doctors of all kinds had lived in Louisiana at the start of the twenty-first century, surely Katrina would have taken a different path. Of course.

"Are you crazy?" my dad asked, without waiting for an answer or recognizing the literal validity of his inquiry. "Just two more years and you are done. Take time off then. You will regret this. What are you going to *do?*"

"I'm going to finish writing my book," I responded. Shortly after 9/11, disgusted by the misrepresentation and demonization of Islam and Muslims in the media, I began writing my first book—a series of vignettes about different young Muslim Americans (all of whom were peaceful, liberated and relatable, and none of whom had anything to do with 9/11 either—just to be clear). I called it *War on Error*, in an effort to both tackle the errors about Islam that infected the minds of so many Americans at the time and expose the so-called War on Terror as the misguided, fear-driven fiasco it was.

"Are you kidding? How do you know anyone will publish it? A book saying good about Islam? No matter how wonderful you write, there's too much prejudice. Be reasonable. What does Matthew say?"

"He supports me. He thinks it's a good idea. And I *am* being reasonable. In fact, I've never been so reasonable. If I spend another minute in the law school, I'll kill myself. I *need* this. I can come see you guys over Christmas, and I promise I'll go back to school in the fall.

"But I need to travel to interview a bunch of the people for the book. And I promise someone will publish it. Americans are interested in this stuff now, and there isn't as much prejudice in publishing."

"I don't mean it in bad way. I love Jewish people,"—oh shit, here come the conspiracy theories—"but you know many Jew, they don't like Muslim, and in most publishing places, they are in charge. Why they would want to publish this kind of thing? They don't believe it. They think we are terrorist."

"Ahmad, you're crazy," I said, regretting my words the moment they exited my mouth.

"*Vai*, you talk to your father this way? I pay for all your school, I give you everything, and you say *this*? *Fekr meekoneey man adam neestam*? [Do you think I'm not a human being?]"

"No. I'm not saying that, Ahmad. I'm sorry. I'm just saying the whole world isn't run by Jews."

"Did I say that? I didn't say that. They are wonderful people. Some of them, they just don't like us. Just like some of the Muslims don't like Jews. You have to face reality Melody *jan* [dear]."

"Ahmad, it's not like that. They will like it more, and they *don't* run all of publishing. And so what if they do! They understand what it's like to be discriminated against. They'll support me. They'll be the least of my problems."

"*Azizam* [my dear], even if they publish—and of course they *should*—but even if they do, you can do this *after* law school. It's not a good time."

"I get it. You don't want me to do this, but you'll see. I promise. Just think about it, and we'll talk more later."

We had at least a dozen similar conversations before I finally submitted my leave of absence form to the university. Years later, after my first reading, Ahmad pulled me aside and, referring to his advice not to take that semester off, he said (brace yourself): "I was wrong." I would give up ice cream forever to have caught that confession on tape. It was a first, and despite being admittedly delighted upon hearing it, I soon felt nervous and uncomfortable. This was the first time he'd been wrong in my eyes since I was seven (when he suggested my cousin Mersedeh take off her *roosari* so as to blend in better with her American classmates). Still, I expected Ahmad to be right about most everything—mainly because as a rule, he was. But this second exception soon transformed into a crushing realization—one that's still hard for me to accept to this day: there are no infallible guides in this world, no matter how well meaning.

After taking my leave of absence, Matthew and I spent Christmas with my parents. To clarify, despite the fact that Jesus Christ is a revered prophet in Islam, Christmas has no religious significance for us. We don't think Jesus was born on December 25, and we don't believe he was birthed in a manger. Our take is that he was born under a magical palm tree that rained dates when shaken, a gift from God to give Mary strength for childbirth. So instead of celebrating the arrival of the Messiah on Christmas, we celebrate being on vacation.

Traditionally, on the few occasions we don't go to Siesta Key with the vast majority of the Iranian crew, we celebrated with the leftover ones in Dayton. We rent out Quail Run, a local tennis club, and spend the day playing tennis and eating kabob, rice, turkey and mashed potatoes drenched in way too much butter, as well as other failed attempts at traditional American cuisine. While the menu varies slightly from year to year, tennis is a mainstay. Whether we're in Ohio (indoor courts) or Florida (outdoor courts), the day is consumed with aces, deuces and loves (for the record, I was the queen of loves). This tradition is so entrenched that, as a kid, I used to think everyone played tennis on Christmas.

After New Year's, Matthew returned to Atlanta, and I set off on my own adventure, driving to New England to interview some people for my book. My friend Shireen, a Christian Palestinian, had hooked me up with her friend Sarah, a Sudanese-Egyptian-American bisexual Muslim singer and intermittent pothead who was still an undergrad at Wesleyan. For the sake of my art, in hopes of getting a glimpse into Sarah's world, and for the first time in my life, I engaged in what was all but a graduation requirement at Wes: I smoked pot. For a good Muslim girl who doesn't even drink alcohol, this was a big deal. But it didn't seem like it at the time. I did it impulsively, and despite my noble artistic intentions, Sarah's chapter wasn't the least bit better for it. The substance didn't agree with me. It had me hacking for hours and nearly made me vomit. Plus, it made me staggeringly stupid.

After interviewing Sarah, I headed to New Haven to meet Ameer, a half-Egyptian, half-Korean American-Muslim rapper and Yalie, whom I'd learned about after contacting the Yale Muslim Students Association.

I stayed with Roxana while I was in New Haven, and one day, after interviewing Ameer, alone and on a whim, I got a tattoo. Just like the pot smoking, this wasn't planned. I walked into a popular tattoo parlor across from the Green on Chapel Street, and I approached the front counter.

"Hi. How can you assure me I won't get hepatitis?" I asked, completely serious.

"Oh," Lou (the overly tattooed man behind the counter) replied, laughing, "it comes free with every tattoo."

Then he led me to the back and showed me all the prepackaged needles. Sufficiently reassured, I told the tattoo artist what I wanted: the mathematical sign for infinity, between two M's. Translation: Matthew & Melody forever . . . but on the off chance that he died or we got divorced, it could always easily stand for Melody Moezzi forever. I thought it was perfect. I was clearly out of my mind.

As if the cheese factor of M-and-M forever wasn't bad enough, my choice of location was beyond embarrassing. Right above my ass crack. Yes, a tramp stamp. Lame by any standard. My defense, if you hadn't suspected it already: I was dancing with mania in a way that I hadn't since Montana. Equally intoxicating, it had me making decisions I'd never have made in my right mind. I just thank God I didn't get any other tattoos and resisted the urge to pierce anything.

He drew up a sample:

$$M \infty M$$

I was fine with it, but thank God for Lou.

"It sort of looks like it says MOOM, no? Maybe you want me to do it vertically?" he suggested.

I don't know where that man is today, but he deserves a medal. Having a tramp stamp is embarrassing, but I'm not sure I could have lived with MOOM above my ass crack for the rest of my life.

So he tried again, and I went for it:

M

∞

M

Before he pulled out his ink, I asked him to wait. I wasn't having second thoughts. I just thought it might be a good idea to pray before a stranger started piercing me repeatedly with a tiny needle. By most interpretations of Islam, tattoos are forbidden. You're not supposed to mess with the supposed perfection God gave you. But I figured He'd already given me this giant scar across my stomach, so I was at least entitled to a blemish of my own choosing. It was only fair.

"Is there a place I can pray?" I asked.

"Um, what?"

"Pray. I just want to say a quick prayer before you start."

"Well, you can do it here, I guess. I won't interrupt you."

"You don't understand, I'm Muslim. I pray in a special way. I need a quiet spot where I can do all the prostrations."

I'm pretty sure he still didn't understand what I was talking about, but he pointed to a back office and said I could pray there. I did. Clearly God was too busy to send me a sign that this was an all-around shit-tastic decision.

So, I returned without hesitation.

"Let's do it," I said, sitting backward on a weirdly shaped stool. Luckily, the stamp is small. Still, it's not exactly classy. Matthew was kind enough to say he liked it when I got back to Atlanta, and though he has never hinted otherwise, I still don't believe him. How could anyone in his right mind not hate it? Not the idea behind it or even the fact that I have it (I figure it's always good to be easily identifiable just in case I'm abducted, raped and left for dead in a ditch on the side of the road), but I just can't get over the geography. Could I have chosen a sluttier or less original location? Worse yet, I also somehow failed to notice the two rainbows of stretch marks adorning either side of my butt and lower back. Such things happen when you lose fifteen pounds in a week while you're lying in a hospital bed on parenteral nutrition, and given how rarely I look at my back or butt in the mirror, it's just as understandable as it is unfortunate that I never noticed the stretch marks until it was too late.

In a way though, the ink and the stretch marks framing it, however unsightly, serve as a useful reminder of the most pernicious organs I house, the ones I can never neglect, lest they strike again: my tumor-prone pancreas and my imbalanced mind. So on the rare occasions that I catch a glimpse of my own rear view, I like to remember all the insanity I've overcome, as opposed to all the insanity that remains (not to mention all the trouble my family is bound to have trying to convince someone to give me a traditional Muslim burial).

Driving back to Roxana's house after branding myself for life, I felt happier than I had in years. I had more ideas running through my mind than I could keep track of, and I wanted to call everyone I knew to share them. My grand plans and ideas included joining the circus (Why drive a car when you can drive an elephant?), dancing or skipping everywhere (Why walk when God invented more jubilant means of transport?), buying an ocelot (Why own a housecat when you can own a wild animal?) and the list goes on. But amid all my ridiculous ideas, I also had a few good ones. I decided to add quotes and Qur'anic verses to the start of every chapter in my book (which turned out to be many readers' favorite parts—though I'm not sure what that says about my writing); I came up with what I'm still convinced are two brilliant ad campaigns for Ikea and Apple; and I stopped biting my nails after realizing just how damn disgusting it was.

Herein lies the trouble with madness. How do you sort out the ocelots from the creative breakthroughs, or the elephants from the nail-biting cessation? You don't. They all seemed like equally bright ideas to me at the time. The problem with mania—even the milder hypomania I was experiencing during my visit to Connecticut—is that you can't distinguish genius from crap. And I use "crap" here as a euphemism for straight-up lunacy.

At the time, no one could have convinced me that any of my ideas or behaviors were even moderately irrational, let alone abnormal. That's the other thing about mania. Unless you've experienced and recovered from full-on psychosis, it's nearly impossible to realize that you need help or that you have a disorder. That's why people are much more prone to seek help for depression than they are for mania. I mean, what sounds crazier than going to a shrink because you're too happy? But there's a fine line between eccentric exuberance and madness, and it would still be a few years before I discovered I fell on the latter side of it.

When I got back to Atlanta, I'd written over half the book in less than a month. I was riding high. Until I wasn't. Law school quickly brought me back to reality, and by the last semester, I was swimming in a blinding cloud of white phosphorus.

Thus we arrive where we began, with Dr. Lessor, Stillbrook, ELLIE the elephant, Dr. Forgettable, stale Play-Doh and puzzles galore. I left Stillbrook without a proper diagnosis, and without a long-term treatment plan. Despite growing increasingly manic over my time there, no one bothered to notice, let alone to consider revising my diagnosis. So I left still thinking I had unipolar depression. I left without even a rudimentary understanding of what bipolar was, besides a pejorative reserved for *really* crazy people—certainly not me. This oversight on the part of each and every one of my health care providers there, among a few oversights of my own, helped set me up for full-blown mania and psychosis.

I walked out of Stillbrook with the same false assumption I'd maintained my entire life—that the boundless euphoria and wicked agitation that overcame me from time to time were completely normal, things that everyone experienced. I soon learned, however, that not everyone in the adult world seriously considers joining the circus or buying ocelots. Turns out we circus-loving ocelotophiles are in the extreme minority. Lucky me.

fourteen

hoods and hurricanes

By the time graduation rolled around, I'd been free for six months. Stillbrook and the pathetic suicide attempt that had landed me there were ancient history as far as I was concerned. But ancient history has an impertinent penchant for haunting the present, though I'm grateful it had the decency to wait until after graduation. When I came back to finish my last semester after being released from Stillbrook, some other students asked me where I'd been. I told them I had spent the last few weeks in lockup. I didn't specify where, so the assumption was that I'd been in prison. It seemed preferable to the truth, so I let it stand. I figured it was better being viewed as a tough ex-con than a fragile ex–mental patient. I liked the persona, and assuming it helped me to get through that last tiresome semester. By graduation, though, it had worn its course, and I didn't care what my classmates thought of me. Besides Amina (who in fact later dumped me after what I thought was a witty and amusing maid-of-honor speech at her wedding and what her new dick of a husband thought was a direct insult to him) and Ilham, I had no intention of keeping in touch with any of them.

Before skipping (yes, skipping) up to the podium to collect the papers that would immediately grant me respectable, low-level royalty status in the Persian community, I read through two issues of *Glamour* and an entire *Economist*. I wore a short red-and-white polka-dot sundress that made me look like an overgrown Iranian Minnie Mouse, and Mario (the third-most important man in my life after Matthew and Ahmad; we've been friends as long as Matthew and I have been married; and just to dispel any suspicion, Mario is way gay) shouted, "Melody for president" at the top of his lungs as Amina (who'd graduated a year earlier) hooded me. My parents, Matthew, Christina, Roxana and my friends Edgar and Lindsay were also there to celebrate.

Despite only recently being released from Stillbrook, Angela managed to make it as well. The fact that she dressed up and drove forty minutes to sit in the hot sun for two hours just to watch me collect two pieces of paper meant the world to me. Because I was getting a joint degree, I sat in the way back, behind the Z's, and was one of the last ones to be called. This was perfect, as it meant that the row behind me was filled with civilians, not graduates, and that's where my fan club was sitting. When Angela arrived, I introduced her to everyone. She had only met Matthew and my parents up until then, so everyone else's first instinct was to ask how we knew each other. A moment of silence ensued. There's a sort of unspoken bond among mental patients: you need explicit consent to share anyone else's "status," particularly with normies. Angela and I turned to each other.

Can I tell them? I asked silently by widening eyes as I darted them across the row to meet hers.

Yeah, it's fine, she answered with her signature "fuck it" shrug.

"We met in a psychiatric hospital. We were roommates. She's my favorite crazy person," I replied.

Silence, apart from a hushed chuckle from Matthew and Mario. "Yeah right, Mel!" Angela said, laughing. "You're your *own* favorite crazy person. Is it possible for you to love anyone more than yourself?" Everyone laughed, some more uncomfortably than others, but I was grateful for Angela's crack nonetheless.

"Fine, second favorite. And you can't love anyone else until you love yourself. Just ask Oprah," I added, sticking out my tongue like a six-year-old.

Christina pulled me aside after the ceremony to ask about Angela. By this point, Christina was officially Dr. Girgis, well on her way to becoming a psychiatrist.

"I'm not sure it's so great to be making friends from the hospital. I treat a lot of patients, and they aren't necessarily what they seem."

"Christina, I'm no different. You could just as easily say that Angela shouldn't have made friends with *me*."

"But I don't know *her*; I know *you*. And you *are* different. You didn't get out that long ago, and you're doing great. I don't want anyone else to drag you down."

"Don't worry about it, Girgis. I'll be fine," I said.

Christina is a brilliant psychiatrist, but seeing as how we've been best friends since high school, it's hard for her to view my case objectively. Today she works with victims of traumatic brain injuries at a VA hospital in Illinois, and she's constantly encouraging me to do more therapy and even try psychoanalysis.

"Why the hell would I do that when my best friend is a fucking psychiatrist? I can just talk to *you*," I always say, knowing full well that doing so in a doctor-patient capacity would be both impossible and unethical. She hates it when I say this, which just makes it all the more tempting. Of course, I do see a psychiatrist to manage my meds (as without those, I'm liable to go *really* nuts—the kind of nuts we've all witnessed on street corners around the country since the deinstitutionalization movement of the 1950s and '60s), but the idea of paying a total stranger to listen to my problems and barely say a thing has always struck me as odd. Though I've been in therapy for years at a time, I gave it up completely a few years ago. It's hard to trust a therapist when you've gone to so many others who failed to make even a proper diagnosis. And again, the idea of therapy has just always struck me as foreign. I grew up thinking you talked to your friends and your family when you were having problems. You talked to doctors when you broke your leg.

S oon after graduation, after having my book rejected by over a dozen trade publishers—including one superbly obtuse house happy to publish it if I included a chapter profiling a terrorist (of course missing the point of the book entirely, and more comically, assuming I *knew* a terrorist, as clearly all of us Muslims have terrorists on call whom we can just whip out of our back pockets at will)—I signed a contract with the University of Arkansas Press, which despite boasting a feral pig as its mascot and being based in Fayetteville, Arkansas (as opposed to liberal, forward-thinking, fancy-pants New York City), was happy to buy the book as is, minus the obligatory terrorist.

As far as I was concerned by that point, New York could suck it. Arkansas was a well-respected academic press, and despite my pitiful advance, I was overjoyed. I loved my publisher. He knew a ton about Islam (despite being Irish Catholic), and he totally got where I was coming from. That and he pretty much let me say whatever I wanted.

Not long after the book came out, he called to let me know I'd been nominated for a Georgia Author of the Year Award. I'd never heard of it. Nonetheless, I was ecstatic. I won all the limbo and Hula-Hoop contests I entered as a kid, as well as a few speech and debate tournaments in high school, but I'd never won something big. Sure, I was only a nominee, but that was good enough for me. Still, when I was invited to the awards ceremony, I declined— mainly because it was forty bucks a plate. It just seemed weird to charge nominees and way overpriced. Plus, I was sure I'd lose—I was up against two books on Christianity, and I just figured that in Georgia, Christianity always wins over Islam.

But then I got an e-mail from one of the event's organizers saying I'd won and that Matthew and I could eat for free, so we went. I wasn't supposed to let on that I knew in advance, so I feigned surprise when my name was called and collected the weird glass hurricane vase of an award. Engraved on the hurricane is a map of the United States with the phrase "Georgia Writers" and a giant map of Georgia superimposed over it. Under the map it reads:

44th Annual Georgia Author of the Year Award

June 7, 2008

Creative Nonfiction: Essay Category

Melody Moezzi

War on Error:

Real Stories of American Muslims

Suddenly, I wasn't just an author. I was an *award-winning* author. Granted, it wasn't a Pulitzer or a Nobel, but it was a start. Plus, I loved that the acronym for the award was GAYA and that I now had all these fancy embossed gold stickers to slap on the covers of my books. It's amazing how much validation you can get from some stickers, a paper certificate and an engraved hurricane.

Just as Matthew and I were about to leave, I felt a tap on my shoulder. I turned around. It was Angela. I hadn't told her about the ceremony, but she'd read about it in the paper and showed up. She gave me a big hug and we took pictures. I swear she was happier for me than I was, and I swear I was happier to have her there than I was to win the award.

"Shit, girl," she said between her teeth, as she stood beside me, smiling wide for the camera, "you've come a long way from puzzles and strip searches."

"Not that long," I replied. "I'm still hanging out with you, aren't I?"

"Touché."

part
four

fifteen

hooping for peace

I dumped Dr. Lessor shortly after leaving Stillbrook. Even if not for his failure to properly diagnose or treat me, there was also my inability to look him in the eye after the embarrassing pocket-knife incident. Plus, having graduated from Emory, I couldn't have continued seeing him even if I were masochistic enough to want to.

A bigger person might have taken pity on him and called it even—a bloodstained carpet for a dash of negligent health care. But I'm not that big. As far as I'm concerned, a champion sumo wrestler isn't that big, and I ought to be all but beatified for not suing him. I may as well have spent my Tuesday afternoons talking to a Cabbage Patch Kid for all the good he did me.

Still, after disposing of Dr. Lessor, who played the increasingly rare role of both psychiatrist *and* psychotherapist, I was now in the unfortunate position of having to shop for two new mental health providers: one new drug-dealing M.D. and one new head-shrinking Ph.D. Given it's nearly impossible to find a psychiatrist who also does regular psychotherapy these days (thanks to insurance companies that pay significantly more for fifteen-minute "med checks" than they do for forty-five-minute therapy sessions), psychiatrists have little financial incentive to do much more than dole out scripts.* And it's worth mentioning that the kinds of medications they prescribe after spending just fifteen minutes with a patient can cause some serious, perhaps enduring, and often unsightly side effects about which patients are frequently uninformed. Things like seizures, tics, drooling, blackouts, diabetes, obesity, vomiting, memory loss, "fogginess," tardive dyskinesia (characterized by potentially permanent and pronounced involuntary movements like limb-flailing, rapid blinking, grimacing, tongue protrusion, lip-smacking, -pursing and -puckering, and a whole host of other distressing, purposeless motions), and even a worsening of the types of conditions a given medication was prescribed to treat, like mania, depression and/or suicidality.

That said, many medications work brilliantly with minimal side effects. Nevertheless, if you're the one involuntarily drooling or persistently sticking out your tongue or flailing your arms and legs, it's hard to take comfort in that. One such drug made me so suicidal I actually attempted to kill myself, and others have introduced me to the joys of slobbering, temporary tics, explosive diarrhea, "word retrieval" problems (the highlight here: forgetting the word "fork"; that was the last straw), unexplainable and unwelcome weight gain and loss and a unique, all-but-intolerable brand of restlessness that made me want to tear off my own skin. All this

---

* Gardiner Harris, "Talk Therapy Doesn't Pay, So Psychiatry Turns Instead to Drug Therapy," *The New York Times*, March 5, 2011, http://www.nytimes.com/2011/03/06/health/policy/06doctors.html?pagewanted=all.

to say, I've grown increasingly cautious when it comes to selecting a psychiatrist and agreeing to take certain medications.

Case in point: I've never taken lithium, despite the fact that it's the "gold standard, first-line treatment" for bipolar; I fear the cognitive deficits, weight gain and kidney problems that can accompany it. Call me vain. Call me kidney-obsessed. I just can't get past the possibilities. I'm deathly afraid that one day I'll agree to start taking it or some other medication—or worse yet, have it administered to me against my will in a hospital—and then immediately morph into this fat, foggy, drooling diabetic on dialysis.

So, I made it a point to interview a boatload of psychiatrists and psychologists before picking the right ones. Still, I fucked up. Again. I can't say how or why, but I can say that since then I've relied more on my friends and family for support and only seen a psychiatrist about once a month for what I consider necessary med checks.

Ultimately, I abandoned psychotherapy because I finally accepted the fact that I suck at it. Maybe I'm just not well adjusted enough or Westoxified enough or trusting enough for it to work for me. Whatever the case, I don't expect I'll be going back anytime soon. I have friends; I have a husband; I have parents; I have a sister; I have a real and ridiculously extended family, and I've garnered far more insight and comfort from them (free of charge) than I ever have from a shrink.

Still, as skeptical and suspicious as I've become of most mental health professionals, I know enough to continue taking the one mood stabilizer that has worked for me—partly out of fear and partly because my friends and family won't let me get away with *not* taking it. They (and I) know all too well that medication is a necessity for the type of bipolar disorder with which I happen to be blessed. Plus, I've known way too many others who've gone on their meds, gotten better, thought they were cured, gone off their meds, then deteriorated. And as a rule, the longer they spent repeating that cycle, the more damaged (cognitively, emotionally, physically, intellectually, financially, et cetera) they tend to be. And I'm damaged enough as it is.

But I admit that at times I'm tempted. Since my diagnosis, however, the threat of falling into a trap that trite and reliving my worst depressive or manic episodes has been enough to keep me popping my pills—at least thus far. I may be *particular* about the kinds of medications I take, but I'm not dumb enough to think I can treat a chronic mental illness with yoga and wheatgrass enemas.

The psychiatrist I ultimately chose—mainly for his impressive credentials and calming demeanor—ended up prescribing me yet another antidepressant. It turns out it was one of the antidepressants *least* likely to induce mania, but given the fact that I was already genetically predisposed to it, it didn't matter. I went crazy anyway. Yet again, I was the exception.

The psychotherapist I selected turned out to be just as calming and credentialed as Dr. Lessor, and equally clueless. I hate to sound like I blame these generally good and well-meaning souls for all my troubles. I don't. I fully acknowledge that had any one of them even mentioned bipolar as a possible diagnosis, I likely wouldn't have believed them. Up until that point, all I knew about bipolar disorder I'd learned from watching Billy on *Six Feet*

Under—the perverted degenerate in love with his sister, who stalked her, tried to cut a tattoo out of her back and did a whole bunch of other creepy shit. Sure, *Billy* was bipolar. *I*, however, was just unconventional, marching to the beat of my own *tombak*.

As such, I would have to go fully nuts to acquire the solid, indisputable evidence I needed to accept any such label. I wouldn't buy into a diagnosis like that without full and thorough discovery. Anything less would be unreasonable, unfair, *unlawyerly*. This was the first of many occasions upon which my law degree seriously fucked me. Two years after leaving Stillbrook, I once again found myself on a locked ward, closing out 2008 with a bang followed by a long series of whimpers.

An infectious Obama-mania took over the planet that year, and I was overcome by it. Like so many around the world, I was giddy over the possibility of an Obama presidency. So I did what any reasonable activist would do. I started an organization to help raise funds for his campaign. Then I did what one increasingly manic activist would do: I went about acquiring as many Hula Hoops as possible, as well as a venue at the Democratic National Convention that would allow me and all my disciples to spend an entire day Hula Hooping to support a presidential candidate who appeared to support peace. It seemed like a *duh* effort to me—so much so that I was astonished when (after extensive Googling) I discovered that no one had already come up with the idea. I mean, was there any better or more obvious way to achieve world peace than by gyrating in place in an effort to keep a big "O" swirling around your waist?

————

We *have* to go to Denver," I told Matthew the second I found out no one else was doing the whole Hula Hoop thing. He was at work.

"Why?"

"Are you kidding? Duh! The *convention*! I have an idea. You're totally going to love it," I said.

"Sure I'd love to go to the convention, but what's the idea?" he asked.

"I'm going to call it Hula Hoop for Peace. I've already contacted Wham-O. They claim to have invented the Hula Hoop, but really it's an ancient practice. The Greeks used it for exercise. Did you know that?" I didn't give him a chance to answer. "But yeah, it looks like one of their top dogs is Iranian—actually it's totally obvious from her name. I forget it, but it screams *irooni*. Anyway, I left her a message. I'm sure they'll want to donate Hula Hoops. It's free publicity for them! This is going to be *huge*. We have to build a website."

"Slow down. You're serious?" Matthew asked.

"Of course! Don't you think it's *brilliant*?" I asked, ignoring his confused tone, expecting him to immediately jump on board.

"It's *interesting*," he said hesitantly. "I mean, it's creative at least."

"But it's totally obvious. Don't you *get* it? The circle of the hoop is an 'O' for 'Obama,' and we can hold up signs that say 'Don't bomb Iran.' There are *two* O's in that. It's perfect. Obama is our best chance, and his name starts with an 'O.' It's a *sign*."

"Yeah, didn't think of any of that. Dude, you're so weird—I

have no idea how the hell your brain works, but who knows. Let me think about it, and we'll discuss more when I get home."

"It's not *weird*. It makes so much sense. It's crazy no one else is already doing it. I'll show you some drawings when you get home, and you'll get it. You'll *love* it. I promise."

"I'm not saying weird is bad," he offered, "just don't go off the deep end. I'll look at your drawings. I can't believe you called that company."

"Believe it, bitch!"

I couldn't wait for Matthew to get home. When he did, I miraculously managed to convince him it was a good idea. I wove together all kinds of arguments, but it wasn't all that hard to persuade him. Though unconvinced that hooping for peace was the best idea in the world, he was down for witnessing history, so he agreed to make the trip.

A couple weeks later, after securing a venue on the campus of the University of Denver, recruiting several dozen supporters, being featured on hooping.org and receiving a cease-and-desist letter from Wham-O (who was not only unwilling to provide free Hula Hoops, but insisted I stop using their "Hula Hoop" trademark name for my organization), we headed to Denver. Unwilling to go through the hassle of fighting Wham-O's diluted trademark (even though any reasonable court in the country would strike it down in a second), I changed our name to "Hooping for Peace" and set out to buy as many Hula Hoops along the twenty-two-hour drive as my Camry could fit. We must have visited at least a dozen Walmarts.

The biggest bonus of the convention's being in Denver was the fact that Romana lived there. We could hoop to our hearts' content and also see her, Robert and the kids. She clearly thought I was crazy for doing what I was doing, but she was polite enough not to make a big deal about it. She didn't realize how close I was to the edge. No one did. I'd always been "eccentric": the only lawyer-turned-artist in a family of physicians, the weird kid who staged protests aimed at the ice cream man, the adult who slit her wrist in her psychiatrist's waiting room. As far as everyone else was concerned, I was just odd, and my only mental illness was a resolved case of suicidal depression brought on by a bad drug reaction and the stress of law school. No one suspected I was flirting with the high end of the bipolar spectrum, let alone about to consummate the affair. Even my dad, who mentioned the possibility of manic depression a couple years earlier, was now reformed. He dropped his case when I told him that he was being ridiculous and that maybe *he* was bipolar.

Thus, I continued my crusade, having just enough sense not to mention to anyone that I actually *believed* I could bring about world peace by Hula Hooping. While only a handful of people attended the full-day hooping event, I ended up getting a lot of media attention for my antics. The day before the official, planned Hooping festivities, I Hula-Hooped for six hours straight in the middle of a patch of pansies and snapdragons in front of the Colorado State Capitol. There was a giant photo of me in the *Rocky Mountain News*, along with a plug for the organization and a caption reading, "Melody Moezzi, an Iranian American, Hula-Hooped for more than five hours to bring awareness to the growing conflict between the United States and Iran at Civic Center Park in Denver Sunday, August 24, 2008." I did interviews with Univision, Laura Ingraham, local news stations and several documentary filmmakers. News of my activities hit *The Guardian, Middle East Online* and the Payvand Iranian Newswire. In short, for that one week in August, I was the most famous hooper in the world. I didn't give any thought to how inane I looked, Hula Hooping in a long, flowy pink leopard-print dress in what was likely the most hopping park in the country that day. Matthew was with me the whole time, and given the fact that I love and wear that dress frequently (sane or not) and that I seemed to actually be raising awareness for my cause, he grew increasingly supportive. It's amazing how much credibility a few television, film and radio interviews can get you.

It all went to my head. I'd certainly achieved far more impressive feats in my life, but at the time, it seemed like this was the pinnacle. Again, all the while I maintained the secret conviction that my "work" would in fact incite world peace. Granted, it takes a certain degree of irrationality to be an activist of any kind, whether it's with a Hula Hoop, a pen or a law degree. You have to really *believe* that you can effect change, that *one person* can make a difference, *all* that stuff. I still believe it, and I always will.

But Hooping for Peace was different. It was my first step into the land of full-blown mania. As I watched, with tears in my eyes, as Barack Obama accepted the Democratic Presidential Nomination, I too accepted my own nomination. I had been tapped for greatness. Soon, I would be a prophet. Soon, I would be a queen. Soon, my delusions would devour me.

sixteen

don't worry, be happy

We left Denver the day after the convention ended, with a hundred Hula Hoops and a bunch of "Yes We Can" posters in the trunk. I was indefatigable: bouncing and dancing in my seat, singing along to Nas and Tupac's "Black President," crying, grinning like a madwoman, driving too fast and, most of all, talking.

With Matthew in the passenger seat, sleeping mostly, my mouth ran wild, desperately trying to keep up with my head. I didn't mind that he was knocked out. Talking to myself was fine by me. Besides, I had Nas and Tupac to keep me company. I was loving them: singing along with Tupac's disbelief from the grave: "Although it seems heaven-sent / we ain't ready / to have a black president," and Nas's response on the ground: "Yes we can / change the world."

"It's happening, Matthew. It's *happening*! No one thought it was possible. *I* didn't think it was possible. Iowa, and now *this*! Did you *see* him? Did you *hear* him? He's perfect! And he's not just a lawyer; he's a Constitutional law professor! Not a damn *bizz*-ness man with a fake southern accent riding Daddy's coattails. Seriously, it matters *so* much that he's self-made and that he knows the Constitution and the court rulings. It's not just that he isn't a moron and can pronounce 'nuclear.' He's brilliant, charming, young, handsome. And he knows his shit. He knows the law; he'll stop all this collateral damage, close Guantánamo, end the war. The world will finally respect us. After eight years of disgrace and disaster, they'll see that the American people are smart and that it's our *leader* who was the imbecile. Just like in Iran. The world is changing. Without an enemy here, Ahmadinejad has no one to fight and no reason to be reelected. We'll be able to take direct flights to Tehran! My mom says you could do that before the Revolution. Can you imagine not having to go through Frankfurt or Amsterdam or London or fucking Baku? You can finally learn Farsi! I can hang out with my grandma, cousins, aunts and uncles in peace. No more twelve-year-old assholes with rifles running around the streets, stopping us to ask if we're siblings or strangers, sisters or whores; no more breaking up parties and weddings, and no more having to bribe their punk asses not to; no more dress codes or censorship or sexist bullshit. There will be real law, fair law, actual *rule* of law in Iran. We'll be able to do and say and wear whatever the fuck we want. The whole *world* will change. And we're going to be such a big part of it. Huge! It's *our* generation that will bring Obama to power, and *our* generation that will kick Ahmadinejad out. *We're* doing it! Seriously, anything, fucking *anything*, is possible in this country. You just have to work and pray and work some more. Trust in God, but tether your camel, right? This is us finally tethering our fucking camel for once. Who said that? Rumi? Hafiz? Mohammad? The Qur'an? Whoever said it, it's right."

I was more than euphoric. I was hypomanic. Translation: I wasn't completely crazy, but I was well on my way. Hypomania is the most beautiful land I know—it puts chocolate, sex and narcotics to shame. Given the opportunity and the assurance that elevation and oxygen levels would remain constant, I'd stay there forever. I know of no other place where you can keep up so much energy without sleeping or eating, finish in a day what would take most people a week, abandon so many of the self-esteem issues that prevent you from meeting your full potential, be the life of the party, guiltlessly increase your participation in "pleasurable activities" and engage in so many more "goal-directed" behaviors. Why give up all that productivity? Why lose that sense of invincibility? Why *ever* come down from that?

My least favorite bipolar mantra, after "It's just like diabetes," is "What goes up, must come down." No matter how many times my experience has proven it, part of me is convinced that there must be some way to safely set up permanent residence in Hypomania without any repercussions. For one, I did it in Montana. Plus, satellites and space stations can go up without coming down. It's at least *possible* for gravity to lose.

So, why live in accordance with some stupid song we sang in elementary school as we lifted and lowered a giant red parachute? If I remember correctly, that song suggested not only that "what goes up, must come down" but also that we "ride a painted pony" and "let the spinning wheel spin."* How can I trust anyone promoting that kind of cruelty to ponies? And who the hell uses spinning wheels outside of nineteenth-century child labor mills?

---

* "Spinning Wheel" is a ridiculous song by Blood, Sweat & Tears (written by band member David Clayton-Thomas), released on their self-titled 1969 album. I don't think they intended for it to be used in elementary school gym classes.

Still, I've never been able to maintain any type of ideal low-grade mania for more than several months at a time. With the sole exception of Montana, my hypomania has always morphed into something worse. It's insanely fun while it lasts, but then it just gets insane. Like throwing a killer party in your head where you're the only one invited. But when that party ends, there's always some colossal mess: a mess that only you can clean up and a mess that makes the fall that much worse.

A month after returning from Denver, I was scheduled to speak and do a book signing at the Clinton Presidential Library in Little Rock—all as part of a traveling art exhibit funded by Queen Noor of Jordan. It was called (brace yourself for some painfully colonialist language here) *Breaking the Veils: Women Artists from the Islamic World*. In the minds of the event organizers, despite growing up almost entirely in Ohio, I still fit the profile. I figured why not run with it. It was about time Dayton took its rightful place in the Muslim world, and I was happy to do my part. Plus, they were paying me handsomely, putting me up in the fanciest hotel in Little Rock, and Mario agreed to drive up with me, which made it more vacation than speaking engagement.

Most important though, this was a huge deal for my parents. They became citizens just to vote for Bill Clinton, and it was the first time they ever donated to a political campaign. To them, my getting invited to speak at the Clinton Library was just as good as being elected president myself. Ahmad must have called a hundred times to give me ideas for my speech and, of course, fashion advice.

"Make sure you dress conservative—professional. Pull your

hair back, out of your face. Maybe cut it—it looks so nice short. You have such a beautiful face. Why you always have to hide it? And oh, I think you should talk about what a smart thing he did in Bosnia. Tell them how you went to Dayton Peace Accord at Wright-Patt. They will like that. I know you know what to say better than me. I'm so proud of you, Melody *jan.* Whatever you say, you will do great. Always remember the story of the meat."

My first ever reading and book signing took place in Dayton, and before we left the house to go to the bookstore, Ahmad pulled me aside. I could tell he was about to drop a poem or anecdote, possibly both. He has at least one of each for every occasion. I have no idea how many poems he knows by heart, but my guess is hundreds at least.

I can't overemphasize the role of poetry in Persian culture. It is more than an art form in Iran. It's a national pastime—like baseball in the States, but bigger. One of a handful of standard government channels consists of a continuous reel of poems. There'll be some still shot of a flower or a field or a mountain in the background and a poem scrolling down the screen on top of it. And weirder still is the fact that people actually *watch* this channel, even though they likely have the entire book of poems somewhere in the house—possibly even sitting on top of the television.

Not having had the benefit of the Flower & Poetry Channel growing up, I've always been pretty bad at understanding Persian poetry. It's like a completely different language compared to contemporary colloquial Persian, full of big words from centuries back. Sort of like Shakespearean English, but worse. It annoys the hell out of Ahmad that I don't understand perfectly, but he translates for me anyway. The story about Rumi that he shared with me on the night of my reading, however, was in his own words, so it required no translation. And unlike so many of his other poems and stories, this one made immediate sense to me.

One day the great thirteenth-century Persian Sufi poet Rumi (whom we refer to as *Molana* or "The Master") visits his teacher, friend and guru, Shams. Shams instructs Rumi to get a colander and fill it with raw, bloody, ground meat. Shams then tells him to put that colander on top of his head and walk through the central bazaar with it, all the while letting the blood and meat drip down his face. Rumi, being a loyal and devoted student, follows Shams' instructions and comes back to him the next day. Shams then tells Rumi to return to the bazaar and ask around to see if anyone noticed him. No one did. Ahmad's conclusion: "You see, everyone is so worried about themself that no one even notices something as crazy as that! It doesn't matter if you make mistake, Melody *jan*— no one will notice. But I know you will be perfect. I could never do such a speech."

This couldn't be any further from the truth. Ahmad is in fact the king of speeches. He just prefers to give his one on one, without a microphone, over tea.

I could easily have focused on Iran at the Clinton Library, but in the end, I spoke more about Muslim Americans than Muslim Iranians. I always feel the most American when I'm asked to speak as an Iranian and the most Iranian when I'm asked to speak as an American. So, I spoke from the perspective of an Ohioan, keeping *Molana* and his ground-beef hat in mind. I was a hit.

After Little Rock, I was planning on following the exhibit and doing another lecture and signing at its next stop in Mississippi, as well as leading a writers' workshop in Atlanta as part of winning the Georgia Author of the Year Award. Following years of relentless toil, disappointment, persistence and rejection—not to mention mountains of unabashed ignorance and Islamophobia from editors and publishers—I was finally getting to do and say what I wanted. As a writer and an activist, as a Muslim and an Iranian American, as a lawyer and a loudmouth, this was *exactly* where I wanted to be. People were genuinely interested in what I had to say, and they were actually paying me and giving me awards for saying it. This was what I had worked so hard for, and I was determined to keep it up.

Somewhere between the convention and Obama's election, however, things fell apart. I never made it to Mississippi, and I never led that writers' workshop. By November, I was watching the returns of the election on a crappy analog TV, my ass stuck to a plastic-covered couch on a locked psychiatric ward.

By the time I got home from *Breaking the Veils*, I was exhausted. I had been running at a frantic pace for the past two months, and I needed a break. Apparently, so did my mind. I spent the next month in bed, sinking into an ever-deepening abyss, occasionally getting up to shower, but mostly trying to sleep as much as humanly possible, wishing I was dead and eating nothing but take-out, mint chocolate chip ice cream, popcorn and the occasional Fruit Roll-Up. As always, Matthew was concerned and sympathetic, but not too worried because he was accustomed to my depressive episodes. They often stop by for an unwelcome visit in the fall, but they tend to fade by December, if not sooner. Neither of us thought too much of it.

That fall, however, was different. My depression didn't fade. It vanished. Overnight. I was moping and wallowing and eating Papa John's in bed one night, and by the next afternoon, I was singing and dancing, possessed by an inexplicable euphoria. In less than twenty-four hours, my mind had transformed into this unstoppable Happiness Factory, churning out more ideas, plans and aspirations than I could keep up with, all of which I was convinced were entirely reasonable, immediately achievable and incomparably brilliant.

Of course I can cure cancer, eradicate hunger and broker a lasting peace in the Middle East. Just give me a week. First, I have to clean, paint and redecorate the house, write several new books, apply for a few dozen patents and give away all my earthly belongings. That shouldn't take more than two or three days. And then I can spend the rest of the week on cancer, hunger and peace. More than enough time.

By the end of Day 1 in the Happiness Factory, production was growing exponentially and demand was through the roof. Little did I know that the bubble would soon burst, à la Enron, AIG and Lehman Brothers combined.

That afternoon, I played Bobby McFerrin's "Don't Worry, Be Happy" on repeat for hours on end, and by the time Matthew got home from work, I was Bobby's disciple, following his instructions to the tee: not worrying, being happier than I'd ever been and singing that song "note for note" at the top of my lungs, complete with Bobby's signature vocal percussions. To say that Matthew was shocked to find me this transformed would be a gross understatement. Still, he was relieved, even excited, to see that I'd finally gotten out of bed, taken a shower and emerged seemingly intact from my month-long funk. Cautiously, so as not to break the spell, he asked how this was possible, how such a metamorphosis could occur so quickly.

"You're like Gregor Samsa in reverse. Instead of a roach,

you've turned into Tigger on crack. And overnight. Don't get me wrong—it's great. But how did you do it?"

"I don't know. But, I'm better. *Waaay* better. It's like everything is glowing, and I'm the sun."

After a month of extreme depression and minimal human interaction, I was ready to talk. And I did. Nonstop. I jumped from one idea to the next without so much as a breath or a coherent transition. The thoughts soon began to overwhelm me, and I couldn't have decelerated if my life depended on it. I was on the verge of my first full-blown manic episode and psychotic break, but neither Matthew nor I had any idea what mania or psychosis meant, let alone that I was exhibiting all the telltale signs. Matthew kept asking me to slow down, but I insisted that he was the slow one and that *he* needed to speed up or just listen closer.

I had so many ingenious things to say, and I couldn't say them fast enough. When Matthew began to fall asleep on the couch after hours of listening to my inexorable pontification, I was beyond irritated. I kept waking him up in more and more annoying ways. At first, I'd just shake him, but eventually, I moved on to spraying him with one of the water bottles we used to train Olyan, and finally, to jumping on the couch cushion next to him and shouting, "Earthquake!"

"Don't you realize what you're missing?" I insisted after the first earthquake. "This is brilliant. *I'm* brilliant. You have to listen."

"Please, Melody, can't we do this tomorrow?" he begged, rolling over on the couch.

"No!" I insisted, pulling him back around to face me. "What if I die tomorrow? What if *you* die tomorrow? Then you'll miss it, and you'll regret it! You know, it's pathetic that you don't know how our legal system works, that no one knows how it works. You *need* to know your rights. I'm going to teach you about the American justice system, so much of it is so counterintuitive—and unjust. That's why all the people who insist on taking the stand in their own defense, who think they'll be found innocent just because they are, always end up in jail. The lawyers use it as a chance to get into their heads and establish *mens rea*—even if it's not there. You remember what *mens rea* means, right?" I gave him no chance to answer. "Guilty mind. And who the hell doesn't have a guilty mind about *something*? The point is, when you're a criminal defendant, you should *never* take the stand in your own defense—unless you're Gandhi or the Dalai Lama or some shit, but even then, it's a risk." Matthew was asleep again. I incited another earthquake.

"Damn it, Mel! Stop it! I need to sleep. I can learn this all later. You need to sleep too. Just take an Ambien already." I was still standing on the couch looking down at him. He may as well have been speaking Hungarian.

"Aftershock!" I yelled as I continued jumping on the sofa until he finally agreed to sit up and listen just a little bit longer.

"Seriously," I continued, "you have to know the system to work the system. No one ever bothers to learn how it works until they find themselves stuck in it, and with the Patriot Act and all the bullshit Bush is pulling, you may need to know this stuff one day. They know you're a convert. They're probably listening in on your phone calls. You know how regular Americans look at that shit. How it scares them and weirds them out. You remember how even that Iranian girl called you John Walker Lindh when she found out you converted? And she was educated. She was a fucking doctor *and Iranian* and that's how *she* sees things. Forget

Dubya and Condo-fuckin'-leezza! Why did I get this?" I asked, referring to the legal pad I was holding.

"Who knows? We need sleep. Please, let's just go to bed," Matthew pleaded, gazing up at me in desperation as I paced around the room waving my legal pad in an effort to remind myself why I'd picked it up.

"Soon. Soon. I promise." He was facing me, trying to keep his eyes open for fear of another aftershock. "Oh yeah, that's what the pad is for: you need to know the law. Charts will help. Flowcharts. Remember that. These racist Islamophobic hick bastards might be after you one day. It's not like you're immune just because you're white. You're still Muslim; you still married a Muslim Iranian. You've got to know your rights. Seriously. And lucky for you, I have this huge body of knowledge from law school that Ahmad and Jazbi paid so much money for. Don't you want to know it too? And it's *free* for you! Are you listening? Are you listening? What was I saying?"

"Tomorrow, Melody, tomorrow. Please!" Matthew pleaded. I ignored him.

"Okay, here's a piece of paper. Copy this down so you don't forget. We'll have to start with the distinctions between civil and criminal courts, and you should know a little about administrative and military courts as well. And then you need to know how the appeals process works. If I die or if they arrest me or you and take us to Guantánamo or some shit—if you get into a car accident and the bastard decides to sue. People can sue you for *anything*. It can be completely baseless, but by the time you prove it, you've already spent all this money on legal fees. However you look at it, you'll need to know all of this eventually. Okay, let me draw you a chart. . . ."

Having taught sixth grade in Atlanta's inner city for two years, Matthew has more patience than a Buddhist centenarian. I can think of no other explanation for why he didn't grab me, pin me down and forcibly shove an Ambien down my throat the moment I mentioned flowcharts.

I tried to keep him up all night drilling civil and criminal procedure into his head—that is, when I wasn't going off on any number of random tangents. I was convinced he could learn in one night what had taken me three years. When he left for work the next day, he'd gotten only a couple hours of sleep. I hadn't gotten any, but I was wired, riding the sunrise like a roller coaster about to run off the tracks.

seventeen

call the travel channel

Before he left, I promised Matthew I'd try to sleep: "I'll even take something if I have to." After considering the idea, however, I quickly discarded it. I felt so good that I figured instead I could just organize all of my drugs. Being the daughter of two physicians, I have a sizable pharmacy, full of samples and medicines I never take but save for "guests" or "emergencies."

I emptied all the pills out onto the Persian rug gracing our living room floor. I was planning on color-coordinating them—entirely overlooking the fact that afterward I'd no longer have any way of telling them apart by name or purpose. Without Matthew there to keep an eye on me, I talked to myself, and soon, to other imaginary people. Over and over again, I had long conversations with them, then stumbled upon a fleeting moment of clarity realizing there was no one there, only to quickly disappear into fantasyland again.

When Matthew came home, the floor was littered with pills. It was hard to spot them thanks to the intricate patterns on the Nain.

We kept stepping on them and getting capsules stuck to the bottoms of our feet. Still, I refused to let Matthew clear them away.

"Stop!" I shouted, crouching over the stockpile of meds with my arms stretched out over them. "I have a plan! It's brilliant. I promise. Don't worry about it."

"Are you serious? How do you know which is which? It makes no sense." Matthew was annoyed.

"Colors, Matthew, colors. I know what *all* of them are! That's why you can't touch them. It's going to be great. *Great!*"

Matthew has always been able to calm me down, and not just me. He has an uncanny ability to soothe most people and other animals. But by that point, nothing and no one could get me to chill, not even Matthew.

When he asked me to explain my system for organizing the pharmaceuticals, I couldn't. I tried, but by that time there were about three hundred other thoughts crossing and crashing into one another in my mind, all at a million miles a minute. They wouldn't stop. Repeatedly, I'd start a sentence, but then flooded with so many other thoughts and insights, I'd forget what I started saying before I could finish. So I'd just move on, full speed ahead, to the next thought. Soon, I stopped making any sense at all.

My new unbounded zest and exuberance, not to mention my nonstop talking and increasing irrationality, were all taking a toll on Matthew. As my only full-time witness and victim, he was growing exhausted and it showed. Soon after he got home that night, he fell asleep watching me sort my nameless pills.

With Matthew passed out, I'd lost my audience, something I desperately needed. So I called Mario. Mario was the first friend I made after moving to Atlanta. At the time, he was working at

Outwrite, the city's most popular gay bookstore, and as a hot young gay black man in Atlanta, he was always getting hit on.

I used to study at Outwrite (which partly explains my shitty grades), and one night Matthew came to pick me up. Before he came to my table, he stopped by the counter to order a coffee. Probably shocked by the fact that Matthew wasn't already hitting on *him*, Mario proceeded to hit on Matthew. Overhearing their exchange, I went up to the counter and grabbed Matthew's arm.

"Um, he's mine," I said, laughing and flashing Mario my wedding ring.

Ever since, we've been tight. He's the one who drags my ass out of the house when I'm too depressed to move. He's the one who comes over, banging on the door in the middle of the afternoon when I stop answering calls and e-mails. And I have no choice but to answer, because he has a key. If I don't open the door, he'll march right in, announce that he's come to steal me away, and he'll do it too. But while Mario was all too familiar with both Depressed Melody and Hyper Melody, he had never met full-blown Manic Melody before that October night.

Mario always knows which clubs have the best music, and he's also my favorite shopping and dancing partner on the planet. He respects and adores New Order, Cavalli, the Pet Shop Boys, Gucci, The Smiths, Versace and Depeche Mode as much as I do and, like me, he can dance or shop for hours on end without a break. So, calling Mario was a no-brainer, which was lucky for me because my brain was nowhere to be found. Matthew woke up just long enough for me to tell him where I was going and with whom. He was relieved and more than happy to hand me over to Mario for the evening, hoping that all I needed was a night out on the town to release the mountain of energy I'd built up over the last month of moping and that he might be able to get some much-needed sleep.

When Mario picked me up, his convertible was packed with a bunch of girls whom I'd never met. They were all about a decade younger than us; the youngest didn't look a day over eighteen. I took this as an open invitation to share the wisdom of my years and the last few manic days with the unsuspecting lasses, and I didn't stop sharing the whole time they were in my presence.

The moment I got in the car, I insisted we stop at a McDonald's drive-through for a Happy Meal. I barely touched it and ended up hiding it under my halter top in a haphazard, though successful, attempt to smuggle it into the club. I could tell that I was annoying Mario and that the little girls weren't taking to me much either, but I didn't care. I just wanted to get in with my Happy Meal, and if that meant I had to embarrass them by doing my best impression of a misshapen pregnant lady, so be it. After my McFetus and I made it in, I took a seat at one of the few open tables near the dance floor and assumed my standard dining position: crossed legs, Indian style. I didn't care in the least that my skirt barely covered my ass standing up. I carefully spread out my fries and chicken nuggets on the table. The prize was a plastic hippo that said, "All righty, boys!" and "You know that's right!" when you slapped its butt. Despite the plainly racist overtones, I loved it and played with it all night.

After neatly arranging my dinner, I could eat only a few fries and one deformed chicken nugget. Food was a waste of time. I needed to *dance*! I spotted Mario at the corner of the dance floor and worked my way through the crowd to get to him. Upon arrival, I swung my arms around him, and he picked me up, twirl-ing me around to the beat. We tore up the dance floor as usual, but I kept bumping into people and blaming *them* for it. "Watch where you're going, fat-ass!" "Learn how to dance, ho!" "Get out the way, fool!" If it weren't for Mario, there would have been some serious bitch-slapping, hair-pulling, face-scratching, and possi-bly even ass-kicking that night. And given my inexperience with the world of extreme club cat-fighting, I'd have been sure to lose.

That night, for the first time ever, Mario was ready to leave before I was.

"C'mon, Mario!" I whined. "We've only been here for like an hour, and two of the girls aren't even ready to leave yet! They'll be stranded."

"We've been here for over three hours, Melody, and they're not coming home with us because they're hooking up with some guys they met. It's almost three a.m. Everyone's leaving. Matthew will be worried. Go get your hippo. We're going home, doll."

By then Mario knew there was something seriously off with me. After he dropped me off, I started cleaning and organizing the laundry room, pantry, closets and cabinets, as well as redeco-rating the house, moving furniture I had no business trying to lift. When Matthew woke up, only the bedroom looked the same. Me, the kitchen, the living room, the bathroom and even the balcony were all in complete disarray. There were random tools and paint cans in the kitchen, contact lens cases and solution on the balcony, stacks of books in the bathroom and, of course, more pills on the living room floor. I was covered in glitter from some Christmas ornaments I'd cleared out of the laundry room; my hair was several inches shorter in places, and I was sporting perma-nent marker "tattoos" of flowers, quarter notes, treble clefs and capital cursive *L*'s all over my left arm. Again, Matthew begged me to sleep as he left for work, and again, I lied and assured him I would.

Looking back, it seems strange that he'd have left me like that, but then again, this wasn't the first time I'd gone nuts cleaning and reorganizing the house or myself. And I convinced him that my disheveled appearance, like that of the house, was part of a greater plan. I'm always making new plans and adjusting and restructuring my life, self and surroundings for maximum efficiency. Matthew had seen me cover an entire wall next to my desk with rejection letters; spend hours wrapping shoe boxes with carefully selected pages cut out of magazines; drive from Atlanta to New Mexico alone for a week on a whim; and frequently type up and edit ever more elaborate lists of seemingly ridiculous and/or unattainable life goals—from "trapeze artist" to "contortionist" to "Supreme Court Justice." To him, this simply seemed like more of the same—only the volume was higher. He had no way of anticipating what my actions signified or portended.

That afternoon, I called everyone I could think of to tell them about all the wonderful new discoveries I'd made over the past few days. Some favorites: "Live like you're always on vacation. No suits, no collared shirts, no worries." "Don't worry about debt. God doesn't care what the VISA or MasterCard people think of you." "Never wear a watch. Go ahead and be late!" "Give everything away. To save your soul, you must rid yourself of stuff."

No one was nearly as excited about my manic bits of wisdom as I expected or commanded them to be. Frustrated with their apparent failure to recognize or appreciate my genius, I drove to Publix and spent over four hundred dollars on groceries we didn't need and never ate: Oreos, Doritos, Snickers bars, Ho Hos. A cornucopia of empty calories and saturated fat. Yet while I seemed to have tons of time to buy all that junk food in preparation for my new disgustingly hedonistic lifestyle, I couldn't find any time to eat it. I hadn't slept for days, and I hadn't eaten anything since my Happy Meal.

After I got home, I called Matthew to fill him in.

"Oreos? Really, Melody? Oreos? You know they have lard in them, right? Lard from pigs. You know that, right?"

"Whatever, Oreos make me happy. I'm only going to eat and do whatever makes me happy from now on. If *you* want to be happy, then *I* need to be happy, and Oreos make me happy. *Deal!* Besides, I have more important things to discuss. Are you listening?"

"Sure. What is it?" he asked with trepidation.

"You need to quit your job and come home. Are you listening? We have a lot of money now. I got a job writing for the Travel Channel, and we're moving to Italy."

"Whoa, what? Slow down. I didn't even know you were applying for a job with them. And where did all this money come from?"

"Lottery. We won the lottery. Hurry up. Quit your job and come home now!"

Matthew says this was the point at which he knew for sure that something had gone terribly wrong inside my mind. I've never purchased a lottery ticket in my life. I'm against lotteries on principle, and Matthew knows this. Plus, he'd just spoken with Mario, who'd inquired about the possibility that I'd taken up drugs. Like me, Mario doesn't drink or use drugs. Together, we'd make Nancy Reagan proud—apart from the gay, black, Muslim and Iranian parts. Still, while Mario knew that drugs weren't exactly my style, he, like Matthew, was running out of explanations for my bizarre behavior.

"Melody, let me call you back," Matthew replied.

I didn't believe that we had won the lottery at the time. I just believed that we should start living like we had. Within a few hours though, I did start to believe it. I was also sure that I had pancreatic cancer and only a year to live and that I had to find Matthew a new wife before I died. My trip was turning sour. Not even Bobby McFerrin could save me now.

With a front-row seat to all of this insanity, Matthew was freaking out in his own data-obsessed way. He started taking notes again. At first it was just because I kept demanding he write things down for me. My ideas were flying way too fast to stop and find a pen and paper myself. Besides, every time I tried to write something down, I became so preoccupied with improving my penmanship that I forgot what I wanted to write in the first place.

Once I told Matthew to quit his job, he kicked the note-taking into overdrive. These notes, however, weren't meant to record my brilliant ideas. They were meant to record my insanity, to present as documentation later. I have a giant accordion folder full of them, some recording my ideas and others recording Matthew's. The later ones are more organized, more like the notes he took before I went to Stillbrook, and they're dated on full-sized sheets of paper, mostly torn out of legal pads. The earlier ones are scattered all over the place—on Post-its and the backs of envelopes and magazines, anything within reach at the time.

On the back of a card from the Clinton Center, allegedly from Bill himself, thanking me for speaking at his library and signing a copy of my book for him:

> Melody forgets everything. She says I'm a bad listener.
> Increasingly belligerent.
> Call the State Department. Something about NASA.

On a pink Post-it with a half-bloomed stargazer lily and a quote from Helen Keller on it, "We can do anything we want to do if we stick to it long enough":

> Get Roxana a job in Atlanta.
> Write lists only in Farsi and Spanish.
> Live like you're always on vacation. Do what you want.
> Do everything for a reason. Study happiness.

On the back of a donation request bearing the photo of a bald pediatric cancer patient from St. Jude Hospital:

> Be consciously selfish. Slow down. Do it right the first time.
> Slow down to be faster. Study mindfulness.
> Keep more non-perishables. Get a Ph.D. Improve vocabulary.
> Learn Italian. Write at least one book a month.

On the torn-out title page of Huston Smith's *The World's Religions*:

> She's talking so fast, not making sense. She keeps saying,
> "Are you listening?"/"What was I saying?" She can't remember
> anything!

**Call her doctor and parents. Why won't she take anything to
sleep? Hasn't slept for days. Force her to sleep.**

On the Farsi side of one of Matthew's countless homemade
vocabulary notecards that reads "Don't go" on one side and "*Naa-
roh*" along with the corresponding Persian script on the other:

**Make her eat. What is this? She won't stop talking. Slow her
down! Sedative?**

Matthew was home within an hour after I told him to quit his
job. Lucky for me, who would desperately need the insurance said job provided in just a few hours, he didn't quit. Nor did
he buy us tickets to Rome (for the Travel Channel) or Amsterdam
(in case I got really sick and chose to pursue euthanasia) as I had
demanded. Instead, he tried to convince me to go to the hospital.
He had called my psychiatrist and psychologist and every other
doctor who mattered: my parents, Romana and Christina.

By that evening, Matthew had collected half a dozen concur-
ring medical opinions that all boiled down to one directive: Get
her ass to the hospital *now*. The consensus was that I was in the
midst of a manic episode, highly delusional and possibly psychotic.

I refused to believe any of this. If anything, *they* were the
crazy ones. I was fine, *better than fine*. I insisted that I didn't need
to go to the hospital. Instead, I went into the kitchen, pulled out
a knife and asked Matthew if he wanted to "go out" together. I
thought it would be a fun and romantic way to ensure that we'd
never be apart. Unsurprisingly, Matthew wasn't down for the

whole Romeo and Juliet bit. He politely declined, took the knife away from me and called 911.

When the police officer arrived, I took one look at him and decided I wanted to be a cop as well.

"Your shoes are padded. It's like wearing heels. They probably give you at least an inch. I would look so hot in that uniform. How do you become a cop?"

"I'll tell you all about it later, but for now, why don't you get your things together and come with us to the crisis center?" the officer said.

"Crisis center? Is someone sick? What's wrong? Did something happen to Mario? Is he okay?"

I don't remember anything I said or did at the house after that, but Matthew does. Apparently, I locked myself in the bathroom at one point and refused to come out. Upon exiting, I started handing various prescription drugs to the officer. My pharmacy was still scattered all over the living room floor.

After two hours of stalling, I finally managed to pack a giant suitcase and a carry-on and eventually got into the car. I was packing for Europe, not the hospital. The cop let Matthew drive me, but he insisted on escorting us there. As we followed the sirens, Matthew told me we weren't going to see Mario.

"This is for you. We're going for *you*."

"You're kidding. You've got to be kidding. In case you've forgotten, I'm a fucking lawyer, Matthew. I know my rights. You can't commit me against my will. Let's just go to the airport now. We'll get a ticket and go straight to Rome. They have great suits. Remember? You can buy a ton of new suits. The Travel Channel will reimburse us for all of it. Just call them. I know they will."

"Sure, Mel. Let's just make this one pit stop," Matthew said, keeping a calm facade despite his growing panic. He had no idea what I was capable of, and for the first time ever, he was genuinely afraid of me.

"Fine. Just to check on Mario. Then we're out. He can come too if he wants. We could buy a villa or something. But not in Tuscany. That's so overdone. Sicily. Do they have villas in Sicily?"

"Sure they do. Of course they do. You'll be fine. You'll be fine. Don't worry. You'll be fine."

"Duh! What's wrong with you? I *am* fine. It's Mario you should be worried about. What if he got in a car accident? I always told him that damn convertible was a death trap."

Matthew tried to focus on the road, praying I wouldn't grab the wheel or try to get out.

part

five

eighteen

naked in the crisis center

You can't expect a full-blown, balls-to-the-walls crazy person to accept reason. And that was me—entirely mad and staggeringly unreasonable.

When we got to the crisis center, I refused to get out of the car. I kept organizing all the stuff I'd packed and frantically taking notes. Eventually, the counselors there had to come out to the car to collect me. After about an hour of coaxing, they managed to get me into the building. The cop was long gone by then, and it was only me, Matthew, two counselors running the desk and two security guards at the front entrance. It was roughly three a.m., and though I couldn't remember the last time I'd slept or eaten, I wasn't the least bit tired or hungry. Rather, I was hyper, agitated and one hundred percent convinced I didn't belong there.

The thing about being crazy is that you don't *feel* crazy. You need no explanation for anything you're thinking, feeling or doing. It all seems perfectly sane, ingenious even. I really *believed* that I had single-handedly discovered the secret to life, that I had all the most important answers. I really *believed* that I was dying and that we had suddenly become disgustingly rich. And more than anything, I really *believed* that nothing I was doing was remotely irrational.

The medical term for this lack of insight, a common symptom of mania, is "anosognosia." Thinking you're crazy is a good sign. It means you're still thinking. When full-blown, acute insanity sets in, however, it carries a ruthless thoughtlessness with it. I had no idea that the mind was able to defenestrate so much, so quickly. Tact, certainty, reason, conviction, intellect, insight: all straight out the window, all unsuspecting victims of uncompromising gravity, all splattering onto the ground like giant decomposing jack-o'-lanterns. A hailstorm of merciless, genetically modified, carefully carved pumpkins plummeting into concrete at thirty-two feet per second per second. It's no wonder that before the introduction of Thorazine and other antipsychotics, many manic patients died of physical exhaustion.*

During my time at the crisis center, my lack of insight wasn't tiring me. It was, however, exhausting everyone around me. I may as well have been trying out to be the next poster girl for anosognosia. If there were such a thing, I'd have booked the gig for sure. The tapes from that night would've made for the perfect PSA.

"This is your brain. This is your brain on psychotic mania. No drugs necessary. Any questions?" And the frying egg would be saying, "I'm not in a frying pan. I'm a chick, and I should be hatching shortly. What's that smell?"

I kept telling Matthew and the staff that I was happy to sign myself in, but whenever someone handed me the clipboard full of

---

* Frederick K. Goodwin and Kay Redfield Jamison, *Manic-Depressive Illness: Bipolar Disorders and Recurrent Depression*, 2nd ed. (New York: Oxford University Press, 2007): p. 725.

forms to sign, I chucked it across the room. Hard. Then I started hitting Matthew and insisting that he never listened to me when that was *all* he had been doing over the past few days. I was so sure he couldn't hear me that I resorted to drastic measures to get him to listen. I stripped naked, thinking this would somehow force him to hear me and see me for what I was—which in my mind at the time was the most brilliant, rational and stunning creature on the planet.

"There goes my shot at running for public office!" I yelled into a security camera, laughing.

One of the counselors finally got me to put my clothes (a bright turquoise Hello Kitty tank top and pink velour J.Lo sweatpants) back on. I continued to loiter around that waiting room for hours, refusing to sign myself in. When the counselors finally realized I'd never sign in voluntarily, they called an ambulance to come and take me to the hospital. Just before the ambulance got there, I started accusing Matthew of things I knew, even in my deluded state, he'd never done and would never do—all in front of these strangers. I told one of the security guards that Matthew regularly raped and beat me. I waved my fists in Matthew's face and repeatedly punched him in the arms and chest. I yelled at him to get away from me, but I couldn't stop lunging at him. And he just took it. He didn't try to defend himself or argue with me.

He tells me now that all he could do at the time was pray that it was all a dream. When he didn't wake up, however, his only choice was to try to calm me down, to stop me from hurting myself or anyone else, and to somehow get me to sign those damn forms.

By the time the paramedics came in the ambulance to transport me, I was completely out of control. As they took me away on a stretcher, Matthew watched from the parking lot. He stood outside the back door of the ambulance, helpless while I cursed at him from inside, telling him I hated him and wanted a divorce. I had to get him to hate me. It was imperative that he ditch me as soon as possible, while he was still young, fit and handsome, so that he could land a suitable second wife by the time I died. And what better way to make him hate me than by publicly slandering, attacking and humiliating him.

One of the counselors from the crisis center was in the parking lot with Matthew as he watched the ambulance pull away. She had heard my raving tirade and was kind enough to pull him aside after they'd gotten me into the ambulance.

"We see this all the time, you know," she told him. "Don't worry. She doesn't mean any of it. She just needs some medication. You know, Robin Williams is bipolar."

He has no idea why she felt the need to share the Robin Williams part, but admits that at the time he appreciated the attempt to ease his mind, no matter how bizarre. From the outside, he says I looked and sounded like a total stranger. I can't overemphasize Matthew's calm, patient and levelheaded nature. He never raises his voice, and in fifteen years, I've seen him cry only a handful of times. He's more than a rock—he's a boulder. Nothing fazes him. This, however, did.

Still, on the surface, he was as cool as a bucket of cucumbers. Despite his utter lack of experience with mania or psychosis, he seemed to get that this wasn't me talking—that it was just a sick and diseased brain that had slipped into an alternate universe. Anyone else would have gone at least a little crazy himself. But not Matthew. As extraordinarily worried as he was, he knew that there had to be some valid scientific explanation for all of this—that there had to be charts and graphs and tables full of relevant data that he could look to. So, true to form, he kept his shit together. Completely cucumber-esque.

By the time I made it to the hospital, I was in five-point re- straints and crying. I had accepted the fact that I was dying, but the thought that death would require me to leave Matthew alone on this godforsaken planet was overwhelming. Still, I was on a mission. I had to find him a new wife. I started scoping out the emergency room for worthy candidates. None of them was nearly hot or cool enough for him. And they were all treating me like some rabid vermin, with visible fear and disgust.

Though I guess I can't really blame them. Between sobs, I was screaming and pulling violently at my restraints, that is, when I wasn't telling everyone around me how to improve him or herself.

"You know, if you just lost forty pounds or so, you'd be so pretty," I told an emergency room nurse. "Why would you con- tinue to live like that? And your earrings are hideous. Here, take mine. I don't need them. I'll be dead soon."

I was offering some stranger a pair of antique 22-karat gold earrings that I'd received as a wedding gift from my beloved Aun- tie Fati. They were my favorite earrings. No use hanging on to material things though, I thought. It's not like I could take any of them with me.

"Listen, I can't take your earrings. You hold on to them. We're going to take you to a room where you can't hurt yourself."

"Hurt myself? Do I look like I'm hurting myself? You're the ones hurting me, not to mention hurting yourself, carrying around all that extra weight. You repulse me."

I wasn't making any friends. The overweight nurse put me in

a room with a mattress on the floor, some sheets, a blanket and a camera in the ceiling that followed me wherever I went, not that there was anywhere to go.

The door had a small window looking out into the hallway. It was almost exactly the size of my head, but square. There was no clock and the lights were always on, so I had no idea how long I was in there. I could only tell the time of day by the kinds of meals the orderlies brought in. If there were eggs, bacon or grits involved, for example, then I knew it was morning. All the while, they injected me with ever-increasing doses of Haldol.

"You need to sleep. You'll feel so much better. Trust me," a nurse said.

"*Trust you*, you sick fuck? You just locked me in a box alone with nothing but a mattress and a tiny window, and you want me to *trust* you? Go to hell!"

I was begging anyone who came in the room for a book, not that I could have sat still long enough to read it. The Haldol wasn't doing anything to calm me down, partly because I didn't *want* to calm down and fought the drug as hard as I could. When I first got to the hospital, the nurse immediately made me pee into a cup to run a tox screen. She was expecting to find crack or meth in my system. She didn't. I was as clean as the sidewalks of Singapore. You could have sold my piss outside Betty Ford. The only chemicals I was responding to were courtesy of my own brain.

Before that day, I always thought it would be enlightening, even fun, to spend a little time in prison. Just like Malcolm. As historical figures go, Malcolm X is my ultimate. Up until then, I was convinced that, like him, I too could genuinely benefit from prison. I don't think that anymore.

Still, I tried to be strong and respond like I imagined Malcolm would. Having lost control of my mind, however, I was pitifully unsuccessful. I had packed my tattered copy of his autobiography, and I asked for it, thinking it would help. It's my go-to book whenever I feel weak or defeated, and locked in there alone, I figured it was the next best thing to a human companion. Something familiar. Something I'd read at least a dozen times. Something from home.

But no books allowed. Only me and my mattress. My only visitors were orderlies bearing plastic trays full of revolting fare and nurses bearing giant syringes full of Haldol. The first of these nurses had to get a security guard to hold me down for my initial injection.

"I'm allergic to Haldol," I lied, "and I'm a lawyer. You can't do this! This is assault and battery and false imprisonment. I'm going to sue the pants off y'all. You'll regret this. You'll lose your jobs, and you'll be penniless. I'll sue you for every last fucking cent you have. Even if you have property tied up in a corporation, I'll get the judge to pierce the fucking corporate veil on your ass. You probably don't even know what that means, you fucking morons! It means I'll screw you for everything you have and then some. I hope you and everyone in your family gets cancer. You'll regret this. I promise you will!"

"Hold still," the security guard insisted, pinning me down on my back with what seemed like zero effort. The nurse stuck the syringe in my arm, and it was over. I stopped fighting the injections after that.

I was desperate to break out of there, but there was no obvious escape route. The doctors, nurses and orderlies were super cautious every time they opened my door, and several security guards occupied the hallway. There was no way I was getting out. So, I set my sights on getting someone else *in*—someone without the singular aim of feeding or drugging me. I called through the window and into the camera asking for someone to come in and sit with me. Just another person to talk to or hold my hand. Even a small pet would have sufficed.

I was no longer having fun. There are different types of mania. Some are expansive, grandiose and euphoric, while others are restless, agitated and hostile. Mine was quickly transforming from the former into the latter.

nineteen

no more screaming

Beyond the different and potentially overlapping "states" of bipolar disorder, when I was diagnosed the *DSM-IV* also specified several separate "types" of bipolar: Bipolar I, Bipolar II, Cyclothymia and, get this, Bipolar NOS or "not otherwise specified."* Then there's a plethora of possible add-ons: rapid cycling, ultra-rapid cycling, seasonal pattern, postpartum onset and the list goes on.

My official diagnosis, confirmed by over half a dozen "second" opinions, is "Bipolar I," also known as "Classic" Bipolar. It's considered the most severe form of the illness. Still, something about the diagnosis, even now, delights me. Just like my A+ (read:

---

* The *DSM*, or *Diagnostic and Statistical Manual of Mental Disorders*, is the so-called bible of psychiatry. It is published and periodically updated by the American Psychiatric Association, and as such, it is most commonly used in the United States, though it is also used in other countries to a varied extent. The fifth edition is due out in May 2013. The *DSM-IV* was published in June 2000.

A-plus, not A-positive) blood type. All these designations, all these *words*, have positive connotations, and they make for such perfect and promising metaphors. Being timeless, getting the best grade, going first. What could be better? I'm hardwired to see all of these as desirable, top-notch traits. It's the result of a philosophy drilled into my head from birth, the strong and unshakable belief that by working hard and getting the best grades, anything is possible. If it means you have to be a little crazy and delusional to reach your dreams, so be it. After all, delusions aren't really delusions if you realize them.

I believe in the power of words, signs and suggestion, and *One* and *Classic* sound pretty damn auspicious to me. So screw the *DSM* and its need to destroy perfectly good words. I prefer to believe these terms favor me, that they're signs, and that they mean what most dictionaries say they do.

I know that my analysis here is about as unreasonable and unscientific as Scientology, but it makes sense to me. Still, denial is a hallmark of bipolar disorder. Despite the fact that I readily and publicly admit I have the illness, part of my experience with it includes a persistent battle between convincing myself that I have no such chronic mental illness and admitting to myself that I do.

Maybe I'm okay.
Maybe this is all made up.

Maybe it's just a way for doctors
and pharmaceutical companies
to take me for a ride.

This is just my personality.
I feel fine now.

versus

I've been sick before.
I've tried to kill myself.

I've seen and heard things
that weren't there.
I've believed things that
weren't true.

I've taken my medication and
gotten better.

I've skipped my medication
on occasion and gotten worse.

I've witnessed others do so
with the same results.

That "I feel fine *now*" is a killer. The medications for manic depression can work wonders. I've seen it in others, and I've experienced it myself. But therein lies the problem. People feel better and then convince themselves they no longer have the disorder. Then, they go off their meds. The rest of the story is so hackneyed, I won't even bother. But a huge part of treating bipolar requires believing that it's a real illness—and what's more, admitting to yourself that you have it. For those prone to delusions in the first place, it's not the easiest thing in the world to do. And the "sane" world doesn't make it any easier.

If you could diagnose bipolar with a CAT scan or a blood test, I expect it would be both easier to treat and much less likely to evoke so much shame and embarrassment in its victims. But you can't. At least not yet—though scientists have been working on developing a blood test in recent years.* Still, bipolar disorder isn't like cancer—not in the way it's diagnosed, and certainly not in the way it's viewed by health care professionals and society as a whole.

If you have cancer, you get flowers, visitors and compassion. If you have a mental illness, you get plastic utensils, isolation and fear. If you survive cancer, most people consider you a hero and inspiration, and they tell you so. If you survive a mental illness, most people consider you a feeble-minded degenerate and an embarrassment, and they wouldn't dare tell you so. Although, they seem to love telling everyone else you might or might not know. It's more juicy gossip than medical misfortune. No one's making a

---

* Ming T. Tsuang et al., "Assessing the Validity of Blood-Based Gene Expression Profiles for the Classification of Schizophrenia and Bipolar Disorder: A Preliminary Report," *American Journal of Medical Genetics Part B: Genetics* 133B, no. 1 (2005): 1–5.

killing selling "Bipolar Survivor" wristbands or "Schizophrenia Survivor" T-shirts.

The walls were closing in on me. I was terrified and desperate to get out of isolation. I tried to pray, but I couldn't remember the words to prayers I'd repeated nearly every day of my life for years. I couldn't even remember the proper prostrations. Sure, I could pray in my own words, but I wanted the comfort and familiarity of the Qur'anic verses—the words and motions I shared in common with over a billion others around the world, the inimitable rhymes and rhythms of Divinity, the devotions that distinguished me from my captors. Forgetting my prayers was like losing a compass in the middle of a vast, dark wilderness. The day had begun with Beatrice leading me through paradise, and now here I was in hell, unable to recite the simplest prayer, with Virgil nowhere in sight. How quickly fortune, favor and fantasies can turn.

Unable to gather more meaningful words to recite, I tried to sing songs. But I couldn't remember any of those either. I know the entire score to *My Fair Lady* by heart. I've sung those songs since I was a kid, but I couldn't remember any of the lyrics, or melodies even. I couldn't even remember the lyrics to "Don't Worry, Be Happy," which I'd sung at least a hundred times over the past three days.

Somehow, though, my legal knowledge was still intact, and I was more than happy to share it. As all my other wisdom and education deserted me, the law became my sole source of solace, my only hope in a hopeless struggle to regain freedom and dignity.

"I'm suing all of you for false imprisonment and intentional infliction of emotional distress! You injected me with drugs against my will. That's not just malpractice: it's *battery*! Maybe even *criminal*. I'm a licensed attorney. I know my rights. You can't do this!" I yelled at the walls.

Matthew says he could hear me screaming from the waiting room. He says that was the hardest part: hearing my incoherent cries and knowing he could do nothing to stop them. By then, the doctors had confirmed what everyone already suspected: I was experiencing a psychotic break brought on by acute mania. Apparently, if you let mania go too long or too far, it's not uncommon to enter the land of psychosis. And at the moment, I was a resident alien there, in the course of applying for full citizenship.

Meanwhile, I finally found a song to sing, or rather, scream. It wasn't consistent or euphonic, but it was something.

"My name is Melody Moezzi—M-E-L-O-D-Y-M-O-E-Z-Z-I. My Social Security number is two-eight-five . . . [and yes, I yelled the whole thing out loud—not as if anyone there would *want* to steal my identity]. I'm an attorney and a member of the Georgia Bar. This is false imprisonment. I'm being detained against my will. I know my rights! My name is Melody Moezzi. . . ."

When I realized none of the doctors or nurses cared how loudly I screamed, I considered alternatives. The room wasn't padded or sound-proofed, and it was surrounded by several others like it. I'd seen them on the way in. Maybe there were other patients in there, and maybe they could hear me. I took a shot.

"I know that I'm not the only one stuck in here," I yelled, banging on the walls. "If anyone else can hear me, knock on the walls."

The knocking began. A spark of hope. I then came up with a way to really piss off the guards.

"Everyone, let's all squat in the middle of our rooms and poo at the same time. We're in this together!"

At the very least, it was an effective way to get some attention. Two guards immediately came in and pulled me up off the floor, before I could even pull down my pants. Then the back wall retracted into the ceiling, like a garage door. There was a sink and a toilet. They led me in and told me to go to the bathroom. They couldn't pull the wall back down the whole way because it would have cut off my knees when I sat down on the toilet.

"This is some pretty shitty architectural planning, you know. And besides, I don't need to shit. Well, I guess I can pee. Turn around."

They wouldn't turn around.

"Just go."

"Well, stop *watching* me!" I demanded.

"If you want to go, go. If not, we're closing the door."

"You mean the wall? Give me a second, you sick fucks. I hate all heterosexual men. You're disgusting. You're probably getting some sick pleasure out of watching this. Why the hell else would you work in a place like this? I hope you die."

"Are you done?"

"Turkeys are done. People are finished. Didn't you go to *school*?"

"Okay, you're through. Pull up your pants. We're closing the door."

I complied, and the wall closed.

"Okay now, are you going to defecate on the floor?"

"Not with you watching me, I'm not."

"Well, then, we'll be right outside, *watching you.*"

"Can't one of you stay and talk to me? I'm really lonely. I feel so isolated."

"That's why they call it isolation, honey," one of them said. He looked at the other one and they both chuckled. If I had a gun, I don't doubt I would've shot them both then and there. But they had the guns—or at least that's how I remember it. Whatever the case, they had the power, and all I had was a mattress.

I'd never felt more helpless in my life. I tried to comfort myself by thinking about all the things I would do when I got out. I'd get a ton of tattoos, cut off all my hair like Audrey Hepburn in *Roman Holiday*, travel the world thanks to my new imaginary job with the Travel Channel and follow each and every impulse, no matter how fleeting or irrational, before I died. All I needed to do was find a way out.

But I kept doing crazy shit, giving my enemies even more reason to keep me locked in. Things like taking off my shirt and pressing my breasts against the window in an effort to get someone's attention (which only made the guards permanently pull down the shades on my sole window), chucking mashed potatoes and bacon across the room, refusing to eat and trying to incite mutiny by encouraging my fellow inmates to join in on my hunger strike and embrace the power of poop.

I wanted someone to talk to. I would have settled for even a hallucination, but no such luck. You can't *will* hallucinations; that's sort of the problem with them. They're there when you don't want them, and they're never around when you do—at least in my experience.

So I went back to the window and started knocking, desperately trying to get someone's attention. With the blinds down, no one could see me. If I could just get someone to sit with me—to remind me that I was real and assure me I wasn't going to die in there, or if I was, that at the very least, I wouldn't have to do it alone—then maybe my panic and terror might have lifted a little. I wanted a witness. At least then, Matthew would have some solid evidence for his killer wrongful death suit after I was gone. As long as I was alive, I would have welcomed even a mildly hostile visitor with open arms—just to have another soul in the room. The guards were right. There *is* a reason they call it isolation.

Anyone who thinks solitary confinement isn't cruel and un- usual is either a masochist or has never experienced it first- hand. Even for just a few hours, it's intolerable, *especially* when you're mad. And if you're not crazy to begin with, it's a great way to get there. Studies have shown that solitary confinement can and does induce insanity in some cases. Besides the depression, anxi- ety and rage that you'd expect with prolonged seclusion, there's also the potential for hallucinations, impulse control problems, as well as impaired memory, concentration and cognitive func- tioning, even in individuals with no prior diagnosis or history of mental illness.[*]

So, why the hell would anyone even consider using it as a *treatment* for insanity? The way I see it, it's not just counterpro- ductive, it's moronic—dare I say, *insane*. Why not use laxatives to treat diarrhea or garlic to cure halitosis? I've heard arguments

---

[*] Stuart Grassian and N. Friedman, "Effects of Sensory Deprivation in Psychiatric Seclusion and Solitary Confinement," *International Journal of Law and Psychiatry* 8 (1986): 49–65; Grassian, "Psychopathological Effects of Solitary Confinement," *American Journal of Psychiatry* 140 (1983): 1450–1454.

claiming that people don't remember most of what they experience when they're psychotic, and thus putting them in isolation isn't so bad. They'll forget it soon enough.

I didn't.

I still have nightmares about it, and I still dread the very real possibility of finding myself in isolation once again, with guards and nurses who refuse to look at me or answer my questions, for fear of catching whatever I have. I've never been the object of more vicious indifference in my life, and I've never felt more invisible and worthless.

No matter how hard I banged on my tiny window or how vociferously I yelled into the camera in the ceiling, no one came. Eventually I got tired and gave up, and after God-knows-how-many injections of Haldol, I finally took a nap. Not a long one, just long enough for my captors to deem me sufficiently stable to transport to Ashwood, the nearest mental hospital.

But no one told me I was going to Ashwood. I was sure I was being set free. My mom had flown down from Ohio, and she and Matthew were waiting for me outside the isolation room. I had already made all kinds of plans in my head. We would go to brunch, and I would spend the rest of the day getting a haircut, shopping and being tattooed. When I found out this wasn't happening, I was livid. I immediately began screaming and flailing my limbs, hitting and kicking anything or anyone within reach—until, yet again, nothing and no one was within reach. I was freezing, curled up in a ball in a corner of my cell when I finally took a crack at my only viable escape route: sleep.

But before I could drift off, someone let Matthew in the room. He sat down on the floor, wrapping the blanket tightly around me, and told me everything would be okay. I was so happy to see him. It was time to tell him the truth.

"I have something to tell you," I said. "I didn't want to say anything because I didn't want to hurt you, but I'm dying. I have pancreatic cancer and about a year to live probably. Call Dr. Weinstein. He'll tell you. I can't be in here. I need to be in Italy, to be traveling the world *with you!* I don't have time for this shit. I'm dying! Do you get it now? I know I must have looked crazy, but I'm not. I'm just dying. Now you have to get me out of here." I was sobbing and using my blanket as a handkerchief.

Apparently Matthew had already overheard me tell one of the paramedics about my cancer. He had called my gastroenterologist hours before he was allowed into the isolation room, by which point, he knew full well that my pancreas was fine.

"I *will* get you out, but first, they're going to take you to Ashwood to make sure you're okay. It's protocol. You won't be in there for long. Just until we can sort some things out."

"Fuck protocol! Why are you doing this to me? And why don't you even seem to care that I'm dying? Where is my mom? Where is Roxana? Did you call her? She has to come down. Why aren't more people here? Where is my dad? My sister? I need them here." Tears poured down my face.

"Of course I care, but let's be sure before we jump to conclusions. They told you that you had cancer once before, remember? They were wrong then, and I'm sure they're wrong this time, too. You're past the five-year benchmark. And I talked to Romana. She's talking to the doctors. She's doing everything she can. We're all trying to help you. It'll be okay. I promise."

That was the longest conversation I'd had since arriving at

the hospital. Matthew kept rubbing my arms and assuring me they'd get me out any minute.

"Any minute" took a few hours, but with Matthew in the room, I was finally able to calm down long enough to get some sleep. When I woke up, there were two paramedics in the room, asking me to get onto a stretcher.

"I can walk," I said.

"No, honey," one of the paramedics told me, "it'll be easier this way."

I climbed onto the stretcher, and before I could protest, they had me in restraints again. Then I lost it, screaming and cursing and of course threatening to sue everyone. Matthew had to leave because Romana was calling. She heard me screaming in the background and told him to get my mom out of there.

"This isn't good for you," she said. "You shouldn't have to hear all of this."

She was right. It wasn't good for anyone to hear any of it. Besides, there was nothing they could do. Matthew and my mom left me with the paramedics, who assured them that I'd be at Ashwood shortly.

I don't remember what happened after that, but I do remember that when I got there, my throat was so sore I could barely talk, and my wrists and ankles were red and swollen from trying to break free from the restraints.

Once you've gotten naked in public, tried to stage a shit-in while in solitary, chucked clipboards and mashed potatoes at strangers, and convinced yourself that you've won the lottery, work for the Travel Channel and have terminal cancer, it's hard not to believe that there's something highly unusual about the way your brain works. After I managed to get the hell out of isolation, I had time to start accepting this reality, and once I did, a few weeks later, I finally began to improve.

My family did everything in their power to ensure that I got the best care and medication available. They read all the books and articles they could get their hands on, determined to become experts. My parents consulted with all the psychologists and psychiatrists they knew and several they didn't. More than anyone else, though, they consulted with Christina, who in turn consulted with her professional colleagues and other resources. Romana and Matthew were relentless researchers. Matthew filled a giant binder with all of their findings, and he continued to take notes, especially when he talked to the doctors.

Mood Stabilizers:

-Lithium: can be toxic and dangerous, but gold standard; tremor/coordination problems, thirst, weight gain—sounds like it sucks, but doc keeps saying it's great.

-Valproate or Carbamazepine . . . a lot of them cause weight gain

-Antiseizure/anticonvulsant drugs are classic bipolar drugs

-Lamictal/lamotrigine—Romana says it's the best; Christina says it's good.

-Abilify—antipsychotic?

→ Atypical antipsychotics (less side effects) v. Typical (Haldol, etc.).

Melody hates Haldol. Makes her crawl out of her skin.

→ *PRESUMPTIVE DIAGNOSIS: Bipolar 1: mania/
depression; explains a lot—just a name; she's always
had crazy highs and lows, just not this bad. Chronic;
no cure, but good treatments. Must take drugs!*

*Can family come to group sessions? When can we come
see her?*

*How long will she be here? Can we make her stay if
she doesn't want to?*

He didn't write down the answers to these questions, but he
got them soon enough, after he and my mom met me at Ashwood.
At first, we were yet again separated by walls, and I was still yell-
ing on the other side—though, by then, I wasn't nearly as loud
thanks to my exhausted vocal cords. Still, I wouldn't shut up until
hours after they finished signing me in and were gone for the
night, until I had gotten a few more hours of sleep and until the antipsychotics finally started to kick in.

At the top of the next day's notes from Matthew's discussions
with the doctors, my mom and me, he wrote:

*No longer psychotic. Still some delusions. Looks
confused.*
Keeps asking same questions. Forgets things.
Still manic, but meds are working.
No more psychosis. No more screaming.

twenty

ward ignored

I'd broken my pledge. At Stillbrook, I said "never again." But here I was, *yet again*, on another psych ward, officially a veteran. Still, I insisted I didn't belong there. As far as I was concerned, this was all just some colossal cosmic mix-up. Consumed by denial and delusions, I fully believed I was a prophet with a direct line to God, that I was one of Obama's top advisers, that I was a millionaire and, most of all, that this was all an elaborate scheme by the Bush administration to keep me out of politics and destroy my reputation.

Matthew dutifully documented my phone calls from Ashwood while I was there. I want to say they're embarrassing, but I'm trying to get past that now—to believe that his notes provide insight purely into a disease and not into me. But no matter how much I'd like to, I still don't fully buy it. Separating the two is about as easy as splitting an atom. Making it trickier still is the fact that statistically speaking, I'm highly likely to experience another manic episode (if not several) somewhere down the line.

Bipolar disorder is a chronic illness. As such, even with the best medications, no one can guarantee I won't experience more manic or depressive episodes in the future. Furthermore, with each new episode, it becomes increasingly likely that I'll experience another one. That's what doctors mean when they say it's "treatable" but not "curable." Reruns are generally a fact of life with manic depression, and as with most reruns, they're never as good as they were the first time around. The hallucinations tend to get uglier; the voices nastier and the knives more tempting.

The key to treatment is prevention, and the key to prevention is awareness. Possessing neither, my only hope was intervention. But I didn't believe I was sick and thus I wasn't about to submit. As far as I was concerned, my diagnosis was about as valid as geocentrism. Acceptance was a galaxy away.

So instead of attending groups and "engaging," I demanded to use the phone and staged sit-ins, hunger strikes and full-blown tantrums when I was forbidden to do so. Still in the eye of the storm, I couldn't see past the flying debris. Once I got to the phone (yet again, there was only one), I always tried Matthew first. While I vividly remember my protests and my demands to *use* the phone, I do not remember the content of any of my phone conversations while I was at Ashwood. Still, they were many, and long. From one conversation alone, Matthew recorded the following:

> *Ok, stop. Listen to me. Can you stop for a second? —Over*
> *and over, frequency goes up.*

> *master plan*

228

> *Ok, you know what? . . . then total tangent*

> *Listen to me for a second. Ok, listen. (time/space*
→ *no sequence)*

> *Melody, stop + think.*

> *Keeps asking me my age + her birthday*

> *"Is that correct?"*

> *I have a plan for my life, and I am dragging you*
along kicking + screaming.

> *I'm racist . . . blue-haired/ blond-eyed devil*

> *I am crazy.*

> *Sanity is relative*

> *Am I the devil?*

> *I love science . . . Spalding Gray . . . Swimming to*
Cambodia

> *I love Garrison Keillor. Ok, I like them both . . .*

> *When did Spalding Gray kill himself?*

> *Move to London. England is the devil. I hate your*
mom. I don't hate your mom.

> *This is all a lie. I've made this all up.*

> *We have all the $ in the world. Imagine you had $1m. This is all a lie.*

> *Violin article about abortion.*

> *I hate women.*

> *I hate heterosexual males.*

> *This is all a lie.*

> *I tried to kill myself.*

> *It appears I have a job with the Travel Channel.*

> *I want to take every state's bar exam.*

> *The worst is behind me.*

But the worst was yet to come. I was sure that the staff at Ashwood hated me, that they hated *all* the patients. The truth, however, was even more disturbing. Much like those who treated me while I was in isolation, the providers at Ashwood were staggeringly indifferent. So much so that I ultimately began calling them the Indifferents.

I started out on the Stabilization Unit, and within a day, I advanced to the Female Adult Unit. Nothing was expected of me on the Stabilization Unit, but the Female Adult Unit had rules. Most were nearly identical to the ones at Stillbrook, but two quickly became a serious nuisance:

PATIENTS ARE NOT ALLOWED TO LEAVE THE BUILDING WITHOUT A DOCTOR'S ORDER.

[At Stillbrook, a nurse's order sufficed.]

STAFF MAY DETERMINE IF THE PATIENT'S BEHAVIOR IS APPROPRIATE FOR LEAVING THE UNIT FOR ACTIVITIES.

[Though this was also true at Stillbrook, their interpretation of appropriateness was more generous.]

In short, I was a prisoner. *Of course* my behavior was inappropriate. Why the hell else would I have landed there in the first place? Still, the Indifferents had sole say over where I could go and when, and I sensed they enjoyed the power trip. The little sunlight I was permitted was always tainted by a giant cloud of cigarette smoke. If I've learned anything from my stays in psychiatric hospitals, it's that crazy people *love* their tar and nicotine. So, I had no choice. If I wanted my daily dose of Vitamin D, I would have to endure both the stink and the mildly elevated risk of lung cancer.

To make matters worse, most of my belongings had been seized upon my arrival. Their rules and regulations were even more suffocating than the secondhand smoke. No "sharps," no drawstring pants, no shoelaces, no belts, no mirrors, no nail polish, no makeup, no perfume, no money, no radios, no "recording devices," no cell phones, no laptops. Essentially, no fun.

Once again, I was stuck with puzzles and Play-Doh, but this time I didn't even make any friends—at least as far as I can remember. My memory was absolute shit while I was there. Perhaps it was the antipsychotics, perhaps it was the mania or perhaps it was the constant humiliation. I can't be sure.

Whatever the case, I *do* have my hospital records, and they speak for themselves. (Note, there's no way I could include as many [*sic*]s as would be appropriate when citing these records, so I have left them out. My hope is that you'll be able to figure things out within the context despite the abysmal grammar, spelling, and punctuation.)

HISTORY OF PRESENT ILLNESS: Melody is a 29-year-old, married, middle Eastern female who comes in with an acute mania . . . The patient was disorganized, flight of ides, tried to disrobe in the lobby at Care of Crisis [Correction: I did], and stated that she is an attorney and plans to sue Ashwood hospital for being here. Suicidal ideation with plan to jump off a building. The patient is delusional, but denied delusional thoughts, but still says she wrote a book [Correction: I did] and wants to find her husband and [correction: a] wife. Pleasant now little recall of last night and recognized. She was psychotic last night, but not now . . . she has a delusion that she is also a lawyer [Correction: I was and am].

RACE: MIDDLE EASTERN INDIAN [Correction: not Indian.]

CHIEF COMPLAINT: "I got manic."

Presenting Problem(s): "I AM A WRITER, AN ATTORNEY.
I DON'T ENJOY PRACTICING LAW IN THIS COUNTRY.
[How and why these are "presenting problems," I'm not
sure.] I WANT TO CHANGE MY NAME TO SOMETHING
LIKE F YOU SO THAT I LAUGH EVERY TIME I SAY IT
BECAUSE I HATE MYSELF AND I WANT TO DIE.
BECAUSE I NEED MORE JOY IN MY LIFE BECAUSE
PEOPLE WANT TO HEAR ME SPEAK—I LIKE TO HOOLA
HOOP AND I HAVE BEEN HANGING OUT WITH OBAMA
SO I AM HERE FOR POLITICAL REASONS."

Precipitating Events: Pt is exhibiting manic behavior. No
sleep in three days attempted to undress at the crisis center
in the lobby. [Correction: again, I did.]—SUICIDAL WITH
PLAN TO JUMP OFF BUILDING—DELUSIONAL—
BELIEVES SHE IS AN ADVISER TO BARACK
OBAMA, BELIEVES SHE IS A LAWYER, AUTHOR, OWNS
AN ORGANIZATION "HOOLA HOOPING FOR PEACE" TO
RAISE MONEY FOR THE CAMPAIGN. [Correction: Apart
from the "adviser to Barack Obama" part, the rest is true.]
STATES SHE IS HERE TO FIND A WIFE FOR HER
HUSBAND BECAUSE SHE IS GOING TO DIE OF
PANCREATIC CANCER PT REPORTS HEARING
"VOICES AND SEEING THINGS"—HAS NOT SLEPT IN
10 DAYS—IS HYPERVERBAL, DISORGANIZED,
GRANDIOSE.

ADMITTING DIAGNOSIS:

AXIS I: Bipolar disorder not otherwise specified.
[Correction: I'd already been diagnosed by nearly a dozen
other doctors with a "specified" type of bipolar—namely,
type I.]

AXIS II: Deferred.

AXIS III: History of pancreatic cancer. [Correction: I never
had cancer; my tumor was benign.]

AXIS IV: Social and environmental problems [whatever the
hell that means].

AXIS V: Global Assessment Functioning: 21 [A score of 1–30
means a patient is a "candidate for inpatient care."]
My "delusions" about being a lawyer are consistently
documented throughout these records. That is, until the day
before my discharge. The following note appears in the file:

Delusions: No (Yes) (Describe): ~~Believes~~ she is a lawyer.

This was the sole correction to my error-ridden file. Nowhere
did anyone correct any assessments regarding my "delusions"
about being an author or a hooper, which makes me think the Indifferents had serious delusions of their own. To say that these
records are ~~disturbing~~ fucking horrifying would be ~~an under-
statement~~ outrageously charitable.

Not only could staff members easily have asked Matthew or my parents to help distinguish my truths from my delusions, they could have just as easily Googled me. At the very least, they'd have found my book on Amazon, along with several dozen articles about my work in various reputable publications, as well as many of my essays and articles. If they had any fact-checkers on staff, I expect they'd fit in marvelously at Fox News.

The power dynamic that exists at Ashwood, and at countless other deceptively innocuous-sounding facilities like it, is insurmountable. The "providers" are in charge. The "consumers" are subservient. It's like a mini-dictatorship. Just like Iran, without the rice or *roo-saris* and with way more pork and Play-Doh. Besides these small distinctions, however, there's little difference between the power structure of the so-called "Islamic" Republic of Iran and so-called "treatment" facilities like Ashwood Hospital. Sure, Ashwood doesn't have a Revolutionary Guard or a Supreme Leader per se, but it has its *own* guards and leaders, who, I dare say, can be just as brutal.

I'm not arguing that providers ought to believe everything we tell them as consumers. Of course not. What I *am* arguing, however, is that they need to hear us out, check their facts and treat us with basic human dignity and respect. It doesn't sound like much, but such changes would mark tremendous advances were places like Ashwood willing to adopt them.

I'd like to believe that being released soon after the staff realized I was a real, honest-to-goodness attorney was just a coincidence, but I doubt it. No one likes to be sued. And it turns out that good lawyering and mental illness are not mutually exclusive.

In all, I was at Ashwood for only three days, though it felt like an eternity. Upon leaving, I was still far from well. Nevertheless, I "knew my rights," and I was determined to rot in them, at least for a little while. Though it may *appear* that my J.D. fucked me once again here, I refuse to believe it.

Everyone in my family tried to keep me at Ashwood. They begged me to stay and stop threatening the hospital. But I wouldn't budge, and given I was no longer actively psychotic or suicidal, they had no legal grounds for keeping me there.

In hindsight, I expect I'd have recovered faster had I stayed and kept taking the heavy doses of antipsychotics they were pumping me with, but I'm glad I didn't. Had I achieved "recovery" at Ashwood, I'm confident that I would have had to pay for it with ever-increasing units of human dignity, and I'd much rather decay in a prison of my own creation than recuperate in someone else's.

I would recover on my own terms, in my own time.

twenty-one

going back to ohio

Who needs a babysitter at twenty-nine? Me.

When I left Ashwood, my mind was still swimming with nonsense. There was no way I could be trusted to sit still for five minutes, let alone resist pursuing every stupid idea or impulse imaginable. So Matthew stayed home from work to babysit me, making sure I took all my pills on time, hoping that eventually the chemicals would work their magic and bring me back to reality, back to health, back to him.

The few times he left me alone for more than a couple minutes, I escaped, taking nothing with me. No money, no cell phone, no meds. Fortunately, he always found me within a few hours, but during those brief periods of "freedom," I managed to roam the busier streets near our house, crossing them without looking either way (God protects His prophets, so why would I need to waste time doing silly things like that?); I tried to get on a bus without paying (Why should prophets have to pay silly things like *bus fares?*); and of course I continued to field countless messages from the Divine.

I know we talked about a lot more, but all I remember from our conversations was Him telling me that I was His newest messenger, that I had to get rid of all my earthly possessions and that I'd been chosen to lead a massive political uprising. Against whom, when and where was unclear. The important thing was that I'd been elected by God.

Still, despite my direct line to the Divine, I remained highly anxious and irritable. I cursed drivers who almost hit me, shoved strangers who happened to be in my way, kneeled down to yell at an infant in a stroller, telling her to "shut the fuck up," and kicked her mom in the shin when she told me to get the hell out of her baby's face.

To the outside world, I was just another lunatic talking to herself, assaulting mothers and berating babies. To me, I was a spiritual and political prodigy.

Today, I see other mentally ill individuals (mostly homeless) on street corners all over this country, and I'm overwhelmed with fear and empathy. Under slightly different circumstances, I could just as easily be them. Before I lost my mind, these people were all but invisible to me. After, I saw them everywhere.

As a result of the mid-twentieth-century drive toward deinstitutionalization, countless mentally ill patients were left to fend for themselves. The idea behind the movement was a noble one: integrate people with mental illnesses into society by replacing residential mental health facilities with outpatient community-based ones. The problem, however, was that there weren't enough community-based facilities, and many patients still needed long-term care, as they were not yet suited for "reintegration." Consequently, the number of homeless mentally ill skyrocketed, as did their rates of incarceration. Today, hundreds of thousands of

Americans with mental illnesses are homeless (many of whom also happen to be veterans) and the Los Angeles County prison is now the largest mental health facility in the world. In short, deinstitutionalization failed.

B y November, less than a month after being released from Ashwood, I found myself on yet another psych ward. This time in Ohio. After a week of babysitting, Matthew was exhausted, and besides, he had to go back to work. So my mom took me to stay in Dayton for a while.

I lasted only a few days. The twelve-hour drive, which normally takes only eight, was excruciating. I tried to jump out of the car a couple times; I couldn't sit still in the passenger seat or backseat, and there was no way anyone was going to test how I'd do in the driver's seat. My skin wouldn't stop crawling.

The medical term for this is "akathisia." But it ought to be called "vicious agitation that feels like a relentless swarm of merciless, parasitic worms crawling under every fucking square inch of your skin." Sure it seems long, but it could always be shortened to VATFLARSOMPWCUEFSIOYS. It shouldn't be *that* hard a sell, given how much doctors love concocting cryptic, ridiculous names for every condition and procedure imaginable. The official name for my pancreatic surgery: a mid-pancreaticojejunostomy with a Roux-en-Y anastomosis. I rest my case.

The VATFLARSOMPWCUEFSIOYS was excruciating. As she drove, my mom tried everything in her power to calm me down. She played relaxing classical Persian CDs. When that didn't work, she played more upbeat tunes and danced in her seat, encouraging me to do the same, hoping it'd help tire me out. It didn't. She had to stop every hour or so on account of my VATFLARSOMPWCUEFSIOYS. I either ran in place, or jumped up and down, or just shook like a maniac. She insisted I do everything right next to the car and consistently encouraged me to ignore the weirded-out passersby in the various parking lots we visited and do whatever I had to do to feel better, spectators be damned. And she watched me the whole time to ensure I didn't run away. Matthew warned her about that.

Anyone else would have at least tried smacking me or dousing me with cold water. I know *I* would have. It's absolutely mind-boggling how much mothers are willing and able to endure at the hands of their own ungrateful offspring.

I bolted into the house the second we pulled into the driveway. My mom took a nap while my dad took on the task of babysitting. I'd packed my highest-end Hula Hoop, and after retrieving it from the car, I spent the next few hours hooping in the piano room. For years, my poor parents paid ridiculous sums of money on piano lessons. Romana and I rarely practiced.

After I spent about an hour hooping, talking to Ahmad and making minimal sense the whole time, he suggested I try playing some piano.

"Piano?" I responded. "You must be kidding. I don't know why you kept paying for our lessons. We were never going to be Christina Ho." Christina was the star of every concert. All of Mrs. Wasson's students who actually cared about piano wanted to be her.

"Christina who?"

"No, *Ho*, not *Who*." Clearly she'd had much more of an impact on me than on him.

"I don't know this Ho. Maybe you want to take a nap?"

I started laughing hysterically and chanting *Who, Ho, Who, Ho, Who, Ho* as I hooped.

Ahmad was the one who really needed the nap. Besides the fact that I was exhausting him, it was his routine. As long as I can remember, he'd come home from work every afternoon, turn on CNBC and fall asleep after watching about five minutes.

"*You* can take a nap if you want. I'm fine here," I told him.

"Are you *sure?*" he asked tentatively. Ahmad isn't nearly as patient as Jazbi, and without his naps, he's even more impatient, not to mention cranky.

"Yes, I'm sure, Ahmad! I'm not a ten-year-old!"

"Okay, then, wake me in an hour. Your mom should be up soon anyway."

It turns out, however, I *was* a ten-year-old—or at least, I had the impulse control of one. The second he fell asleep, I sneaked out and started driving back to Atlanta. I'd barely made it to Cincinnati when Ahmad called.

"Come back *right now!*" He was livid.

"You can't force me, Ahmad. I have rights. I'm not a child."

"I'm going to call the police. I tell them you stole the car. You have no money. What are you going to do when you need gas? We have credit card from your wallet. You have nothing. Come home!"

A tiny ray of clarity sneaked in from behind the dancing gummy bears in my brain and, miraculously, I gave up. I tried to turn around, but the gummy bears were fighting back, sticking together and clogging up the spaces between my synapses. I couldn't remember how to get back. I'd driven from Dayton to Cincinnati and back hundreds of times, but this time it felt like I was driving to Mars. Ahmad tried to help, giving me step-by-step directions, but he may as well have been speaking Icelandic. I ended up driving to a gas station off the highway and asking an attendant for the address. I gave it to Ahmad, and he drove there so I could follow him home.

I was back for only a few hours before my parents suggested heading to the Haven Hill Hospital psych ward. I agreed, mostly because I thought they might be able to get my VATFLARSOMP-WCUEFSIOYS under control.

The thing about Haven Hill, though, was that my dad worked there, so I expected him to be crazy embarrassed. (*I* was.) But he didn't seem to be—at least not as far as I could tell. According to my records, I was admitted to the seventh-floor inpatient psych unit "on an emergency basis because of rapid decompensation . . . experiencing insomnia, racing thoughts and irritability." My diagnosis at Haven Hill differed significantly from the one I'd received at Ashwood. More specifically, it was accurate—noting that I had bipolar, type I, a history of pancreatitis and high cholesterol, as well as low potassium levels and a touch of tachycardia.

Under the "ASSETS" section of my admission form it says, "The patient is cooperative and invested in treatment." As agitated and manic as I was, this was true for the most part. I was slowly beginning to accept that there was something seriously wrong with me, and I wanted to fix it. Though this insight was erratic, it grew stronger.

When my parents left the ward, it was late. I couldn't sleep, so I began reading the few dated magazines I could find. Most were pet-, garden- or sports-related, and although I've never been particularly interested in any such genres, I was transfixed, as if every article had been written for me and *only* me. I've been missing out, I thought. All these years God was sending me messages in the pages of these ridiculous publications, and I didn't know it.

I committed to subscribing to all the top garden-, pet- and sports-related magazines the second I got out.

"It's time to sleep," one of the nurses told me as she pulled an ancient *Cat Fancy* out of my hands.

"But I'm not tired. I'm fine sitting right here. Can I have the magazine back?"

"I'm sorry, honey, but you need your sleep. I'll get you something to help if you like."

I don't remember if they gave me anything when I first got there, but I imagine so, as the VATFLARSOMPWCUEFSIOYS had improved. I wasn't tired, but I was able to sit still and remain "appropriate"—quite an achievement given the circumstances. So I didn't fight her—partly because I'd gained a little more control over my impulses by then and partly because I was afraid she'd find out about the messages in the magazines and take them away for good.

"No, I'll be fine," I answered. "Where am I sleeping?" As I asked this, I looked up at the nurse, and noticed a guy drooling and watching television behind her. I took my first good look around the ward at that point, quickly realizing for the first time that it was coed. I'd never been on a coed ward before, and I wasn't excited about it.

"Shit! You can't expect me to *sleep* here. I'll get raped. *Gang*-raped. Why the hell are there *men* on this ward? Everyone here is crazy. How do you know they're not all rapists?"

"We do checks every fifteen minutes. You'll be fine. I promise. And they're not rapists."

"You don't know that. Most rapists never get caught. Plus, it takes just five minutes to get raped. Maybe less. I took back the night in college. I met tons of girls who were raped. Don't you

know, like, half of all men are rapists?" I'd clearly pulled this ridiculous statistic right out of my ass, but I genuinely believed it at
the time.

"We can leave your door open, and if we hear anything, we'll
be in there right away. No one has ever been raped on this unit. I
promise you'll be fine."

I didn't believe her. As she led me to my room, I started bawling uncontrollably—until I met my roommate. I'd seen her when I
first walked onto the unit, and when the admitting nurse told me
there were no private rooms available, I immediately asked to
room with her. She was young, beautiful and looked like the san-
est person in there. My best prospect by far.

"This is Sophia," the nurse told me. "She'll help you get settled
in." That's when I first noticed she was pregnant. No one would be
so cruel as to rape a pregnant woman, I thought, and as her roommate, I immediately felt immune by association. I stopped crying.

Sophia showed me where the towels were and introduced me
to the most ridiculous shower I've ever encountered.

"You press this button, and the water turns on. But it only
stays on for about thirty seconds. Then you have to press it again.
The first run is pretty cold, but then it stays warm for about another three or four pushes."

"You mean you only get two minutes of warm water?" I asked.

"If you're lucky."

"Jesus Christ!"

"I know," Sophia said. "I think it's because they think you'll
drown yourself or something. I don't know how anyone drowns
themselves in a shower with a giant drain and no tub, but that's
just how things work here."

Sophia stayed up with me that entire first night. We swapped horror stories. She told me about her worthless ex-boyfriend who beat the crap out of her and how she slit her wrists four times with a butcher knife.

"Luckily, I didn't cut all that deep. I only needed stitches on one of the slits."

My story felt lame by comparison.

"I know there's something wrong with me," I shared. "But no one beat me up or anything. My husband is amazing; so are my parents. I have no excuse."

I expected Sophia to look down on me for this (spoiled little rich girl with no real reason to be here), but she didn't.

I headed to group with Sophia the next morning bearing low expectations. They were met. Overall, it was nothing new. Besides a bit more focus on rage and violence on account of all the men there, it was pretty much the same old spiel—abused as a child; alcoholic mother, father, self (or all of the above); trouble with the law, et cetera. Confessions regarding the latter prompted me to share some legal insights, which quickly made me the most popular girl on the ward—with everyone except for Scott, a former sales manager who insisted I was a CIA spy. A few of the patients actually formed a line in front of me after group ended. They all wanted the same thing: to get out. Despite informing them that I was licensed to practice only in Georgia, they wouldn't leave me alone, which wasn't really the end of the world because I loved the attention. Still, I wasn't crazy enough not to limit my liability. I didn't make them sign releases or anything, but I did cover my ass.

"I'm happy to talk with you," I said calmly to the handful of patients who'd approached me, "but you must realize that I *do not* represent any of you in any way and will only be sharing my opinions—*not* legal advice.

"Now," I continued, pulling up my oversized purple, polar-bear print pajama pants in an attempt at professionalism, "who's first?"

They all raised their hands enthusiastically—apart from one elderly woman toward the back, who was staring at the linoleum.

"You," I said, pointing at her. "Do you need help?"

"Oh, yes, dear, but I can wait."

"No," I said, "you're the oldest, so you go first. Respect for elders, you know. What's your name?" The rest of the crowd politely dispersed when I said they could approach me later. We sat at a table at the back of the television/playroom.

"I'm Myrtle," said my new nonclient. "My husband is keeping me here. He thinks I'm going to kill myself. But I'm not. I want to get out." Myrtle was in her eighties at least, but she had a young voice. She was shy for sure, but there was none of the crackling in her voice that so often accompanies old age.

"Well, Myrtle, why would your husband think that?"

"I took a lot of pills last week. I kept forgetting that I took them, and I guess I took too many. I wasn't trying to *kill* myself. I just forget how many I've taken sometimes."

"I see," I said, delighted that someone there would value my opinion. "So you've been here a week?"

"Yes."

"Well, that's too long to be held against your will in *any* state. Usually it's two or three days, tops. So long as you're not a threat to yourself or others, they should let you go. Just try to look as sane as you can and don't talk about hurting yourself or anyone else."

"Of course not. I don't want to hurt *anyone*."

"Good. Just tell everyone else what you're telling me, and you should be out in no time. Besides, it doesn't sound like you're crazy like us. You probably just have Alzheimer's or something."

"Oh no, dear. It's not *that* bad," she said, mildly offended.

"My apologies, Myrtle. I'm sure you're fine," I replied dismissively, still too nuts to realize how insensitive I'd been. I then noticed Ahmad out of the corner of my eye. "If you'll excuse me," I said. "I see my father over there. We can continue this later."

Ahmad was walking onto the ward from the back door behind the nurses' station when I got up. Though there were strict visiting hours, they didn't apply to me. By that time, my dad had worked at Haven Hill for over twenty years, so lots of the doctors and nurses knew him. He'd even delivered some of their babies.

Ahmad gave me a big hug, grabbed my head and kissed me on both cheeks.

"Sit down," he said, opening a paper bag full of bagels and Danish. "Eat something."

"I can't eat. I have to ask you some things," I said.

"Look, I got chocolate flavor," he said.

"Maybe later. Ahmad, I need to know what's really wrong with me."

"*Azizam*, nothing is *wrong* with you. We told you what's happening. You have what is called bipolar—manic depression, they used to call it. The medication you're taking is the best. It will start working soon, and you will get better. How is it here?"

"It's okay I guess. They took my glasses, though. Can you ask them for my glasses? Or at least my contacts?"

"Of course. I'm sure they'll give them to you soon," Ahmad replied.

"The showers are crazy. You have to push this stupid button. It's like being in a *deh* [village] or something. I may as well be showering in a bucket. I don't know if they can help me here."

"Give it chance, *azizam*," Ahmad said, laughing. "They know what they're doing. I know these people. Oh, you are excited to watch Obama win tonight?"

"I completely forgot. It's Election Day already?"

"Yes. I just *know* he's going to win." Ahmad beamed.

"Really? You think so?"

"I bet you a hundred dollar. No, five hundred."

"Eh! What kind of *mosalmoon* [Muslim] are you?" I asked, laughing. "I hope they'll let us watch. I'm so happy I voted early."

"I'm sure they will. I'll talk to them." He did, and they did.

So it was that I watched Obama win the election I'd hooped my heart out for from a locked psychiatric ward—sans glasses or contacts, in a pair of blue Hello Kitty flannel pajamas, on a grimy orange-juice-stained, plastic-covered couch, surrounded by Republicans, crayons, coloring books and stale crackers. The first Y chromosome I'd noticed on the floor, the drooling kid watching TV when I first got there, was now shuffling back and forth down the hall behind me as I watched the returns.

"If Obama wins," he said, "all the babies will die. Abortions everywhere."

"I'd get a hundred abortions if it meant he'd win, you fucking idiot. Shut up, and go drool somewhere else," I told him. He didn't listen. He just kept shuffling and talking about dead babies.

One of my few fellow liberals on the floor was an older white nurse named Ella. She was big into CODEPINK, and she'd gone to see Obama speak when he came to Dayton. Ella liked me, and I liked her back. Unlike many of the mental health providers I'd encountered before her, Ella was neither careless nor condescending. She gave me a radio once when I asked to listen to music; she told me to listen to it quietly in my room and not to tell anyone. She held my hand once and told me I was beautiful. And she called me by my name and always looked me in the eye. Thank God for the Ellas of the world.

When the CNN anchor finally called the election for Obama, Ella and I started jumping up and down and high-fiving each other. She even hugged me—something the nurses aren't supposed to do. But our joint celebration lasted less than a minute. No one else was nearly as elated. Ella went back behind the nurses' station once our hug was over, but I continued my celebration solo.

"Did you hear that, Bubba?" I asked the disturbed, drooling shuffler. His name wasn't really Bubba, but I thought it suited him. "All those fucking babies. Dead! Isn't it *fantastic?*"

One of the nurses overheard this outburst (it was hard not to; I was all but screaming) and offered to sedate me.

"I'm sorry; I'll stop," I responded. "Can I use the phone?"

"No, Melanie," she replied.

"It's only to call my dad," I said, managing not to correct her. "You know, Dr. *Moezzi*. He told me to call him." It was a lame appeal, but it worked.

"Well, just for a minute," she responded.

I ran to the phone and dialed out. Ahmad picked up.

"Melody *jan!* Did you see it? Did you see it?" I could barely hear him. There was a party in the works. I started to tear up.

"Yes, I saw. It's amazing. I wish I could be there with you guys. Or with Matthew."

"Me too, *azizam*. When you get out, we can celebrate. Now you go to sleep. I come see you tomorrow. I love you."

I tried to call Matthew after that, but the nurses wouldn't let me. They told me to go to bed and that I should be grateful they'd let me stay up so late in the first place.

The saddest part about being on a locked ward isn't being locked in a strange and sterile place. It's being locked *out* of the rest of the world.

Steven, a Vietnam vet on our floor, had asked if he could vote that day. One of the nurses laughed at him. This man had served his country and was now paying a huge price for it, and yet he wasn't even allowed to exercise his most basic civil right.

CNN kept flashing this number across the screen for people to call and report if they'd had trouble voting or witnessed any voting irregularities. I wanted to call and tell them about Steven. But then I realized how futile it would be. Imagine: "Hi, CNN, I'm a bipolar Iranian girl on the seventh-floor psych ward of Haven Hill Hospital in Dayton, Ohio. There's a patient who fought in Vietnam here, and they won't let him vote. Oh, and he's pretty sure he's Jesus Christ." So yeah, I didn't call.

Shortly thereafter, however, I did start visiting the CNN Center in Atlanta on a fairly regular basis. Not knowing anything about my psychiatric hospitalizations less than a year earlier, producers happily booked me as a sane and knowledgeable commentator on issues related to Iran and/or Islam. With every new interview, I felt myself gaining a little credibility, and with each new ounce of perceived clout, I imagined that the next time I ran into another Steven, I might be able to amplify his voice just enough to get someone on the outside to listen.

Upon leaving Haven Hill a few days after the election, I was sure that any shred of credibility I had left was shot to hell. I couldn't imagine anyone ever taking me seriously again. Having accepted this new reality, I took it upon myself to focus on the one person with whom I had a chance of regaining some credibility: myself. That's not to say I wasn't still a total mess when I left the hospital. I was. But I was a mess with hope, and thanks to some miraculous medications, I was a mess who no longer thought God was talking to her through the pages of *Cat Fancy*.

part

six

twenty-two

clear blue stormy skies

How I got back to Atlanta is a total fucking mystery to me. Had I no one to fill in the gaps, I couldn't be sure whether I'd traveled those five hundred miles via Toyota or unicorn. Matthew insists it was the former, and this not being a choose-your-own-adventure, I'm left to take his word for it.

Apparently, he flew up to Dayton to fetch me shortly after I was released from Haven Hill. Quickly recognizing I was about as fit to operate heavy machinery as I was to solve the Riemann hypothesis, he opted to drive the whole way back. Though he remembers significantly more about the trip than I, he still recalls little. I take this as an indication that the journey was much more tolerable than the ride up, but then again, I can't be sure.

Since Stillbrook, my manic and depressive symptoms had grown consistently worse, and with them, so had my memory—perhaps my mind's way of protecting me from reliving all the ridiculous things I'd done courtesy of its faulty wiring. While there are certain vile experiences I vividly remember, there are many I don't. Likewise, while there are specific tender moments I keenly recall, others escape me. I'm haunted by this amnesia. It's like a double-edged pocketknife that can just as easily cut blood vessels as blood oranges.

My first clear memory after returning to Atlanta was setting foot onto the "campus" of Clara Vista. With the solid support of the rest of my family and Christina, Matthew signed me up for the outpatient day program there. He also managed to land me a generous "scholarship." This meant (because our insurance denied my claims—maintaining that I was sane *enough* after my two expensive inpatient stays) that we would have to pay only about a hundred dollars per day instead of three hundred.

Clara Vista was idyllic, particularly compared to my last hospitalization (not to mention the two preceding it). The grounds were pristine. There was music, art, basketball, volleyball, yoga, a talented chef on staff and a greenhouse. More important though, nearly all of the staff members seemed genuinely concerned and invested in my recovery. It was nothing short of a revelation.

But I was still a mess: fragile as freshly blown glass and absolutely incapable of stillness. My skin taunted and tortured me. I felt as though I'd received a full-body epidermal transplant—only I was rejecting the organ. I did whatever I could to manage the restlessness, but little worked. I bounced on one of those absurd inflated exercise balls during my entire intake interview; I Hula-Hooped and practiced high kicks in the gym during lunch, and I left sessions every five minutes for "pacing breaks."

But I had started an effective medication regimen at Haven Hill—a bona fide miracle, as it takes years for many patients to find the right cocktail. As a result, by the second week, I was able to sit still for an entire hour at a time. By the third, the shaking, pacing and bouncing had diminished considerably. I looked almost normal. Not to say that I *was*—the disquietude and agitation were far from gone. Still, I'd learned to better manage them, constructing an invisible cone around my neck like the ones they put on dogs to stop them from infecting or reopening their wounds after surgery.

I began to accept and understand my diagnosis at Clara Vista. I wasn't happy about it, but I wasn't entirely devastated either. Finally having a name for what was happening to me, for the extreme vacillations in mood that I'd experienced for well over a decade, was more of a relief than anything else. And knowing I wasn't alone made the diagnosis almost tolerable.

So fighting my natural instincts to file an appeal, I accepted the unanimous verdict I received at Clara Vista. Determined to learn more about it, I took to reading all the bipolar-related books Matthew had already purchased and finished: *Bipolar Disorder for Dummies*, *Bipolar Disorder: A Guide for Patients and Families*, *The Bipolar Disorder Survival Guide*, *Take Charge of Bipolar Disorder*, *The Complete Idiot's Guide to Bipolar Disorder*, *An Unquiet Mind* (my favorite) and at least a dozen others. The more I learned, the more I came to accept the reality of my situation.

Realizing that I'd never be free from my "disorder" and that treatment would require constant vigilance and daily medication was like having a thousand rugs pulled out from under me. As I more fully considered how much I'd put my family through—and how much I might put them through in the future given the recurrent nature of manic depression—I came to a painful conclusion: it isn't fair to expect any nonblood relation to stick around for something like this. So I sat Matthew down and gave him permission to leave me.

"You didn't sign up for this," I said, holding back tears. "I totally get it if you need to leave. I wouldn't hold it against you for a second."

"Are you kidding?" Matthew replied. "I knew you were crazy from day one. I'm not going anywhere. You're stuck with me."

In total, I spent six weeks at Clara Vista. Every weekday from 9 a.m. to 2:45 p.m., I was there—attending individual sessions (with my counselor, a staff psychiatrist or dietitian), as well as group sessions involving everything from woodshop to spirituality to art therapy to circuit training. When Ahmad first came to visit, he said it was like a resort and that he'd love to check in if it weren't so damn expensive.

Still, as striking as Clara Vista was, it *wasn't* a resort. Resorts, for example, generally don't require drug tests. As a teetotaler who'd never used an illicit drug in her life (save that one miserable encounter with marijuana at Sarah's place), I'd never feared drug tests. Today, they terrify me.

Before Clara Vista, I never thought to thoroughly hydrate in anticipation of a drug test. That was something only *real* drug addicts did to cheat. Turns out, however, the more dehydrated you are and the less urine you produce, the more likely you are to present with a false positive.

So when I handed the nurse my cup with barely any pee in it, she asked if I could produce more. After telling her I'd given it my all, she "guessed" it would do.

I tested positive for cocaine.

"You must be kidding! I mean, it sounds sort of sexy and all, but it's not *me*. I don't even know where the hell you *get* cocaine. Do they sell it at Publix? I don't even *drink*. I'm *Muslim*."

"Well," the nurse replied, "it's *possible* it's a false positive. Why don't you come back tomorrow and we can do another test.

You may want to drink more water this time. You're clearly dehydrated—having so little urine and it being so dark."

Despite disparaging my piss, she seemed nice enough. The next day, however, she wasn't.

"So, here you go. Let's try again," she said, handing me another cup.

"Could I get a glass of water?" I asked. I tried to drink more that day, but I woke up late, and mornings have always nauseated me—so much so that I rarely eat or drink anything before ten or eleven to avoid throwing up. It was nine a.m.

"Sure," the nurse replied. She came back with a half-filled Dixie cup.

Even after the Dixie cup, my "output" was pitiful, but yet again, supposedly sufficient. She tested it once more. This time, it came back positive for cocaine *and* methamphetamine. I couldn't help but laugh.

"Seriously, this is hilarious! I mean, why would I go out and do *meth* knowing I'd be having another drug test today? Plus, my skin is flawless, and look," I said, flashing her my widest Julia Roberts grin, "I have all my teeth. And even if I *were* a drug addict, I would hope I'd be classy enough not to resort to *meth*. I watch *Intervention*. That shit is *crazy*. Seriously, I've never done drugs in my life. I told you, I don't even *drink*."

"We're going to have to do a hair test, then. Unless you can admit you have a problem. Denial is the number-one sign of addiction. Admitting you have a problem is the first step toward recovery. It's nothing to be ashamed of. You're here to get well, and to do that, you have to be honest with yourself, and with us. Otherwise, we can't help you."

I wanted to throw up.

"I'm telling you, I'm *not* a drug addict," I said, now thoroughly annoyed.

"Whatever you say," she replied. "Here's the paperwork and instructions for the hair test. You can talk to the secretary about setting up an appointment."

I quickly realized that the angrier I got and the more I denied it, the more I looked like a drug addict. So for the next week, I attended NA meetings—arms folded, eyes rolling—until I took the hair test that ultimately vindicated me.

As irritated as I was about the whole ordeal, I was determined not to let it get to me. Plus, everyone seemed pretty apologetic and understanding about everything, so I let it go.

I continued to attend my group and individual sessions, and began to thrive. I started interacting more with the other patients, but not beyond hellos and a few hugs here and there. I complimented them on their outfits, paintings, sculptures and poems, and they did the same for me. But I made no deep friendships. There were no Maries or Angelas there.

I used to believe that all crazy people had a hint of genius in them—or at least a handful of extraordinary insights. I don't believe that anymore. Many of the psychiatric patients at Clara Vista may very well have once been highly intelligent, but after repeated bouts of mania, depression and/or psychosis, some of them were barely communicative. Still, I tried to relate and imagine those patients as they might have been before their minds were hijacked.

There were a few artists and poets, but none of them spoke much. There was another lawyer, but he was too depressed to be entertaining. And there was even a handful of other "minorities" (a black girl, a Korean, a few Jews), but that was it. My attempts at humor and commiseration were generally lost on them.

I once told a drug addict seeking legal advice that I wasn't really a lawyer, but rather an organ trader who had no interest in him on account of his contaminated organs. He didn't laugh, but to my credit, a short-lived rumor spread. Another time, I suggested that a serial suicide attempter—one who'd tried over a dozen times—consider taking up a cause next time: "You know, Vietnamese-monk style." No one laughed, and I was asked to leave the group.

Beyond my morbid sense of humor (read: defense mechanism), I expect two other matters helped keep my fellow wounded at a distance: my prostrations and my pristine pleura.

While at Clara Vista, I happily and unabashedly whipped out my prayer rug and chador whenever I felt like it. I prayed in the gym, in the hallway, on the lawn—pretty much wherever I found enough space or inspiration. I suspect it weirded some of the others out. Even crazy people have their prejudices.

A kid named Blaine (supposedly the son of a prominent politician) had a habit of talking to me while I was praying—even after I politely asked him not to, explaining it was disrespectful. I ignored him as much as possible. (You're supposed to disregard distractions during prayers—phones aren't answered, cats aren't shooed away, humans aren't smacked when they start calling you a terrorist, et cetera.) Eventually Blaine got physical, pushing my shoulder once as I bent forward. At that point, I broke my prayer— my lame justification being that it was nobler to defend my faith before such an affront than to ignore it.

"Blaine, if you *ever* touch or talk to me again, I'll tear out your fucking kidneys and sell them to my terrorist friends. And I'll report you. Now back the fuck off my rug." He stepped back, and after that, he never looked at, touched or spoke to me again. I'd like to think it was the former threat that frightened him most, but I'm pretty sure it was the latter.

At any rate, Allah wasn't making me any friends—though I can't blame Him alone. Apart from my regular *salat*, something else set me apart: my absolute disgust for cigarettes.

Not ingesting tar and nicotine into my lungs meant that I was immediately left out of the biggest and most fascinating clique at Clara Vista. I tried to chat the smokers up during and in between groups, but our conversations never got far, as they were absolute slaves to their addictions. To their credit, they were always kind enough to invite me to the courtyard to continue our discussions. But it was I who couldn't bring myself to suffer the stench—not even for the sake of engaging conversation.

Still, despite not belonging to any proper clique, I was amiable. I smiled at people, I made an idiot of myself in yoga and drumming, and I shared in group. I made a serious effort—more than ever before. I was committed. So much so that I even earned a Certificate of Appreciation for "successfully integrating and becoming more involved in the community."

"Congratulations!" Matthew said when I showed him the award that night. There wasn't a hint of sarcasm in his voice, only genuine elation. It simultaneously delighted and freaked me out. I laughed. "Seriously. This is a big deal." I could tell he was about to cry—again, a phenomenon I'd only witnessed about a half dozen times and one that I was determined to avert.

"Yes, yes," I said, batting my eyes and striking my best movie-star pose. "I have a bright future ahead of me as a professional mental patient. We must update my LinkedIn account at once."

"I don't care," Matthew replied. "I'm putting it on the fridge." And he did. (Right next to a slip ripped out of one of Ahmad's prescription pads: "Name: *Melody and Matthew*; Rx: *I love you, Twice a day*; Signed: *Ahmad Moezzi, M.D.*")

I've never felt more like a total loser and an overwhelming success at once. It seemed silly to put this ridiculous "award" on our fridge while my college and graduate degrees collected dust under our bed. But I was thrilled and gratified to have it there. Retrieving my mind has been hands down the hardest feat I've ever faced—collecting my various diplomas was a walk in the park by comparison—but it seemed bizarre to be so proud of my award (even with its accompanying gift certificate for a free coffee from Java the Hut). Nevertheless, I was then, and I am now.

I still have the voucher. I couldn't bring myself to redeem it— something about that slip of paper just seemed way more valuable than a cup of coffee. I keep it and the award in a folder with my Georgia Author of the Year certificate and my fifth-grade Young Author's Award. The only other thing in that folder is a 9x5-inch card with the heading:

ALUMNI CELEBRATION
"STARS of CLARA VISTA"

It's a program from November 21, 2010, for "Surrounded by Joy: A Community Service of Worship." My name is listed as one of three "Alumni graduates" sharing "testimonials."

That day, some two years after my "graduation," I shared my

story in public for the first time. I've always felt comfortable speaking in front of large groups, and by that time, I'd already given tons of lectures before much larger and seemingly more daunting crowds. Nevertheless, when it came my turn, I was terrified. I could barely stand up and nearly tripped over the microphone cord.

But I made it to the podium, and despite a few long pauses to accommodate tears, I testified. It was a short yet thorough testimony, and it changed my life. After that, I gained the courage to continue sharing my story, to continue shedding my shame and to continue speaking out against a heavy cloud of suffocating stigma, one that has consistently loosened its grip with every new public testimony.

When I finished speaking, Matthew all but jumped out of his seat. He started clapping like a madman, and the rest of the crowd followed suit. Still, the road from graduation to standing ovation was lined with more manure than marigolds.

twenty-three

#iranelection

By the *Nowruz* (Persian New Year marking the first day of spring) after "graduating" from Clara Vista, I had only a few months of sanity under my belt. My skin was still as thin and porous as papyrus—but it was a clean leaf, with no worms or insects crawling on or beneath it. I fed it a steady diet of starch (a "mood stabilizer") and paste (the wisdom of a small, caring Guardian Council led by Matthew). Slowly responding to this nourishment, I matured into an obstinate papier-mâché, pomegranate piñata— full of tiny scarlet seeds that, given the chance, would no doubt irreversibly dye everything they touched. Durable, but a piñata nonetheless. One strong blow, and I would have bled out, leaving only stains and the stench of fermented fruit in my wake.

The Guardian Council worked tirelessly to prevent such exsanguination—coating me with superglue at every chance. "Have you taken your Lamictal today?" "You need to sleep more—take this Ambien." "You need eat more—take this *aash* [thick bean and noodle soup]." "You need to get out more—take this car."

By the time millions of Iranians poured into the streets of

Tehran to protest the bogus reelection of President Mahmoud "There Are No Gays in Iran, The Holocaust Is an Exaggeration" Ahmadinejad, the Council and the Lamictal had staged a revolution of their own.

The ice-cream man, Amnesty, Bosnia, Denver and my countless letters to (and now accusatory articles about) world dictators were all preparation for this: a chance to fight for my *own* country, my *own* people, my *own* past. Watching those historic events in Iran, I immediately thought of my high school calculus teacher.

One morning I arrived late to class because I was hanging up signs announcing an Amnesty meeting about human rights in China. When I presented my excuse, Mr. Young smiled and said, "Child, you were born for the sixties." I believed him for over a decade—right up until the moment I saw the streets of Tehran packed with more people than could fill the Ohio State football stadium ten times over. I'd been born at the right time after all—even if the place was still a bit iffy.

I dove headfirst into the pro-democracy, opposition Green Movement. I wrote and published pieces about the Movement wherever possible, and I ran my mouth about it on every radio and television station that would let me—from Air America to Voice of America to CNN to Georgia Public Broadcasting. I published so many pieces for the *Huffington Post* that some friends started calling me *Khanoom* [Lady/Ms.] Arianna.

And I discovered Twitter. I didn't even know what a hashtag was before that summer, but I caught on quick, following the #iranelection feed like a lifeline. I learned whom to trust and whom to suspect, following the former and blocking the latter; I called contacts inside Iran to get intel and confirm or deny rumors on the feed, and I tweeted most of what they told me.

Still, watching from afar as the other children of the Revolution rose up was excruciating. This was *my* generation, kids just like me, born in or after 1979—only their parents hadn't left; they actually grew up in Iran as opposed to just stopping by over summer and winter vacations; and they had no American passports or Costco memberships. They were the real deal. I was just a dual citizen, sprinkling sumac on my Big Mac.

I admired and envied them. I wanted to buy green T-shirts and bandannas in bulk, fly to Tehran and join them in the streets. I also, however, wanted not to be arrested. Of these competing aims, the latter won out. On the whole, Iranian prisons make American psychiatric hospitals look idyllic. Were the allegedly Islamic Republic to have its way with me, I'd be mad again within a week. Probably less. So I continued to speak out from the safety of my home in Atlanta, the "city too busy to hate."

One night, I was invited to do a short live interview with Don Lemon at the CNN Center. A young woman, Neda Agha-Soltan, had just been murdered in the streets of Tehran, and her death had been captured by a camera phone. It was all over YouTube and had just gone viral. Sitting in the makeup room as a heavily pierced stranger straightened my hair, I watched the shaky video footage of Neda bleeding to death in the middle of the street, her eyes wide open, thinking, My hair is straight enough; that's enough eyeliner; just mike me and get me to the studio already.

Don was polite and clearly expecting a levelheaded bobbing head. Instead, he got me. While I've certainly churned out more than my fair share of written and spoken commentary over the years, I've always done so as an activist first and foremost. That means that when I see people dying in the streets, I don't just voice analysis. I voice anger.

I was sure that by creating martyrs like Neda, the mullahs had signed their own death warrants, and I used that interview to say so. "Now that you've created these martyrs," I concluded, "forget it! The people will win." My voice cracked a little, but I didn't cry. By the next day, I'd received well over a hundred messages of support through e-mail, Facebook and Twitter—from every continent save Antarctica. I also received nearly a dozen other media invitations. And a call from my sister.

"After Roxana [my niece, seven at the time] saw you on TV, she asked me, 'Is *Khaleh* [Aunt] Melody going back to Iran to *fight?*' She was totally serious. It was hilarious. Honestly, though, you can *never* go back now. You know that, right?" Romana said, more telling than asking.

"Well, yeah, not as it is *now*. But the more we speak up, the more likely it is that things will change, and then we can all go back to a *free* Iran. Things are changing."

"I don't know, Melody. I wouldn't get your hopes up," Romana said, always the voice of reason.

But I did get my hopes up. I kept writing; I kept speaking; I kept tweeting; I kept praying. I couldn't stop. Matthew took note.

Maybe you should slow down a little," he told me one night after a radio interview. I was losing my voice.

"There's no time, *azizam*," I retorted. "It has to be *now*. You *know* how important this is." And he did. He sincerely respected what I was doing and why I was doing it. The whole Council did.

They were insanely proud of me. I had become a mini-celebrity in the Iranian-American community, and particularly for my parents, watching from some five hundred miles away, this meant I must be fine. Their friends were all congratulating them on the fine specimen they'd raised. They even received a card from an Ohio congressman commending them for raising such an upstanding citizen. Both tribes had confirmed my competency, Ohioan and Iranian alike.

But the papier-mâché was cracking, and Matthew was the only one close enough to notice.

"I know this is important, Melody, and I'm so proud of you," Matthew responded. "But you're putting too much pressure on yourself. Remember where you were a few months ago."

"How the hell could I forget?" I snapped. "You ask me every fucking minute if I've taken my meds. You check my pill bottles. I know you do. I'm not *crazy*. This is just who I am. I've *always* been like this."

"I'm not *saying* you're crazy. I'm just saying you need to take better care of yourself. You know stress triggers mania, so you need to reduce your stress. Get out of the house. Take a break. Do some yoga or something."

"Thank you, Deepak Chopra."

"Call me whoever you want, but seriously, Melody, you can't keep staying up at night, trying to stick to Iran hours. You're not in Iran. You live in *America*. You need to get off the fucking computer once in a while. I'm not asking you to go Amish or anything. Just take a break. The National Black Arts festival is coming up," he said, waving a copy of *Creative Loafing* at me. "You've always wanted to go, and we've never been. Let's go."

"I don't have time for black arts! Don't you see? I'm doing

Persian arts. We can do black arts after Iran is free. We can go set up our own black arts festival in the middle of Azadi [Freedom] Square if you want. But now I need to focus on *Iran*."

"I get it," Matthew responded, straight-faced. "You hate black people. I married a racist. That's cool." I laughed. He laughed. We never went to the festival. I did, however, agree to see my shrink.

I recruited a new psychiatrist shortly after leaving Clara Vista. And this time, I did more research than ever before. I e-mailed a well-known psychiatrist in Atlanta—an oft-cited expert in the local and national media—and asked him to see me. At the time, however, he was too busy with mice or rats or some other vermin to attend to humans, so he recommended a local clinical psychiatrist who he insisted was just as good: Dr. Wendy Green.

After a little Googling, I learned the following: she graduated medical school with honors from the University of North Carolina; she completed her psychiatry residency at the University of Pennsylvania and she served as chief resident during her final year there. I immediately e-mailed Matthew her credentials. He said she sounded badass and that he prayed she was taking new patients.

The heavens replied, and thus Wendy "Badass" Green, M.D., entered my life. Right off, she reminded me of Romana: serious, smart and striking. She also had a certain sweetness about her— more than Romana, but nothing saccharine, and a healthy sense of humor. Combined, it was just enough to offset the clinical surroundings and the inherently bizarre nature of any such overwhelmingly one-sided encounter. This alone set her worlds above her predecessors. But I'd set a high bar.

Every psychiatrist I encountered after my diagnosis (and there were over half a dozen) suggested I lower my expectations for myself—that I accept my "disability." Dr. Green didn't. She got me.

So when I called her several months after we'd started our sessions, telling her that I was about to do my third national television interview, she didn't immediately assume I was delusional. She just told me that I was wise to call for an earlier appointment given the racing thoughts, insomnia, anxiety and agitation I'd been experiencing.

"Why don't you come in tomorrow?" she asked.

"Tomorrow? Let me see," I began. Matthew grabbed the phone.

"She'll be there. Just tell us what time."

Matthew left work to join me at the appointment. He wanted to talk to Dr. Green himself—partly to confirm that I wasn't losing it and partly to submit that I was. While I'd been keeping busy with high and lofty matters, I'd also been entertaining some more delusional notions as well, including a growing suspicion that I was being watched by agents of the Islamic Republic. Not followed or anything. Just "watched." My response: "It's not paranoia if they really are out to get you."

We left with a new prescription, an antipsychotic: Zyprexa.

"It sounds like an overgrown African land mammal," I told Matthew as we left the office.

"*You* sound like an overgrown African land mammal," Matthew said. "Just go fill the scrip. I need to get back to work. You promise you'll go to CVS?"

"Yes sir," I replied, standing tall and saluting him. He kissed me and left. I filled the prescription on my way home.

I wasn't supposed to take the first pill until bedtime, so I spent that afternoon perusing Zyprexa-related message boards. The most common complaint by far: feeling slow and sluggish. I decided I wouldn't take it. This was a time for cheetahs, not hippos or elephants.

Understandably, Matthew wasn't pleased.

"Melody, you haven't slept in two days! That's not *normal*."

"Yes I have. I got a few hours yesterday and the day before. I'm *fine*. And I have the pills just in case."

"I know I can't force you to do anything," Matthew said, "but it's midnight, and I'm going to bed. I think you should do the same."

"I will," I replied. "Just give me, like, a half hour, and I'll be there. I promise, I *will*."

I wasn't.

Instead, I sat up and tried to write. But my thoughts were racing too fast to compose any coherent prose. I could hear one of the popular opposition chants from the TV in the bedroom: "*Natarsid, natarsid. Mah hameh baham hasteem.*" ["Fear not. Fear not. We are all united."] Figuring Matthew had fallen asleep watching the news, I went into the bedroom to turn off the television. He had indeed fallen asleep, but the TV wasn't on. The chanting was in my head.

Wait, I thought. It's happening. Again. But this time I *know* it's happening. This time is different. I can fix it. I just need to stay here for a while and investigate. I mean, I'm not actually crazy. I *know* the TV isn't really on. I *know* the chanting is in my head. I *know* that's weird. But if I stay here long enough to figure out what's causing this, then maybe I'll be able to fix it myself, without drugs or shrinks. No one's brain works exactly like mine. It's like snowflakes or fingerprints. All I need to do is figure out the formula for *my* crazy. Then I can alter the chemical composition, custom-tailor it. No need to buy some drug mass-produced in a factory somewhere in India when I can create my own haute couture brew. It's like Old Navy versus Dior. A no-brainer!

This would have been a fabulous time to pop a Zyprexa. But again, I didn't. Instead, I kept writing, trying to document every fractured thought in a futile attempt to construct a treasure map to the most fucked-up principalities of my mind. I was convinced that later on, when I was fully with it, I could use that map to travel back to fix my damaged parts.

But just when I thought I was making progress, I was rudely interrupted. By Stalin. Not Stalin himself. That *would* be crazy. Just his statue, floating in the middle of my living room. Then I noticed Mrs. Parker, my fourth grade teacher, standing behind me, looking over my shoulder as I typed. I was telling her to back up when Matthew walked in the room.

"What's going on? Why aren't you in bed? Who are you talking to?" he asked, rubbing his eyes.

I broke into a long, breathless diatribe about how I was going to discover the secret to my own insanity and create an haute couture fashion line to fix it.

"Drugs may or may not be involved. I may need to hire a chemist. Do chemists work pro bono? Can you turn down the TV? It's distracting me."

"Melody, the TV isn't on. And you're talking to yourself."

"Oh, I know. That's part of finding the solution. I know I'm having hallucinations, but because I *know* I'm having them, I'm not crazy yet, and that's how I'll figure out how to *fix* the crazy." It made so much sense to me at the time. Admittedly, it still does on occasion.

"Melody, we *know* how to fix it. Take your meds, sleep, done. There's no map. There's Zyprexa or Ashwood," he said, grabbing my shoulders and staring me down. "Do you *really* want to go back there?"

The threat of hospitalization wasn't enough to get me to abort my cartographi-chemical experiment, but it was enough to convince me to delay it. I took the pill, and I slept for over a day. When I woke, I remembered everything. Stalin, Mrs. Parker, the chants. They were all gone now, but I was petrified.

Maybe I *do* need to go back to the hospital? If you think I should go, I'll go," I told Matthew, tears streaming down my face. "What do you think?"

"I think the medication worked. It did what it's supposed to. I mean, are you seeing anything *now?* Are you hearing anything *now?* Are you paranoid *now?*" he asked. I took a second to consider each question thoroughly.

"No," I answered, relieved but hesitant. "But what does that *mean?*"

"I told you. It means the medication worked," he said, holding my head in his hands and wiping my tears with his thumbs. "The wonder of modern fucking medicine."

"I get it," I said, removing my head from the cradle of his hands. "It just scares me."

"It scares me too. But give yourself some credit, *azizam.* I mean, it's only been six months. You're not some delicate tulip. You're like kudzu." He broke into his best Farsi accent, imitating two of Ahmad's favorite refrains, "You have good gene. You are number v-one!"

I laughed, pulling him closer. "Really? Kudzu? You can't come up with anything better than *kudzu*."

"Nope."

Perhaps he's right, and I am more resilient than I give myself credit for. Or perhaps the rest of the world isn't as stable as I once thought. Perhaps we're *all* pomegranate piñatas, capable of bleeding out without a moment's notice. Sanity isn't promised to anyone, revolutionaries least of all.

All I know is that I haven't seen Stalin or Mrs. Parker since, and I'm glad for it.

Michael Jackson couldn't have picked a shittier time to die. Right as the Green Movement hit its stride and the Zyprexa kicked in, MJ's careless Caribbean doctor became the world's new Ahmadinejad. Global insanity ensued.

Before Jackson's death, all eyes were on Iran. The Iranian people had earned more universal support and esteem than I'd ever seen. With all that encouragement, respect and attention, I was sure things would change. But pop takes precedence—especially in America.

As the allegedly Islamic Republic continued to round up students, lawyers, activists, bloggers and journalists—subjecting them to rape, torture, illegal detentions, show trials and executions—nearly every mainstream American television news outlet ran the same handful of MJ clips on an endless loop.

Many in the media suggested that the Iranian opposition had died along with Michael. Not so. Rather, the media had just stopped paying attention to it, and eventually the movement entered hibernation. I have no doubt that the Iranian people will rise again and that the children of the Revolution, having learned from their parents' mistakes, will bring about a free and democratic Iran.

Whatever the case though, as much as I write, speak, yell and scream about the passion and resilience of the Iranian people, *my* people, I will still never fully fit among them. I remain a hybrid, with my mind and body in America and my soul in Iran. Perhaps insanity is inescapable when you separate a soul from its vessel. Like eggs outside a nest, we must improvise to survive.

twenty-four

stabilized volatility

T hank you for calling Trader Joe's, Josh speaking. How can I
help you?"

"Hey, do y'all have hyacinths?" I ask.

"Hya-what?"

"Hya*cinths*. They're flowers. You usually have them in pots
around this time of year."

"Um, I'm not sure, ma'am. Can you hold for a second?"

I hold for a minute. Josh returns.

"Yeah, I don't think so. But no one really knows what they are,
so you may want to stop by and see for yourself. We have tulips
and daffodils."

"No thanks," I say. Fuck tulips and daffodils.

I hang up and turn to Matthew, who is presently engrossed in
King Leopold's Ghost.

"Matthew, nobody has them. No one at Trader Joe's even knows
what the hell they *are*. What am I going to *do?*"

"Seriously, this is *crazy*. Do you have any idea how devastating the rubber trade was in the Congo? It's nauseating. You've *got* to read this."

"I'm sorry, *what*? Hold the rubber. Did you hear me? I can't find a single fucking *sonbol* [hyacinth], and it's my last *seen* [s]."

Hyacinths, signifying the start of spring, are a mainstay of any respectable *sofreh-eh haft-seen* (literally translated, spread of seven s's), which is the traditional *Nowruz* setting. As the name suggests, it includes at least seven objects beginning with the letter *s* (or *seen*).

All I need is a *sonbol* to complete my otherwise stunning *sofreh*. I have *sekkeh* (coins, for prosperity); *seer* (garlic, for medicine); *sib* (apples, for health and beauty); *senjed* (the dried fruit of an oleaster tree, for love—saved from a million years ago and re-used every year, as they're not exactly native to Ohio, or North Carolina, or North America, for that matter); *serkeh* (vinegar, for patience and senescence); *somagh* (sumac, for sunrise).

I even have a gang of the other supererogatory items that don't start with *seen*: a mirror (for sky); rosewater (for water—regular water, of course, would be uncivilized); candles (for fire); painted eggs (for fertility—sorry to break the news, but Iranians invented "Easter" eggs); a goldfish (for the animal kingdom); my prettiest copy of the Qur'an (for faith), and *Divan-e-Hafez* (his collected poems, for love, beauty and all things Persian). And for still more extra credit, I have an orange floating in the middle of a crystal bowl of water (representing the Earth suspended in space), which is a total bitch because I have to keep swapping out the orange so it doesn't rot.

"Did you call Home Depot? Or Harris Teeter? Or any of the other grocery stores?" Matthew asks, without looking up, still caught in Adam Hochschild's African web.

"I called *everyone*. Nothing. *Nowruz* is in a *week*."

"There are supposed to be some Iranian stores here. Call them," Matthew replies from the Congo.

"I tried. They don't have them yet either. *Sonbol*s were so easy to find in Atlanta! What's with this place?" No answer. I plop down on the couch, lie across Matthew's lap and pout until he starts scratching my back.

We just moved to Raleigh. Matthew got a Harvard fellowship to study the Wake County Public School System. He spends his days mining data, constructing charts and graphs, and advising the district on how to improve student performance. The gig is as noble and numbers-oriented as it is prestigious. He loves it for the digits and the do-gooding, but he could give a shit about the distinction. Still, I both relish and taunt him for it.

Whenever he does something stupid (spills his tea, trips over the cat, pisses on the toilet seat), I sing, "Now that's my *Haaaaar-vard* fellow." He hates it.

As for me, I've been sane for some time now—relatively speaking. I spend my days writing in a small office at a corner desk with a giant framed photo of Azadi Square packed with protesters on one wall and a travel poster that reads "See America First: Glacier National Park" on the other.

I take my Lamictal every morning, and about half a dozen times a year I dip into an "emergency" bottle of Zyprexa—only when the voices or visions strike or when my thoughts start going all Usain Bolt on me. I haven't been hospitalized in over four years. I've even started serving as an advocate for Clara Vista—speaking to donors as a star graduate and scholarship recipient, sharing my "success story" in its quarterly newsletter, appearing in a video testimonial for its website, and even teaching a writers' workshop for current clients. I've also started writing and speaking publicly about mental health as a human rights issue, as well as about the need for greater research and resources. In short, I'm a model mental patient. If Phi Beta Kappa were ever to create a psychiatric consumer division, I'd be one of its first inductees.

But I'm not cured. As a rule, bipolar disorder is "relapsing and remitting." I can be fine for years at a time, but then there'll be this big, comic-book-worthy *BAM!* Even if I do everything right—take my meds, stick to a steady sleep schedule, eat like Dr. Oz, pray like Mohammad and yoga like Madonna—it's still highly likely I'll get sick again.

Given I've experienced nearly a dozen major depressive episodes, one full-blown manic episode and a handful of hypomanic episodes, I'm about as likely to dodge a future episode, statistically speaking, as I am to join the NRA, move to Michigan and start my own militia.

Even over these last four years as an outpatient, I haven't been entirely "well." One major depressive episode had me seriously considering both suicide and electroconvulsive therapy. I even passed all the preliminary tests to qualify for a course of six to twelve treatments twice a week over three to six weeks. Before my first treatment though, the depression began to lift on its own. I can't say why, but I'm grateful, as it spared my brain any extra electrical currents. Still, I may very well reconsider ECT in the future. Should I ever again experience the severe treatment-resistant depression it's intended to treat, I expect I'd give it a go. Christina insists she's had patients who've improved dramatically afterward, though many who undergo ECT complain that it can cause permanent memory loss. Then again, so can suicide.

It's been two years since I qualified for ECT. I'd like to think I've gotten better at detecting and addressing my symptoms early on—and that in doing so, I've gotten better at "getting better." But it's not like I can conduct a double-blind identical twin study to be sure. Whatever the case, I don't expect I'll ever be "cured" of my neurological bipolarity any more than I'll be cured of my bipolar cultural identity. But I do expect I'll manage.

The Guardian Council is as strong as ever. Now that we're in Raleigh, less than a half hour away from Matthew's parents, they've enlisted wholeheartedly as well. His dad, Tom, has pancreatic cancer, and his mom, Jean, is his primary caretaker. We expected that by moving up here we'd be helping them out, playing the parts of the good, self-sacrificing son and daughter-in-law. Turns out, though, they've been just as much of a help to us as we've been to them.

Nevertheless, when we first came here, I was sure I'd hate being so close to them. I still didn't know them *all* that well. My cursory rundown on the Lenards after a few Christmases and Thanksgivings was as follows: They barely go to parties; they wear their shoes in the house; they have only a handful of friends; they go to Mass on Sunday mornings; they eat Yorkshire pudding, and they have no doctorates.

In short, I felt I had little in common with these people. I was wrong. I had their son, whom they'd somehow raised to fit me perfectly. After calling them my in-laws for nine years, I now call them family, because they are. And having my family around since we moved here—even the imperialist British and American sides—has been a huge blessing.

A few months after we moved to Raleigh, I took everyone to *Charshanbeh Soori* (the eve of "Red Wednesday" before the New Year) at the North Carolina state fairgrounds. I didn't know any of the other Iranians there, but I was happy with my crew: Matt, Tom and Jean. They were all so excited about it. Jean even looked up *Charshanbeh Soori* online and printed out a Wikipedia page about it. She read it to me over the phone, asking if it was accurate:

"'Bonfires are lit to "keep the sun alive" until early morning. The celebration usually starts in the evening, with people making bonfires in the streets and jumping over them singing "*zardi-ye man az to, sorkhi-ye to az man.*" The literal translation is "My sickly yellow paleness is yours, your fiery red color is mine." This is a purification rite. Loosely translated, this means you want the fire to take your paleness, sickness, and problems and in turn give you redness, warmth, and energy.'

"So is that right?" she asked.

"Totally. I'm so impressed you looked it up," I replied, truly touched.

"Of course!" she said in her Americanized though still distinctly British accent. "I'm going to memorize the song. Tell me how you say it."

I repeated it in Farsi a few times for her, and when she got to our house, she was chanting it on her own, ready for the fire, comparing it to Guy Fawkes Day. I can't ever remember loving the woman more.

Tom was a little tired from his chemo, but he was determined to go.

"I'm ready!" he said, with as much enthusiasm as he could muster—which, given his normal nonchemo demeanor, is still more than most "healthy" people on a good day.

"You know this is mostly for you, Tom," I said as I tied my sneakers. He did. "The fire is supposed to take away your sickness and give you its radiance and health. There are stories of people spontaneously recuperating from most anything after *Charshan-beh Soori*," I continued. "Everyone says they're myths, but I figure it can't hurt."

Tom smiled and gave me a big hug. "I'm with you, kiddo," he said, tearing up. Terminal cancer brought out his emotional side.

"Come on, let's make a move!" he said, putting the handkerchief he'd just wiped his eyes with back in his pocket. We all constantly tell him that handkerchiefs are disgusting, but he still insists on using the vile things. He'll even offer you one if you so much as sniffle in his presence. If not for the sneakers, the layers of mismatched shirts, the Brooklyn accent and the abiding baseball cap, you'd think he'd walked straight out of the nineteenth century.

We got to the fairgrounds around seven p.m. They hadn't lit the fires yet, so we headed for the food. We'd already eaten dinner, so we just got some tea and Iranian trail mix (dried figs, apricots, raisins, pistachios, hazelnuts, sunflower seeds) and sat at a picnic table waiting for the fires. Soon, they were lit and we queued up. We jumped over a series of flames, one after the other. Then we lined up and jumped over all of them again for good measure.

"Is that all?" Tom asked, flushed after the second round.

"Yeah," I answered. "We can go now. You should be cured. And if not, we've got some mint chocolate chip ice cream at home."

Tom laughed, and we headed to our place for ice cream before they drove back to Durham.

Tom was supposed to be dead over a year ago. The chemo was supposed to make him vomit his brains out. The cancer was supposed to spread to his liver. None of it has happened yet. His doctor keeps calling him an "enigma." I call him stubborn as hell, and I respect him for it.

A few days later, Matthew comes home from work with a Trader Joe's bag in hand. Our newest cat, Nazanin, bolts for it, shoving her head inside.

"I found your *sonbol*," he says, kneeling down next to the bag and petting Naz. "I got two. Both purple."

"Shut *up*! But they said they didn't have them."

"Correction," he replies, "they said they didn't know what they *were*. Big difference."

"Fucking Trader Joe morons. *Thank* you!" I say to him, throwing my arms around his neck and planting kisses all over his face as though he were a soldier returning from war.

"Get off of me and go finish your *haft-seen*, maniac," he orders, pointing at the matching voids on either side of my *sofreh*. I'm a sucker for symmetry.

I pull the pots out of the bag, taking a giant whiff of paradise.

"Go get two gold pots from the garage," I say as though I'm an ER doc demanding units of blood. I paint all generic terra-cotta pots gold. I've also been known to paint frames, chairs, trash cans, trays and pretty much any object I deem mildly unattractive gold. Matthew and Mario are always making fun of me for it. I'll say I don't like a pair of shoes or a couch or a dog, and they'll be, like, "Just paint it gold."

Matthew brings the pots, and I carefully place the hyacinths inside. Each pot has four unruly stems, bowing and slanting like thick purple licorice sticks.

I demand ribbon. Matthew appears with a spool and scissors. I tie a ribbon around each quartet to pull them together and keep them in line. The thing about hyacinths, particularly in pots, is that they refuse to grow in any rational or orderly fashion. They're always leaning or bending to one side or another. The ribbon is meant to keep them in check, to impose order on disorder.

"You know it's a lost cause," Matthew says. "They never grow straight."

"I know," I say, and I tie the ribbon anyway.

ACKNOWLEDGMENTS

There are too many to name, but some stand out. I thank the following brave souls—

To Matthew: You survived and supported me through hell and back, and all you got for it was this lousy dedication and my lifelong devotion. Not enough.

To my parents: I owe you everything.

To Romana: You set the standard. I've never looked up to anyone more.

To Mersedeh: Your example, more than any other, brought me to Islam.

To Tom and Jean: Love, thanks and respect for being my second set of parents and putting up with me just as kindly and courageously as my first set.

To the rest of my Guardian Council: Mario, Christina, Nobar, Roxana, Rushmi, Sanam: You know what you did.

To Ayesha Pande: If it weren't for you, this book never would have been published, and I'd be eating a lot more pasta and Taco Bell.

To Megan Newman: You had the guts to take on a memoir

about and by a bipolar Iranian–American Muslim activist. They ought to name an extreme sport after you.

To Larry Malley: You let me write what I wanted when no one else would.

To Danielle Durkin: You convinced me not to sell myself short.

To Lilly Ghahremani: You helped me from the start, before you even knew me.

To Barry Peters and Larry Schenk: You taught me to write and fight.

To the exceptional health care providers who truly cared and treated me as an equal: God bless you.

To everyone out there with a serious mental illness who hasn't killed her- or himself or anyone else: You give me hope. Much respect and many thanks.